Matthew
BURKE

A rugby life

Matthew
BURKE

with IAN HEADS

A rugby life

MACMILLAN

Pan Macmillan Australia

First published 2005 in Macmillan by Pan Macmillan Australia Pty Limited
St Martins Tower, 31 Market Street, Sydney

National Library of Australia
Cataloguing-in-Publication data:

Burke, Matthew, 1973– .
Matthew Burke: a rugby life.

ISBN 1 40503671 0.

1. Burke, Matthew, 1973– . 2. Rugby Union football players – Australia –
Biography. 3. Rugby Union football – Australia. I. Heads, Ian II. Title.

796.333092

Set in 11.5 pt/16.5pt Sabon by Post Pre-press Group, Brisbane
Printed in Australia by McPherson's Printing Group

Papers used by Pan Macmillan Australia Pty Ltd are natural, recyclable products
made from wood grown in sustainable forests. The manufacturing processes
conform to the enviromental regulations of the country of origin.

*To Kate and my girls – you are what makes
my rugby so enjoyable.*

CONTENTS

ACKNOWLEDGMENTS

Special thanks to Steve Johnson, fan, statistician, rugby expert and historian, who provided invaluable help with his advice on the fine detail of the book, on match dates, scores and footballing nuances – and who did it all with unflagging good humour and enthusiasm. Thanks too to Bob Burke, whose meticulous recording of Matthew's career via a growing library of scrapbooks provided a wonderful foundation for the project, and to Peter 'Fab' Fenton for allowing us to publish his poem 'The Youngest Cub'.

Occasional comments and observations recorded in the book were sourced from the DVD on Matt Burke's life, *Matthew Burke – A Decade of Excellence*. The involvement of all interviewees who generously gave their time in helping tell the Matthew Burke story is greatly appreciated.

FOREWORD

There was never a lot of huff 'n' puff about Matt Burke the footballer. He just got on with business, calm in any crisis and leading the way by his own example. He was a great rugby player for more than a dozen seasons in Australia, and remains a great player today, even though fate has taken him far away from home for the final years of his career.

It was my pleasure to have played a lot of football with Burkes – to have shared some great victories and memorable trips (and some painful losses, too), plus all the other things that a life in top-level rugby can offer. And I can say this with certainty: no captain could wish for a greater ally in the heat of battle than Matthew Burke. You just *knew* he would do his job and that you could rely on him absolutely when the pressure was on. It's great that he has chosen now to tell of his life in rugby in this book. The Matthew Burke story, with its unbelievably long list of points-scoring records and famous matches and tries and goals and laughs and good times off the paddock – not to mention dubious behaviour on the golf course – is a great Australian sporting tale.

Within the Brumbies, there is probably both a sense of relief and some amazement, too, that he won't be lining up with the Waratahs again in 2005 for the Super 12s – having been told he was no longer needed by the team he had played for since 1992. The thing about Burkes and the Waratahs was that every time he lined up against the Brumbies, he played out of his skin. I don't know what it was, but he was always best on ground whenever we played them. Even in 2004, when he had been in and out of the Waratah team to an extent, he was awesome when he came back for the match against us at home, kicking goals from everywhere, making line breaks, creating space for those around him. The class of the bloke shone through, and physically he was probably in the best shape of his career.

When the Waratahs showed him the door in late 2004, it came as a major surprise to the rugby world. At age 31, he had been such an integral part of that team and a major force in NSW foot-ball for such a long time. I understand how coaches talk about the need to 'move on' and to seek out and nurture new talent, and I have no problem with that. But I don't understand, when a player of Matt Burke's experience and quality was still contributing at a major level (as he was!), why any coaching staff wouldn't have wanted him to stay on for a couple more years. From a leadership point of view, so much is lost when a player like him goes. Throughout his entire career Burkes led by example in the way he trained, the way he prepared for matches, the way he attended to injuries, and the way he played. You simply can't put a price on all of that. But it was typical of Burkey, too, that when the disappointing decision came, he just got on with his life, and started to prepare for the next challenge.

I first saw him play in a schoolboys match – Joey's (St Joseph's

College) v Marist College, Canberra – in the early 1990s. Playing at No. 13 (outside-centre), he seemed even then to be on a different level from every other player on the field. Everything looked a bit easier for him; he appeared to have more time than everyone else. It was obvious even then that he was special. Later, we ran into each other at a couple of Australian Institute of Sport camps in Canberra, got to know each other – and we've been really good mates ever since.

My memories of Matt Burke the footballer are many and include some of the most talked-about moments in Australian rugby in the past decade: the famous solo try against the All Blacks in Brisbane in 1996; the goal to win the Bledisloe Cup in the swirling winds of Stadium Australia in 2002; the shocking shoulder injury he suffered as he scored a famous try against New Zealand in 1998.

The Try: It was just incredible, and he did it all himself. But even more impressive to me from that game was a goal he knocked over from more than 50 metres out to give us a clear break on the scoreboard (even though we lost the match in the end). I remember the kick as being like a cannon going off – and the ball was still going up as it crossed the bar.

The Goal: This was so characteristic of Burkes. Minutes before, he had missed a conversion shot he probably felt he should have kicked, after Matty Rogers had scored. But he had learned from that, made the adjustment he needed to make, and backed himself. This was a tough night for kickers in the winds that tend to channel down at the stadium. But he hit this one so sweetly and straight, and won the match. A beautiful kick.

The Injury: It all happened so quickly as he scored a great try against the All Blacks of 1998 at the southern end of the (then) Sydney Football Stadium. And it was one of *those* incidents – the sort that when you see them happen, you never want to see them again on replay. It was a shocking injury, and a great credit to Matt that through all the work he put in he was eventually able to come back to football.

There is so much to remember with Burkes – and I'd imagine that would be the real pleasure for rugby fans who have followed his career: that there are many riches to be considered. His contribution to Australia winning the 1999 World Cup should never be forgotten. His goal-kicking under pressure in the semifinal (against South Africa) and the final (against France) was just magnificent. He scored 24 points one week and 25 the next, booting goal after goal under massive pressure. In the semifinal under conditions so difficult that the ball had to be held on the tee at times, so strong was the wind, he and South Africa's Janni de Beer turned on as great an exhibition of goal-kicking as you'd ever see.

Throughout his career the debate rolled along as to whether he was better suited to fullback or centre. He started out at fullback, but the way the modern game developed, I progressively formed the view that he was better suited at 13. Playing centre suited his running skills, suited the fact that he was a strong and reliable defender and a great communicator. I thought 13 was right for him. He was an ideal leader there, a steadying influence, coordinating the defensive line and calling the shots in attack. He had a bigger influence on a game at 13, I think, than he could have at fullback.

I would sum up Burke the footballer this way: very athletic and strong, really good footwork, great leg drive, hard bloke to tackle, very strong lower body, strong defender, intelligent footballer at all times – and a peerless goal-kicker. It has been a great 'package' for Australian rugby.

The sport will miss him a whole lot – the man *and* the footballer. In the view of many people in the game he should still be playing here, but I know that over there in the UK they regard him as a massive acquisition – a quality acquisition. He will be much loved there, as a player and as a bloke, as he was here.

The messages of his career are outstanding ones for any young rugby player of ambition (or sportsperson generally) – summed up in the overall approach that was always an integral part of him . . . that he just wanted to become better. Throughout his life in football he has never stopped working hard on all aspects of his game. His approach was always 'professional' in the best meaning of the word. The leadership he offered was by his own personal example. His preparation was never less than outstanding – whether it was skill work, physical preparation or care of injuries. As you will read, he confronted – and beat – shocking injuries, displaying great perseverance and courage. The overall message from the Matt Burke story is there for any young player who cares to pause and consider it: if you aspire to play at the top level, and to succeed – this is what you have to do.

The Burke years have been about balance, too. While rugby has been a big part of his life, it's only *one* part; family and friends and other interests are a vital part of the mix. He has been called 'clean cut' – and he is – but he has always known how to relax, have a good laugh and enjoy life. He's been a great ambassador for rugby – an *enormous* contributor, really – and I know for sure that he has enjoyed the journey.

Throughout it all, the good and the not so good, he's remained what he always was – a great bloke. As far as I'm concerned, that's the best thing of all about Matthew Burke.

George Gregan
Sydney, 2005

PROLOGUE

Rugby is like life. You never know the fulltime score in advance or have much idea of what might lie just down the track. But, ideally, you roll with the punches, accept the certainty that there's going to be some bad with the good and a bit of pain along the way, and then draw from it all the positives and enjoyment that you possibly can. This book tells of my own rollercoaster ride through some exciting and challenging years in a game that may, or may not, have had its beginning when a schoolboy picked up a ball and ran with it 180 years ago.

At the start of this project, many matches ago, the game plan was to time the kickoff of the book so that it coincided with a sentimental ending in rugby, with a team that I have loved playing for, the NSW Waratahs. The idea already firmly in my mind was that sometime in the near future I would take off the old blue jumper for the last time, call it quits – and get on with the rest of my life in Sydney.

But that plan was ankle-tapped in the winter of 2004 when the

Waratah hierarchy made a decision to decline to take up an option on my services for 2005, wished me well for the future – and cut me loose. As you will read further along, I was deeply bruised by that verdict. At only 31, I felt I still had plenty to offer the team, in terms of helping to steer a new generation of Waratahs into what (hopefully) would be a great period of abundance and success.

But it wasn't to be . . .

At the closing of the door, I was heartened by the great wave of support that came from people I knew, and from many I didn't know. Yet, as far as I was concerned, from the moment the news broke, it was done – and I just had to get on with business.

As you will read in later chapters, there began at that point possibly the most intense and hectic period of my life. Almost instantaneously with the Waratah cutting-of-the-cord I found myself back in the Wallaby squad, and on bench and match duties throughout the 2004 international home season. Meanwhile, my manager, John Fordham, was in the thick of negotiations that would guarantee a very different career ending from the one I had contemplated. Soon, there arrived a firm approach from the (UK) Newcastle Falcons, home club of England's hero Jonny Wilkinson, which was enthusiastic, warmly welcoming and financially worth-while. I said 'yes'. For my wife, Kate, and me, it meant a time of vast upheaval and change – and all done at something approach-ing the speed of light. But it also meant a new challenge and the chance of a new life experience – and I had never shied away from those in my career.

So it is that a book that was begun in the course of one mild winter, continued in the depths of another, 20,000 kilometres away, with snow and black ice and frozen football fields much under discussion in England's northeast. My plan was always to tell, in as straightforward a way as possible, the story of a fortunate life spent in and around rugby, and hopefully to transport the reader 'inside' the game as best I could.

Fortuitously, I was born in 1973 with certain latent athletic talents, supported by parents who encouraged but never interfered, and who gave me every possible chance to make the most of what talents I had. During the six crowded years I attended St Joseph's College, in Sydney's Hunter's Hill, I hurdled the seasons from cricket, to track and field, to football . . . and back to cricket again. The successes that came later at higher levels had much to do with those balmy days – the routine of expert, repetitive training and the enjoyment of the weekend contest.

Having made my decision in favour of rugby, above the other games I played, the rest, I must say, is something of a dream. It seems not so long ago at all that I was a teenager down at T.G. Millner Field getting ready to play my first game of first-grade rugby with my local side, Eastwood. Yet, the statistics (so meticulously kept by my dad, Bob) that represent the final words of this book tell of seasons rolling on – of three World Cups and 81 Test matches and 878 points for Australia and 115 state caps and Bledisloe Cup wins, of points-scoring records that I'm proud to hold and of more overseas trips than I can honestly believe I've taken. There have been winning goals and tries, near misses, lucky victories, unlucky defeats and agonising injuries. My golf swing, for example, will never be quite what it was, thanks to a shoulder I wrecked one night in 1998 against the All Blacks. But in the big picture, elation and enjoyment win by a mile over disappointment and pain. And throughout my career I played with and against marvellous players and larger-than-life characters – all of whom share these pages.

Overwhelmingly, the twelve-year rugby career of Wallaby

No. 710 has been a fantastic experience. In years ahead, undoubtedly I will pinch myself at the thought of the passing parade of famous sportsmen I played with and against, of the great matches, and of beautiful stadiums filled with the rugby fans of the world. I lived through the game at a time of edgy transition from amateur days to fulltime professionalism – from the days when rugby was a knockabout romp where the post-match socialising was THE big event, to what it became: the tough, structured corporate-backed business/management approach of today. I lived my rugby life through fascinating times in sport – times when the two rugby codes changed profoundly.

And I have loved just about all of it.

I invite you to share my journey on the pages that follow. I will begin exactly where a book about rugby football should begin: with the shrill of the referee's whistle . . . at the very beginning.

Chapter 1

BORN TO RUN

Considering the varied sporting life that was to follow, I guess you could say I was born at the right time of the year. It was in that brief pause between sports seasons I made my appearance on the scene: 26 March 1973 – a time when the cricketers were packing away their whites, and the rugby players were out in the park, running off the summer excesses. I was the fourth and last of the Burke boys of Carlingford, behind Greg, ten years my senior, Troy, eight years older and Paul, six years my senior. That was the whole team – four boys. Unlucky Mum!

Maureen, my mother, was a Londoner who came out to Australia as a ten-pound Pom. My dad Bob was a Sydney boy through and through, educated at North Sydney Boys High and with a clear memory of the trams that trundled through the suburbs until 1961, kids jumping on and off with reckless abandon, Bob Burke among them. My call to enter the playing field of the wide world came at Poplars Hospital, Epping, deep in Eastwood rugby territory.

I was christened Matthew Coleman Burke – and I guess I might as well tell you about the 'Coleman' bit right now and get it out of the way. There is a fair amount of family history in the name, going back to my great-grandfather Joseph Coleman Burke from Liverpool, England, who is said to have met Lord Kitchener in India one day.

Notwithstanding, I have always disliked the 'Coleman' part of my name – and especially so because my brothers used to really give it to me about it. Even at school I never told anyone my full name – it was always 'M.C. Burke'. Blokes would ask me – but they never got it out of me. Then the secret eventually leaked out. It was before one of my first games for New South Wales. I was sitting in the dressing room when a voice boomed, 'Hey, Coleman!' I just sat there, straight-faced. Then it came again – louder: 'Hey, COLEMAN!' I turned around, and it was one of our props, Tony Daly, laughing his head off. A journalist had been chasing a profile on me for the match program, and had, I discovered, rung my dad, who had told him the story. There it was: 'Matthew Coleman Burke – done this, done that: played Under 21s, enjoys rap music and playing the piano . . .' – all that sort of stuff.

What the hell! I can't play piano, and the only rap music I've ever listened to was a bit of Eminem years later. Just then my father, who happened to be present, walked over to me. 'Did you see the article they ran?' he asked. 'The bloke rang me up . . .'

I just blew up. Some people reckon I've been a bit hard on Dad over the years. That was one time when I would have to agree. Dad loves his footy and has been very supportive of me, but I didn't want him speaking to the press on my behalf. I can smile about it these days . . . through slightly clenched teeth. Incidentally, a couple of my mates still call me 'Coleman', and so does my wife Kate, and

Erica, wife of Wallaby captain George Gregan, just for a bit of a niggle and a giggle.

Dad was always a keen sporting man, and there's no doubt that his interest in sport permeated the family. He played rugby league for North Sydney, to President's Cup level, and has always had a soft spot for the old red and black Bears. His brother Denis played first grade with the Bears in the 1960s alongside the famous winger Ken Irvine, during a period when the legendary Brian Carlson was captain–coach for a time and training sessions were said to be short and the post-match pub get-togethers long and robust. Dad was a fullback, and I know he relished the kicking duels that used to be part of the league game back then. He was a good table tennis player, too. The garage in the Burke house had a table where there were many family round-robins and keen battles – and a lot of fun.

My earliest memories are of the family home at 62 Barellan Avenue, Carlingford, a four-bedroom bungalow of generous proportions at the end of a cul de sac, with a big backyard and a pool. All these years later I can still remember the telephone number.

Carlingford at that time was quite rural, and adjacent to the Burke house was a paddock where horses roamed. Nearby was real bushland, too – to where we would trundle a wheelbarrow full of clippings on gardening day. And just up the road was the local park, which I remember as being the centre of my early world. There, with my brothers and a fluctuating army of other boys from around the district, I'd ride my bike and play in the endless games of cricket or touch footy that moved seamlessly from one season to the next. In my mind's eye the park was a massive place. But I drove back there one day not long ago and, you know, it's not so big at all. I had kept a little boy's perspective on it.

Someone asked me once about my earliest memory. On reflection, my *strongest* early recollection was of finding $10.44 just up the road from home one Saturday morning when I was getting ready to go to Little Athletics – something I did from an early age. I asked around among the neighbours, and no one claimed the money. 'It's all yours,' they told me. I have never forgotten it. It was a fortune!

We Burke boys were good mates, although there has been some drift in our grown-up years, as can happen in families. Greg went off to the air force when he was eighteen and I was eight; he lives in Western Australia these days and we talk on the phone from time to time. Troy did nursing for a number of years and was around home a lot, and he and I have always been pretty close. Paul and I had a bit of a falling out in more recent times and are probably not as close as we should be. But it'll be okay, I'm sure – it's just families.

Let me tell you a bit more about the Burke house, where I guess you could say my sporting life began. Apart from the pool in the backyard, there was enough space on the block for a game of cricket. The problem was that Dad was very precious about his lawns, and Mum was precious about her azaleas, and these things had to be seriously factored in when cricket was under way. The game was played out the front, down the thin strip of grass that led to a double garage. There would be angst on some days when Dad drove in from work and the makeshift bark stumps and bails were still standing in the garage entrance, having been quickly forgotten when we drifted away to play something else.

I can picture him when he was four and playing cricket against his brothers . . . and they couldn't get him out. He had a bat and pads almost as big as himself.

Bob Burke

I suspect that my place as the little 'un in the family had a fair bit to do with the sporting life that unfolded for me. My mum tells me that I was up and about very quickly as a kid – walking at about ten months or so. When I think about it, it seems that I was always trying to catch up with my big brothers. Because I was so much younger than them, as well as some of the kids I played with, I got used to losing at games. But I can tell you I never liked it – and I'm sure it instilled in me a deep drive to keep going – to win. I'm that way to this day. I *never* want to lose. Losing in any match cuts very deep with me – even if I don't appear to be hurting that much. That's just a front. In the sort of world that professional sportspeople inhabit, we are under intense media scrutiny and just can't rant and rave and curse after a loss, however bad we feel. You tend to put on a brave and diplomatic public front – then take the real disappointment away to your own little world.

I suppose there is a day in the lives of most fathers and sons – a game of tennis or squash – when suddenly it turns and the father, having won for years, looks down the court and knows that things have changed. The son has gone from competitive to superior – and the world moves on. That sort of syndrome existed with my brothers and me. I was always striving to get up to their standard – and to exceed it if I could.

We all played soccer as kids – plus a variety of other games during those early years of my schooling, at the local Catholic school, St Gerard Magellan, on North Rocks Road in Carlingford. For me in those early days it was soccer in winter and Little Athletics in summer. Then the year before I went to St Joseph's College – and I'll tell you more later of my Joey's experience – Dad put me into rugby, in the Under 11s with Beecroft–Pennant Hills and cricket with the YMCA, in season 1984/85. From the YMCA team I won a spot in the Metropolitan side for what was the first of many sporting tours. This one wasn't quite as glamorous as some that would come later – but it felt very special to be representing my city at cricket in matches in faraway Bathurst, Orange and Mudgee, I can tell you.

Soccer, though, was *the* game and the first sporting love of my early years. Our team, the Carlingford Redbacks, wore the colours of my dad's league team, the Bears – red and black. There are classic photos of young Burke, hands on hips and foot on ball – and with the ball coming up to about my kneecaps. I started playing when I was four – in the Under 6s. I loved playing soccer. It was such a great game for kids, with everyone chasing the ball and getting a whack at it now and then. I remember how chuffed I was to score a tracksuit when I was named 'Player of the Week' at a soccer skills academy at Eastwood one year.

Rugby wasn't even on my horizon in those early days, and so rugby players weren't on the list of my sports heroes while I was growing up. I watched soccer and athletics on television whenever the chance presented itself – and got a great thrill out of the deeds of the champion decathlete, Daley Thompson. He was such a wonderful all-rounder in the toughest event of all, and a bloke who certainly passed the longevity test in his sport. I loved watching cricket, too. I can still reel off 'C'mon Aussie, C'mon' word-for-word.

My first cricket memories are of Viv Richards, Dennis Lillee and Jeff Thomson and other blokes of that era running around: Rod Marsh, the Chappells, Kim Hughes. Later, I fancied that I batted like Hughes – or tried to. Then I'd switch to the left hand and try to bat like Allan Border.

Later, I always enjoyed watching Mark Waugh bat and field. He was such a genius on the cricket field. He was a natural, a beautiful batsman who always seemed to have extra time. I'd never met him until one day at a charity golf event at Terrey Hills, in Sydney, when I was having a yarn to Michael Slater, Mark walked past and threw me a very nonchalant 'G'day, Burkey. How're you going?' And I was thinking, 'Don't call him "Steve"! Don't call him "Steve"! Just be cool.'

I have had a lot of enjoyment from meeting sporting people from other fields – and especially so Mark Waugh. I suspect that plenty of us regard ourselves as genuine 'all-rounders' and fancy ourselves at other games than the one in which we may have made our name. Lots of keen golfers are like that *until* they stand up alongside a pro and see how it's really done.

My best example of that sort of dawning of reality came in a charity tennis tournament I had been invited to take part in one year at Memorial Drive, in Adelaide, sometime after I had to an extent established myself in rugby. In a doubles game I found myself matched against the great Aussie player and Davis Cupper of earlier years, Frank Sedgman. When it came to tennis, the best part of my game was my serve, which I could give a pretty fair thump at times. I lined up against Sedgman, who was considerably advanced in years by then, and pondered what I should do. Should I try and thump one down, the way I usually did? Or, out of respect, should I just lolly one over with a bit of spin applied? In the end I went for the lolly option, the only problem being that in trying to trick it up a bit I managed to connect with no more than the top part of the frame. The ball shot obliquely off the racquet and finished two courts down from where we were playing. There was much laughter, and a red face for Burke. 'Son, whose racquet is that?' Sedgman asked me. I told him it was my father's. 'Give it back to him,' he advised. At that, everyone just *fell about* laughing. Okay, no mercy from now on, I decided. And for the rest of the game I did my utmost to thunder down my serves to the old bloke. It did me no good. The skills he had honed playing at the highest level had never left him.

I have to say that ball sports always came pretty easily to me. I don't mean to sound arrogant in any way – it's just the way it was. Some kids find schoolwork easy, while some struggle. Sport just happened to be my 'thing'. Something like mathematics wasn't. Even today, my dad can work out some maths problems in his head while I'm still fumbling with the calculator. It was logical that I would gravitate towards sport. It was there that I found my niche – something that all of us search for in life, I guess.

Little Aths at the Hornsby Little Athletics Centre kicked it all off for me, way back in the Under 7s in 1980. Saturday mornings were a lot of fun. By 1983 I was competing in the NSW Championships, and there is a record still on the books in Little Aths in my name – the NSW Under 7s 200 metres in 33.1 seconds. It can never be broken, because the Under 7s don't run the 200 metres anymore! It was the only time I ever ran that distance in a race. I ran it that morning, finished, vomited and obviously developed an instant psychological block, which meant that I never had any desire to run it again. Later, at senior school (Joey's), plenty of pressure was put on me to run the 200, but I never did. One hundred and ten metres over the hurdles was absolutely as far as I ever wanted to go. Dad used to give it to me all the time. 'It's only 200 metres, mate,' he'd say. 'Just another 80 or 90 metres on what you normally run.' *No way.*

The funny thing is that once I got into senior rugby, and the training got serious, I was doing 200-metre runs all the time – though I never learned to love the experience, I must say.

At Saturday morning Little Athletics I did the lot – sprinted, hurdled, put the shot, chucked the discus, long jumped, high jumped – and it was a great beginning in sport. But after a few seasons the grind of Saturday mornings started to wear a bit thin with me. Getting up early to go and run wasn't quite the attraction it had been. Mum and Dad have been great through my sporting career, but Dad can get pretty intense about his sport, and eventually it reached a point where I thought I would switch to something else. That's when I went over to cricket.

Sport grew in importance in my life when I went to St Joseph's College in Year 7. My brothers had all gone to Marist Brothers, in Dundas, and then each of them to different high schools. I know that the age gap between my brothers and me made it easier for my parents to contemplate Joey's as a financial possibility for the baby of the family. When I was heading towards Year 7, Paul was finishing Year 12 at Marist Brothers in Eastwood. I still have strong memories of the interview day at Joey's. Frankly, I was overwhelmed by the place in that first encounter; the enormity of it was quite overpowering for a kid of eleven. The place reeked of history and sporting success. I remember walking with some wonderment through the Hall of Fame and looking up at all the photographs. When it came to interview time, the headmaster posed the question: 'Are you a good Catholic boy?' I told him I was. 'And do you know your Hail Marys and Our Fathers?' 'Yes,' I said – and promptly started to recite them. He cut me short. 'No, no. You'll get plenty of chances to do that when you get here.'

So, I was duly accepted, and went to Joey's as a boarder – a big, big change in my young life. Being a boarder was tough early on – but taking the longer view, it was good fun. At first it was like a holiday, then after a week or so I started to get homesick, to miss the things I had known. But the routine is so full-on there – school, training, sport, study – you don't have much time or opportunity to feel sorry for yourself, and before long I was right into the swing of it. We came home on Sundays each week – for a full day or a half-day. It was time enough at least to get your washing done and have a good home-cooked feed. At Joey's *everyone* plays sport; it's the deal. They had footy teams all the way down to the Fs and Gs – so even the maths geniuses got a game. Usually in the front row.

St Joseph's turned out to be the right place for me. There, the three sports then in my life – rugby, cricket and athletics – dove-tailed neatly into the school year. There would come a day in March each year when I'd arrive home and drop off my cricket gear and pick up my athletic spikes. The previous Saturday I would have bowled 20 overs or so in a GPS (Greater Public Schools) cricket match. By the Monday, I'd be in cotton wool as a sprinter. Then, the running season used to nudge up against footy, and around that time I'd always get a bit edgy. But no way were the blokes in the athletics team allowed to go and kick a footy – just in case one of us might pull a hamstring. But on the Saturday as the dust settled on the GPS Athletics Carnival, I'd call past home to drop off my spikes and pick up my football boots. Oh, yeah, it was non-stop sport – the pattern of the seasons at Joey's. Somehow I got through those six years – squeezing in three sports a year – without being injured. The old school in its commanding position in Sydney's Hunters Hill was the centrepiece of my life.

It was hectic. I can still picture my Year 11 maths teacher, Brother Wilfred, doing his best to contend with fidgety blokes getting ready for sports training. School finished at 3.30 pm, and in the footy season we had to get across to the dormitory, get changed and be ready for training at 3.45. Maths was the last period of the day. I remember Mum and Dad coming to the school for parent–teacher interviews and asking Brother Wilfred how I was going. 'Well, he'd be going all right if he was here for the whole lesson,' he replied. And he was right. Five or ten minutes before the end of the lesson I'd be packed up and on the starting blocks – ready to race across to footy training.

You may have got the drift by now that sport dominated my Joey's years. Academically, I was only a middle-of-the-road student – falling short of what I hoped I would achieve when it came to the Higher School Certificate. I was essentially a 'C' student, with a couple of 'B' classes on the list, pretty much in the middle ground the whole way through. History, economics and art were my favourite subjects. Maths was a struggle, although I got through, running at 65–70 per cent. With me, the parent–teacher evenings always produced roughly the same message and it became almost a cliché: 'Matt hasn't applied himself as fully as he could. If he did, he would be a better student.'

Sometimes the two things – sport and learning – would get jumbled up. The defence coach for the footy teams was the elderly Brother Bede, who must have been nudging 80, and who was also a maths teacher. Brother Bede would talk about tackling in terms of physics and such things as the 'arc of the tangent' – and those of us who were less than maths wizards would be sitting there thinking, 'What's going on here?' A more popular theory was that it was easier just to go out and bash someone in a good hard tackle than to analyse it too much.

Despite my own focus on sport, there were reminders at Joey's that school life was about having a sensible balance.

My time at Joey's was six years of always-crowded days – with the game plan no doubt being to limit the time available for young blokes to get into strife. Our days were absolutely chock-a-block – training some mornings, classes through until 3.30 pm, sport until late afternoon, dinner – then three and a half hours of study. If there happened to be some down-time, we'd be out there playing touch footy.

And so it went . . .

I was privileged during my rugby years at Joey's to be a cog in the wheel of teams that built great success, and it was exciting for me to be able to make a personal contribution to that. We grew together as a team through the seasons, and the long tradition of success – and pride in that – at the school was a strong motivating factor for us all. I was lucky to have shared my football days there with a whole bundle of very able players. The list is a long one – all the way from future NSW and Australian representatives such as Peter Jorgensen, Kevin O'Kane and Tim Kelaher – through to David Kelaher (Australian Sevens), John Isaac, Scott Fay, Nick Ghattas, Patrick Ryan and Graeme Thompson. It was a bumper crop – the sort of confluence of talent that can happen now and again in schools and within football districts. In football there is always talk about great teams, great coaches, strong management – those sorts of things; but the fundamental thing in any success is for a team to have the 'cattle'. I think you could say that at St Joseph's College from the mid- to late 1980s, we had the cattle.

I'm not going to dwell on my own sporting achievements at Joey's. Suffice to say that I had the pleasure of sharing in a good deal of success and that the school gave me the utmost opportunity to fulfil the sort of potential that I was lucky enough to have. I played in the centres through my rugby days there, and the switch to fullback, where I was to spend many happy afternoons, didn't come until I went away on the Schoolboys Tour of 1990. On the cricket field, I was a right-arm bowler, batted around five – and liked to give it a thump when the opportunity presented itself. Squeezed in the middle of all that team sport was the track and field season. I ran the 100 metres, the relay, and the 110 metres hurdles, and tackled the long jump and, now and then, the shot put. At a GPS carnival when I was in Year 11, I alternated between the shot put and the long jump pit – running from one to the other to take part: three jumps . . . three shots . . . back for my last three jumps . . . then three final shots. My best 100 metres time at school was 10.82.

At a dinner held around the end of my last school year, Brian Sidgreaves, President of St Joseph's Old Boys Union, said: 'In my 40 years' association with Joey's I would say that Matthew Burke is the most talented all-round sportsman the school has produced.' These were glowing (and humbling) words. But I have to say that the enjoyment was all mine, and that I greatly appreciated the opportunities the school presented. In the sports I played then (and subsequently), I was never seeking kudos. At Joey's, I just loved the games I played and the things I had the chance to do during what now seem to me to be golden years.

My shoulders are long gone now, from my rugby days, but at school I enjoyed playing cricket and fancied myself as a quick bowler with a bit of zip. I took a good lesson one day, though, when we (Joey's Firsts) played a match against Sydney's Petersham Club. In school cricket there was an expectation that you might have a wicket or two in the first few overs. But against a bloke named Mark Atkinson, who became the 'keeper for Tasmania's Pura Cup side, I got hammered all over the park this day. He was lunging forward, and if I dropped short he was carting me over mid-wicket for six. I think it went to about 0–60 after five overs – and I was given a rest. But with the bat that afternoon, against first-grade bowlers, I was seeing it like a watermelon and got 77 not out. That was an occasion when I thought I could go on and be a pretty fair batsman if I wanted to. The next year against Petersham, I scored a duck – but then I picked up seven wickets.

I remember that my one 'ton' in school cricket came in the Under 12s. I scored 103 not out against Scots, was dropped about five times on the way through and was awarded a little bat in recognition.

My premier football moment at school remains one of my top football moments of all time. It came in my final year (1990) against a pretty fair Sydney High team. We beat Scots narrowly, by six points, and then High came out and beat Scots too (3–0) – so a really tough game was anticipated. The intensity of our preparation that week wasn't matched for years ahead in my rugby career – until I got to Test match standard, in fact. Well, we ended up winning the game 74–0 at Hunters Hill – hitting them like a whirlwind early, then going right on with it. Jorgo (Peter Jorgensen) scored four tries, and everything fell wonderfully into place. But along the way there was a moment that all rugby teams dream of – the perfect try. It started from a High kick we fielded on our own side of halfway. The forwards rolled it, mauled it, there were passes inside and outside, a pass from left to right, a pass from right to left – it was tackle, pop, place, clean-out – then eventually to the backline. I was in the line, and it was so picture perfect I can see it now: pass, pass, pass – and eventually from me to Jorgo, and Jorgo over beside the posts. It was *sensational* – the sort of thing you work at, and work for, at training, but so rarely get to in a match. It was magic.

In that try were all the attacking skills we had worked so hard to hone. And maybe it's a bit harsh to say it, but some of the skills that were drilled into us in those endless training sessions were things that some guys at the elite levels can't do today. It was catch, pass right to left . . . catch, pass left to right. The skill development was enormously high, and repetition at training made sure that you had every chance of getting it right. The speed of the ball across the backline in the two years I played first grade at Joey's was nothing short of exceptional. In the blink of an eye the ball would whiz across to the winger, seeming barely to touch the hands. The game has evolved into something different now from what it was, and certainly the defences are far superior at the higher level to what they once were. Today, it's rare to see that classic rugby winger's try of draw, pass, draw, pass – the ball going through the hands at speed – until the last man runs in for the try, just like a perfect training drill.

I believe that that level of skill has been lost to an extent now, even at the very highest level of the game. Sometimes it's taken for granted that, because a player has reached the top level, he has all the basic skills and doesn't need to work, or be coached, on them. But I see it differently. I think *everyone* needs to be constantly working on skills – revising them and making sure they are up to scratch. No coach should take it for granted that a player's got all that is required in the armament. We all need refresher courses. I remember in my NSW years when a bloke named Scott Johnson came on board – a coach with some good and different ideas. One day he asked me, 'When was the last time you were coached?' I looked at him. 'Well, you know, we come here every day.' He persisted: 'When was the last time you were actually *coached*?' And I scratched my head and thought a bit more deeply about it. 'Well, maybe back in the early days . . .'

And remarkably, that's the way it can be today even for footballers right at the top of the heap, although a coach like Bob Dwyer was good at it – the repetition of the simple stuff . . . catch, pass . . . catch, pass . . . the real basics. Players can fall into a trap – accepting that because they *are* skilful, they don't need to work on those skills. I think of rugby league's Johns boys, Joey (Andrew) and Matt, and those early years, which have been much written about, of them walking around most of the time with footballs in their hands. You get the sense that Joey probably *always* had a ball in his hand, just tossing it around – and it sure shows in his football. No doubt many of us who play football were like that in our earlier years. But then you get a bit older and other things come into your life. You might go and have a couple of beers with your mates instead of tossing a ball around. But my belief is that handling the football has to be a very familiar part of your life if you are making the game a career or have any pretensions to excellence. It has got to be around you 24/7.

The professionalism of the rugby teams at Joey's, supporting the school's tradition and expectation of success built up by men like the legendary Brother Henry, was quite amazing. In the teams I played with during my time at the school we won four premierships (one shared as joint premiers), the last two in first grade, and lost only a handful of games. In the final year, our First XV didn't have a try scored against us, just three penalty goals. That last year, 1990, was a wonderful culmination for what could genuinely be described as a great schoolboy side. Counting the trials, Joey's Firsts played fifteen games, and went through undefeated, scoring, in total, 453 points against 49. For me the magic ending to that season, the clinching of the premiership with a 33–3 win over St Ignatius in the final game (Joey's 44th premiership in 103 years), became a prelude to even bigger and better things. I played for GPS Firsts in games in which we beat CHS (Combined High Schools) (24–6) and CAS (Combined Associated Schools) (10–7). I was then selected as fullback in the NSW 1 team for the Australian Schools Rugby Championships in Canberra – and there we won four straight games to take the title undefeated, the first time in sixteen years a state side had gone through unbeaten. From that carnival it was on to the Australian Schoolboys side to face the New Zealand Schoolboys.

My selection in that team to face New Zealand in September 1990 was both a thrill and an honour. Craig Polla-Mounter, bound for an excellent rugby league career with the Canterbury Bulldogs, was our captain. He had played in the previous year's match in New Zealand – and the Aussies had been thumped. We knew how tough it would be . . .

I look back on it now as a milestone event in my football career – the first of many encounters with the team in black. It was also my first introduction to the haka – the intimidating and colourful New Zealand 'challenge to war'. The New Zealanders have played brilliantly on the intimidation factor of the haka over the years. A magnificent piece of theatre that is much anticipated and loved by rugby crowds, that first day at the Sydney Football Stadium I've got to say it sent a few shivers up my spine. We were only schoolboys, and yet when you hear and watch the haka face-to-face, you know it's the real thing. I'm sure I was like a lot of other first-timers in our team that day – feeling the pinch a bit. You ask yourself pretty fundamental questions: 'Do I really want to be out here?' But once it's under way and you make the first tackle, or have the first touch of the ball, you're okay. The mind sort of switches to automatic pilot and you do the things you have learned to do over a number of years. You just play football.

I played in the centres that day against a team that had been destroying all in its path. There was a feeling of heading into 'new territory' because of the quality of the opposition. I remember the start of the game very well – within a minute of the whistle they had fired the ball along the backline and scored a try. I was thinking, 'My God, how many are they going to put on us here?' It was shaping up as a very steep learning curve. But we came back in that game, fought it out hard and well, and won 9–7. I kicked a couple of goals, and played okay although I injured my AC joint in the shoulder. Then halfback Travis Hall landed one from wide out to get us home. Notwithstanding the injury I suffered, I rate it as a very important game. I had taken the step up to a higher level, and I had handled it. It was a mental stepping stone of some importance.

People have sometimes asked me whether it was always going to be rugby. Well, no. In fact, I loved my cricket to the extent that I have regretted now and then in later years not having been around in the days when you could play the two major games, back to back. There was once a history of blokes successfully doing that. But I arrived at a time in elite sport when the seasons were getting longer, when training was starting earlier, and when overseas off-season tours were becoming more frequent. It was a time when it just wasn't possible to be an athlete at a high level in two sports. Near the end of my school days it was all a jumble. I had such success in athletics in Year 12 that one of the track and field coaches at Joey's was adamant that I persevere at the highest level – as a 110 metres hurdler and long jumper. 'Don't leave the sport,' she said. I had won the long jump and 110 metres hurdles for the sixth time in six years at the GPS carnival and run a leg of the winning 4 × 100 metres senior relay team and had greatly enjoyed the experience.

Cricket stayed long in the mix, too. When I played for the Combined GPS team in my last year and took 4–50 in a Possible v Probables game, having not bowled a ball for six months or so, there was some lingering temptation. It all happened at the time I was in line for selection in the Australian Schoolboys rugby tour to England. Tony Lantry, our coach at Joey's, said to me: 'Matt, you would have been picked in the cricket side [the GPS First XI] – no problems, but you're going to England!' Yeah, you could say I was a bit confused by all these sporting temptations at the end of my school days. Mum and Dad may have preferred to see me go on in athletics or cricket, but they never tried to influence my decision.

Three things happened that helped guide me to set my definitive course – for a career in rugby. I was in the gym one day playing hoops with Jorgo and chatting about the Schoolboys tour. 'How good is *this* going to be!' he said of the tour. I was a bit of a home-body, but his enthusiasm set me thinking.

Then, I was talking to Mum one night, and she was thrilled by the thought that I might be heading for England, the place of her birth. She said that it represented a fantastic opportunity for me, and that my selection on tour would also give her the chance to go back to England for a couple of months and see her brothers and sister (which she subsequently did).

At a function held before we left, Tim Horan and Jason Little, who had been in the previous year's Schoolboys touring side, showed some slides of previous tours. By then, I was hooked rock-solid on rugby and starting to think that this game I enjoyed so much might just turn into something pretty big for me.

In those growing-up years I never held any sort of burning life-long ambition to play with the Wallabies. That goal only came later, as my involvement in rugby gathered pace. The first time I saw Australia play a Test match was in that last year at Joey's, when they lost to the French in a close game at Sydney Football Stadium. It was a fiery game, featuring a couple of stinks, and I remember the Frenchman Didier Camberabero slotting a couple of field goal chances. I came away that afternoon with a better and deeper sense of rugby at that elite level – and of the people who supported the game. In school rugby I think you grow up in a fairly insular world, of parents and Old Boys and war cries. Going to the Test match took me into the game's wider world. Given my success at school, and the fact that some bits and pieces had appeared in the press about my potential, I guess the thought was taking shape at the back of my mind that it might be on the cards that I could go all the way to rugby's highest levels, and that it was an aim worth pursuing. I always had enormous faith in my own ability. I felt deep down that I had what it would take to get me through. Added to that, I worked hard at doing things well. I understood from pretty early on that that was part of the deal.

Late in 1990 I packed my bags for the UK and went touring with the Australian Schoolboys. It had been the perfect year . . . and one that I will never forget.

Chapter 2
PLAYING WITH THE
BIG BOYS

The chance to tour with the Australian Schoolboys side to the British Isles and Europe was the opportunity of a young life-time. It was a mighty trip, stretching past Christmas 1990 (we trained in Wales on Christmas Day) into late January 1991– and the depths of the northern winter. We travelled under a fairly heavy load of anticipation, the previous Australian Schoolboys side to tour having been undefeated in fifteen matches. Even as a wet-behind-the-ears seventeen-year-old, I had a sense of the tradition and the expectations. I was familiar with stories of the deeds of earlier teams, and especially those of the 1977/78 'Invincibles', which included the three Ella brothers, Michael O'Connor, Michael Hawker and Wally Lewis, and of the team that preceded ours, which included the likes of Tim Horan and Jason Little. Seven of us from Joey's dominant year made the team of 31. We flew to England, starry-eyed kids far from home and parents.

(Well, for *some* of us; my mum and dad flew to the UK and watched some of the games and had a great time.)

Under the direction of coach Chris Hawkins we worked our way from The Netherlands down through England, Scotland, Ireland and Wales. We ran into blizzards and snow and icy-cold days and nights – and I loved just about every minute of it. I played at No. 13 for much of the tour, although at fullback too now and then. I was 180 centimetres tall (5ft 11in) and weighed 84 kilograms (13st 3lb). (I was to play my later senior football at around 98–99 kilos.) In the tour program my main hobbies were listed as 'skiing and cricket', but my chief pursuits were noted as 'eating and sleeping'.

On our voyage of discovery we kicked off in The Hague, and there I was billeted with a family who couldn't speak English. I couldn't speak Dutch, of course, but somehow we managed, and got on famously. Billeting was a big part of the tour – and that added to the experience, for sure. You never knew where you might end up – and mine went from Millionaire's Row-type houses to quite small and shabby places. But the hospitality was consistent throughout. It was wonderful, wherever we ended up. The experience was what we made of it, and I'm sure the tour as it unfolded became a great life's lesson for us all.

After we had played and beaten the Under 19s Netherlands side 46–0 in our one football commitment over there, we spent a few hours wandering around Amsterdam. That was an eye-opener for a young bloke from Carlingford! We hooked up with a couple of Aussie blokes who knew plenty about the strip clubs and other attractions of the place, of which there are a few, and who were keen to share their knowledge. I think the guys had a lot of fun. I know that *I* did. I wandered the streets, just sightseeing. *Honestly*, Mum!

On the Irish leg, the match against Ulster at Ravenshill will always stay in my mind. It was an encounter dominated by a fierce cold wind that made it a nightmare experience. The wind was a monster – gusting up to 100 kilometres an hour; it was just about impossible to run into it. I can picture Peter Jorgensen heading into the teeth of the gale on a long run on his way to a try. Jorgo looked like he was hardly moving as he battled upfield; but the chasers behind him were in slow motion, too, and couldn't catch him. The try seemed to take forever to score. Kicking was near enough to impossible, too, with the ball taking off at right angles from place kicks even when the kick was from right in front. At one stage I kicked for touch and the ball skewed off the side of my boot and shot sideways. But the wind picked it up and the ball finally found touch 50 metres or so downfield. Genius! We won, 20–9.

The weather turned even more vicious on the day we played the Irish Schoolboys at Thomond Park, Limerick. Hurricane-force 12 winds had hit Britain and Ireland twelve hours before the game. On match day, an icy cold killer wind gusting up to 130 kilometres an hour swept the ground, the rain was horizontal, and at one stage a hailstorm hit. A corrugated-iron roof blew off a house near the ground – and it was like a scene out of *Twister*. We won that match 13–9, but along the way I damaged a shoulder badly enough to have to miss the next couple of games. The Irish had been running a counterattack down the left side, and when the bloke with the ball stepped inside I stuck out my left arm and caught him awkwardly and partially dislocated my shoulder, forcing me off the paddock. The weather was so bloody awful that it was almost a relief to get out of there. Rugby in Ireland is *always* like that, in my experience. On the day you play the match the weather can be guaranteed to be disgraceful. Next day, when you wake up having been bashed or beaten or injured – or maybe all three – it dawns calm and clear. And so it was in 1990 when I woke in a lot of pain, ready for the drive out of the place. The morning air was crisp and beautifully clear, and the sun shone. There were days after that match when I walked around looking like a scarecrow, thanks to the strapping a doctor had woven around my shoulders

It was on that debut tour that I learned that, when it came to the often-discussed topic of Irish jokes, maybe it was all true! The people were fantastic, wonderfully welcoming, but every now and then little things happened that made me smile and wonder. One day I was in the back of a car being driven in reverse by a genial Irishman when I saw a cement pole only a few metres behind us. 'Watch out for the pole!' I shouted. 'Ah,' he said. 'If I hit it slow, it's okay.' And he did. *Crunch!*

One of the boys was billeted with a family in a house in which the shower could barely manage a dribble. 'Just put your hand against the wall and the water will run up your arm and you'll be fine!' they explained in all seriousness.

In retrospect it was a big learning experience and a great tour – although a progressively edgy one because of the state of the world. We were on tour at the time of the first Gulf War, and the coverage of Operation Desert Storm dominated the television. In London they were talking about possible IRA attacks in the streets. The advice to Australians from the government was pretty much: 'Come home if you can.' I remember watching CNN with the family of one of my billets and thinking we might get the call to pack up and go home at any time. Late in the tour we were quite scared and couldn't help thinking about the warmth of a super Aussie summer and having a few relaxing beers down the pub with the boys.

In London we stayed at an army barracks, and the army types there tried to get us to go on a six-mile run and obstacle course two days before our game. We didn't fall for it, fortunately. Soon after our arrival they told us: 'We're having trouble with the IRA at the moment and there is a terrorist on the loose. He could even be inside this compound.' There was further advice: 'Don't leave your rooms, because if we call you and you don't give us a specific call sign back, we'll shoot first and ask questions later!' I looked at my team-mate Michael Misson, whose face had written all over it an expression that said, 'Where's my mum?' To this day I don't know how much truth there was in all of it, but it shook us up at the time. And it certainly ensured that we stayed in our overheated rooms at night. It was so hot that Michael opened a window to let in some fresh air, at which point a soldier with a rifle appeared. 'Shut the window, mate!' he ordered. We didn't argue. In the morning the early wake-up was from a military PT type – words to the effect of, 'Wake up, you Down Under f—s! We're ready to go!'

On Scotland's famous Murrayfield we beat the Scottish Under 19s side 17–12 – a considerable achievement considering the physical differences that the couple of years' gap can represent among teenagers.

At the legendary Cardiff Arms Park, where the singing of the crowd was unforgettable, we whipped the Welsh team 44–0 in one of the most dominant performances of the tour. Brother Anthony (Boyd) had said to me before we left, 'When you win at Cardiff Arms, grab a handful of soil, stick it in a bag and write "Cardiff Arms" on it, and bring it home with you. It will be something to remember.' I did that, and so did a few of the others who had scrabbled around after the match gathering some grass or some of the famous soil. Back home in Sydney, the regulations beat us, of course, and those little souvenirs of the ground never made it through Mascot Airport. It seemed a good idea at the time, though.

Back from injury, I played the second-last game, against an

English team listed as 'Older Harlequin Youth XV', an Under 21 side. We won that game 6–3 at Stoop Memorial Ground in Twickenham. Then we lined up for the final game, the 'Test' against England Schools at famous Twickenham itself, in which we beat 8–3 a team that sported a big, tall pack of forwards. That was fantastic. Victory meant we had achieved a junior Grand Slam, and that was something very special. And to have done it at Twickenham, with its old wooden stand, was fantastic. The place is held in the highest esteem in world rugby!

We had afternoon tea with Prince Charles, visited Anne Hathaway's Cottage in Stratford-upon-Avon and generally went around like the starry-eyed teenagers we were. Overall, it was a brilliant experience and I think that most of the guys would rate it right up there with the very special things they have done in their lives.

There were bad days along the track – such as when our bus was broken into when we were in Cardiff. Some bags were pinched, and for Peter Jorgensen that was very bad news. In the town of Rugby, Peter had done some really solid shopping and had acquired a number of football jerseys. They all went – along with the remainder of his gear – and the rest of us had to chip in with training gear to get him through the next couple of weeks.

I was surrounded by talented players on that trip, and it was a memorable experience both on and off the field. Alongside were players bound for big things – Peter Jorgensen, Scott Bowen (destined to be one of the best No. 10s running around, although the ebb and flow of football politics limited his chances), Craig Polla-Mounter (a great success in the thirteen-a-side code), Fili Finau (destined to be a long-term Waratah and Wallaby) and Stu Pinkerton (who went as far as New South Wales, but wouldn't have been out of place in a gold jersey). The tour was to prove exactly the solid breeding ground for rugby's immediate future that the administrators had no doubt hoped it would be.

I came home to the Aussie summer to confront the profound decisions that needed to be made: What should I do with my life? Which rugby club should I join?

Somewhere at home there is a newspaper cutting that lists my career ambitions on leaving school as either 'landscape architecture' or 'human movement studies'. Before the Schoolboys tour we all had to fill out forms listing our hobbies and ambitions. I just peeked over the shoulders of the blokes sitting near me when it came to the question about likely later career direction. To tell you the truth, I didn't have a clue what I was going to do with my life.

In the end, my sporting achievements helped to make the decision for me. My HSC mark was only reasonable – not high enough (and it was never going to be!) to crack the Australian Catholic University's Human Movement degree course per se. But sporting ability was a factor in qualifying for the course – and it was sport that got me over the line. So, I headed that way, found I could handle the coursework quite comfortably, learned a good deal, grew up a bit – and did two and three-quarter years of the three-year course, before a 1993 tour to North America and France spirited me away right at the end. When I look back on it, my university experience was no more than a pit stop along the way for me. The potential pleasures of university passed me by to a fair extent, as rugby and tours took a firmer grip. I had some fun, certainly, but I embraced the academic life very lightly compared with many people. All the while, my rugby career was taking shape.

The big decision for any schoolboy footballer who has shown some potential or experienced some success is the question of which club side to join. In Sydney rugby, making that choice is a very traditional and enjoyable process – and I went through it in early 1991. Basically, it's as simple as this: each week after training the clubs would put on a keg of beer, and you'd visit the ones that interested you. My experience was of going from Eastwood to Gordon, to Randwick, to Eastern Suburbs, to Wests, to Norths . . . What it was *essentially* was a piss-up. You'd go there and drink their beer and eat their pies, and meet some of the guys. That's how the wooing was done. Maybe it still is – although at the game's higher level in the age of professionalism, things are very different, of course, with negotiations conducted these days by player–managers in boardrooms. Back in the amateur days it was a visit to a club on a Wednesday or Thursday night, a few beers, then maybe back to the pub later with your mates.

Complicating things, although not too much, were some expressions of interest from rugby league clubs. St George showed interest, and Canterbury were keen at the time I was finishing my schooling. The club's CEO, Peter 'Bullfrog' Moore, talked to my father about an arrangement in which they would provide me with tertiary education support, something that Canterbury did a lot of. But I enjoyed my rugby and, although flattered by the attention, I guess my direction and my decision was always going to be to stay. There were later 'nibbles' from league, too, and I was well aware of the success of many rugby players over the years – backs, particularly – when they chose to play the thirteen-a-side game. The newspapers reported rugby league interest in me again in 1992 – Balmain and Norths at that time, I think – and it's true, there *was* some knocking on my door. But I was clear about what I wanted. I was going to play rugby, and already I was thinking 'How good is *this* going to be? Travelling the country, and maybe the world, and just playing footy!'

* * *

Eastwood were always pretty high on my list. I lived in the area, and my brief sortie in junior rugby was in the Eastwood district. But what tipped me over the line was my father becoming a sponsor of the club when I was in Year 12. I couldn't really go anywhere else *but* Eastwood then. I mean, my old man had his name up on the board there – and for me to play at another club wouldn't have been seen to be right. Anyway, it was just down the road – a good club and close to the heart and soul of a young bloke like me who had grown up in the area. And there were friendly faces everywhere – Joey's Old Boys who had made Eastwood their choice, too – Darren Junee, Andrew Cairns, Tim Kelaher, Tim Dalton and Mark Malloy.

We knew of him at Joey's because he was the gun, the coming star. We knew all the clubs wanted him, and the rugby league clubs wanted him. So I took Scott Johnson, who was the captain of Eastwood (I was coaching), to watch a game at Joey's versus St Ignatius. And Matt didn't do a lot in that game. They cut him out a lot in the backline, which surprised us. But we saw that he was good, so we decided that we wanted him here at Eastwood. And I went down with Johnno again to his house. And we just said, 'Look, Matt, you're a local. Three-quarters of a mile away from Millner [T.G. Millner Field], you know.' And Johnno said, 'Look, if you don't come down I'll come and drag you down by the ear, so we'll see you at seven o'clock on Tuesday night. I'll come and get you.' And Matt came.

Of all the players I have seen come out of the school, he had the most natural talents. He was big, he was strong, but he was also very, very well balanced. He could kick with both feet, he passed beautifully, right to left and left to right, which is very rare. Some of them never learn how to do it. Some of the Test players still don't pass very well left to right. He was so well balanced – ambidextrous, if you like – he could kick goals, place goals, with his left foot. I have seen only one other person do that, so we knew he was very special and he went straight to first grade.

Peter Fenton

I have a vivid early memory of going to a Monday night training session with Eastwood, Colts training. I was seventeen and a half and had no expectation of going straight into grade. Anyhow, I went to training and we were doing a drill where you hit, drive and go to ground, and the bloke who was holding the pad – well, I basically hit him for six. We were always told that when you do stuff, you do it 100 per cent even if it's training. But the coach turned around and started giving me a gobful. 'Who do you think you are?' he said. 'You've hurt this bloke.' I just looked at him. 'Mate, it's a contact sport and he's got the pad.' I ended up walking away, thinking 'Nah, you've got to look for better than this. You've got to try and test yourself, and go higher.' So I turned up on Tuesday for training and did the same thing. Then *I* was holding the pad, and got belted out of the way. I remember finishing the session feeling battered, sore and sorry, and thinking, 'This is where you want to be. This is where you can test yourself.' So, I played first grade straight out of school.

I'm happy to this day with my choice of club. Eastwood was, and is, a friendly and accommodating place in the great rugby tradition. They did some shuffling to fit me in to first grade – with Marty Roebuck switching to five-eighth so that I could play fullback. There were suggestions that this was a coaching 'masterstroke' from Geoff Johnson, but I suspect it was also just Marty being helpful – Marty being that sort of bloke and a big influence on my early career.

* * *

I made my first-grade debut for the club in the final trial of the 1991 season, against Sydney University at Millner Field. I managed a try, and we won 21–3. My premiership debut came the next week, on 29 March, when we pipped Gordon 12–7, again at Millner Field, in wet and greasy conditions. I was three days past my eighteenth birthday. In successive weeks I had taken the big step up – and about all I remember is that, most of the time, it was a lot of fun. It's a happy and enduring memory of my beginnings in senior football. That stepping up to grade after the Saturday afternoons in the cerise and blue with Joey's was genuinely enjoyable. To be honest, it wasn't that difficult. With the speed I had, and the skills I'd developed in the Joey's years, I found I was okay. Those things were always going to hold me in good stead. Maybe it was just the enthusiasm of youth – the fact that I loved my footy, knew I had the ability to catch the ball and run with it, and just went out there on a Saturday arvo and did it. But for all that, I quickly learned that to be a teenager newly arrived on the club scene, and one reputed to be of some potential, playing against some of the 'hard heads' of the competition wasn't going to be anything vaguely approaching plain sailing.

My first season with Eastwood, however, was only brief – although certainly memorable, if not necessarily for all the right reasons. Chris Hawkins, our coach on the Schoolboys tour, had taken over at Gordon – and we played them in the premiership opener. I was seventeen and a half, playing with and against mature blokes in their twenties. In that game against the Highlanders, Coach Hawkins had obviously decided that I should be given a good test. This was serious club football, after all, and if they could rattle the new boy – well, they *would*. Early on, five-eighth Tim Wallace put up a bomb which looked like it might bring rain. Playing fullback, I got myself ready, but I hadn't even positioned my foot for the leap when Gordon inside-centre Matt

Glascott pelted through and wiped me out before I had got within cooee of the descending ball. I must be careful what I say about that, as Matt subsequently married my wife Kate's cousin and so is now 'family'! He reminds me of the incident now and then. The ball had barely returned to earth when the stink started. Welcome to first grade! I didn't get to throw too many punches, but I was in there trying!

To stand side by side with your team-mates in such a situation was part of winning your colours, of course – and the process contin-ued in the dressing room. There, it was especially necessary to win the respect of the forwards, rugby forwards being the way they are – so it was a matter of striding into the room after the game, grab-bing your beer and downing it. You might then sit there for as long as an hour or more after the game, swilling beer. For first-season players – and especially GPS boys, I suspect – there was the need to prove yourself as part of the place and one of the boys. The for-mula for that included getting into the culture of drinking plenty of beers.

How much the world of football has changed! Today in the dressing room after a match it's bananas and jelly snakes, and sports drinks and carbo shots to counter any dehydration with rarely a beer to be seen. Back then you just sat and drank as much beer as you could, and by the time you got out on the town that night, you were well under way.

It all took a bit of getting used to, being a teenager among seasoned club players. It was a big learning curve. We played 'drift' defence at Eastwood; at Joey's, we had always played man-on-man. In an early club match against Sydney Uni, I had an embarrassing moment in a cut-out play in the backline which left the ball sitting there, begging to be intercepted. But I was a greenhorn, and a bit hesitant in this, my second, game of club football. Instead of the ball finishing up in my hands, I finished up in no man's land – and the ball went straight to their Rob Egerton, who raced through and set up a try under the posts. Scott Reid, Eastwood captain, turned to me as we jogged back to take up our positions behind the tryline. 'Have you got that sorted now?' he asked icily. I nodded. 'Well, don't let it happen again!' he said. I have deleted the adjectives that accompanied and considerably lengthened Scott's comments.

It was at Eastwood after one of those early games in 1991 that I had a brush with my father on the question of whether or not he (or fathers generally) should be permitted in the dressing room after matches. Dad loves his football dearly, but in serious sport I honestly believe that change rooms should be out of bounds for anyone but team members. Dad had come into the change room straight after the game, and was standing there chatting, with a beer in his hand. I looked at him and said, 'Mate, what are you doing here?' 'I was invited in,' he said. 'Did *I* invite you in?' I asked. 'No, I was invited in by Jacko [an Eastwood stalwart].' 'Mate, this is *my* room,' I told him. 'Your environment is out there on the verandah, having a beer. This is *my* environment, my place to be myself and to get myself organised after the match. I don't want you coming into the change room again.'

When we talked about it later, Dad commented that another player's father had been in the room. 'Honestly, I don't care about anyone else's father. This is *my* domain, and as far as I'm concerned you don't come in here,' I said. And Dad respected that from then on, which was great.

I think he only ever came into the dressing room twice more in my entire career. The first time was when I ripped a hamstring playing in Auckland in 1995, and he came in to check up on me. I remember giving him the big death stare and asking him to leave.

The last occasion came years later, following my 101st game for New South Wales, when he popped in for a beer. 'It's a proud moment, and I'd like to share it with you,' he said, by way of excuse. I was on the table having physio at the time and it didn't worry me too much. But I didn't ease off. 'Mate, soak it up, because you'll be out the door pretty quickly,' I said. After that, he didn't even come looking for me after I busted my shoulder against the All Blacks in 1998.

People reckon I was hard on him. The boys in the Wallabies and Waratah teams used to really give it to me about it. It's just my strong belief that there has to be that family separation in sport. The dressing room is the environment of the sportsman. After I left the room after matches, Dad and I would always have a great chinwag, which we both enjoyed. He gets invited to all the functions, goes to all the games – he gets his enjoyment that way. And that's how it should be, I reckon. Fathers are spectators, not players. And there are things in the game that are sacrosanct – like the change room.

I respected Matthew's wishes and accepted them, of course. And I always enjoyed our meetings after the game when the dust had settled and he was ready.

Bob Burke

Eastwood has been my club ever since that first season of 1991 – but the truth is that I didn't play that many actual *games* with the club over the years, and the guys there are inclined to give me heaps about it. My contemporaries have even suggested straight-faced that I would need a street directory to find the club. In all those seasons I don't think I even got to the 50 games mark. Nevertheless, the on-and-off time I have spent there has been a whole lot of fun.

Sometimes at fullback, though, it's not fun at all – even in club rugby. Such was the day in 1992 when we were playing Manly, and big Willie Ofahengaue (Willie O) peeled off the back of the scrum, bumped off our halfback, bumped off Richard Harry – no mean feat – ran over the top of Steve Tuynman, and came straight at me, the last line of defence, standing virtually on the Eastwood tryline. My thoughts were roughly along the lines of: 'What the hell do I do here?' This was genuinely terrifying stuff considering that Willie had up a good head of steam. Then, the gods smiled. Someone dived and ankle tapped him and I managed to look a bit of a genius when I sort of finished it off and half-tackled him, halting his progress just short of the line. I hate to think what would have happened if he hadn't been ankle tapped. Scary! My dad also has a memory of Willie O absolutely crunching me in a tackle one day. It's not something I want to think about . . .

As a young fella (which I certainly was back in the early 1990s), it was easier to make a team when you were a back. The demands of backline play aren't quite as physical as thundering away in the forwards. But there are players, forwards, who come straight out of school and into first grade and go onwards and upwards from there. At Eastwood, Steve Tuynman was one – a nineteen-year-old playing in the forwards in a tough era, a great player to have alongside. Richard Harry played with us for a while, as a breakaway. He was always a big lad, but he just got bigger – and he was always destined for the front row. In the backs I played with Brett Papworth (Pappy), a character on and off the field. He could really play the game. He had a fantastic step and great field vision. And Marty Roebuck was an important figure at the club and a bloke with great dedication to whatever he did – whether to his football or to his studies as a physio.

My first season at Eastwood was brief because I banged up my shoulder in a match against Parramatta at Death Valley. It was the same shoulder I had dislocated playing for Australian Schoolboys against the Irish at Limerick. We were trailing, and in some desperation on the last play of the game I put up a little chip. Their little halfback, Allan Holman, fielded the kick and I set myself up to put a real good shot on him. But as I hit him on my left side, things went wrong. As soon as it happened I thought, 'God, that hurt!' That night I couldn't even pull the doona up with my left arm. I was in trouble. In the seasons ahead I guess the injury ledger sort of balanced up for me; in six years at Joey's I had had pretty much a clean slate. Now, there was the shoulder injury – with more problems lying in wait for me in the unknown future.

The shoulder problem of the 1991 season took me into unfamiliar territory. I had never missed a longish sequence of football, but now I was out with a crook wing and, after surgery to repair the damage, having daily physio with a friend named Mal Brown. When I got hurt, I had no idea what I was in for. The operation was a big one, and afterwards I had my arm in a sling for six weeks. When I finally came out of the sling I couldn't straighten my elbow. I eventually got over it, but the amount of muscle wastage was quite unbelievable. My mates had a laugh one day when I showed them my shoulder and left bicep. Not a muscle to be seen! It looked like I had never played sport in my life.

I was a young, fit (generally) bloke, and a good eater and fair drinker – and right through the wait to get myself right I kept doing those things. To put it mildly, I finished up as a bit of a Shrek. I was massive – to the point that I couldn't fit into my clothes. For a long time afterwards, I kept a pair of strides I bought during that time as a sort of cautionary memento. Every time I saw them, I'd think: 'I'm never going to get *that* fat again!'

It was genuinely embarrassing. Around that time, once my arm had mended, I scored a scholarship to the Australian Institute of Sport (AIS). I had the distinct impression that the coach down there was looking at me and thinking, 'Is this bloke a prop?' I was supposed to be a fast-running back, but my skinfold tests took me way ahead of some of the forwards. Basically I needed to join the Chub Club, as it's known today, and lose it!

The pause in my career at least gave me a brief chance to taste life outside football. For a short while I did the university thing, partying and staying out like most people of that age do. When I think about it, football took me away from a lot of 'normal' things – from eighteenth birthday parties and 21sts and weddings. I missed a lot of them. There are no great regrets, although it would have been nice to have more of a social life while still playing sport!

There came a day when my old man was driving me to uni one morning and I could feel my belly bulging out over my belt. 'Mate, it's time to get on the stepper,' I said quietly to myself. 'This isn't you!'

My time at the AIS in Canberra (in 1991–92) was a valuable step in my progression as a football player, albeit a bit of a junket. It wasn't as hard as it should have been – and I have no doubt that the guys who go there today work a lot harder than we did back then. I remember the strength and conditioning guys asking us: 'What do you want to do with your sporting prowess?' And the response from blokes like me, playing what was then very much an amateur game, wasn't what it would be today. I settled for one or two weights sessions a week, plus an occasional run. The coaches were pushing the case for four or five weights sessions a week – but there was a theory abroad that if blokes of my age did that, we would have been as big as Arnold Schwarzenegger by the time we were 21. So, we didn't. Only with professionalism did the really hard training yakka come to rugby.

But my experience in Canberra taught me about lifting techniques, nutrition and all that kind of stuff, and that was positive. And I think it helped me through university, because a lot of what we did at the AIS overlapped with my Human Movement course.

In my first two seasons of senior football, the new reality of injuries with which I had to contend probably did me a bit of a favour in a funny way, helping to toughen me for what lay ahead. I gradually gained confidence as I came back after the shoulder problem and an early setback of a fractured cheekbone – and into season 1992 I was playing well enough to win selection in the North Harbour v South Harbour game, and then in the City First side. But I had damaged the PCL (posterior cruciate ligament) in my knee, which left me with a knee that sort of slid backwards and forwards, and I missed that game (replaced by David Knox) – threatening my chance of playing for New South Wales against Fiji. Deep down, I probably realised I wasn't ready to play for the Waratahs at the open level yet. My feelings were very mixed. On the one hand, I was filthy that my chance of a first Waratah jersey was in doubt because of injury; while at the same time I was thinking that maybe it was for the best, and that if the opportunity came again another day I would be a more mature player by then. It was all happening a bit too quickly for me, in fact. In the May 1992 issue of *Australian Rugby News* I was tagged as the 'find of the season' and was even tipped as a 'dark horse selection' for the Wallaby trip to Ireland and Wales at the end of the year.

In my own mind I was only just beginning my journey, only just beginning to make my way. But for all the doubts, the first big chance lay just around the corner . . .

* * *

It was in May 1992 that I made what was a fleeting debut for New South Wales against Fiji at Concord. I think the biggest thrill was getting kitted out. It was like Christmas! All of us received a bag, a tracksuit, a pair of running shoes and a pair of football boots. Big boots, in my case. That was rugby back then – some gear and maybe a couple of free tickets to the game. This was a BIG occasion for me – to be stepping up to play with the likes of Tim Gavin and Phil Kearns and, especially, to be wearing the sky-blue jersey for the first time. But the boots were a bit of a disaster. From the very beginning, I had always been particular about my footwear. Now I had this pair with *plenty* of toe room. 'How the hell am I going to run in them?' I thought.

It had been a bumpy week. Training with the Waratahs at North Sydney Oval No. 2 on the Thursday night before the game I pulled my hip flexor. I could barely run, barely push off the mark – the leg just wasn't working properly. But I kept quiet about it. No way was I going to give up my spot now that the chance had come. So, it was a matter of 'grin and bear it' at the training session and then get some urgent physio to try to get it right.

As for the match itself, it was probably a case of if you'd blinked, you'd have missed me. I was on the bench and, like every first-timer, I was terrified. With about ten minutes to go, I clumped out on to the field in what felt like clown shoes to replace Darren Junee. I don't recall too much about what happened, but I remember being thrilled just to be there. My biggest impression was the speed of the game. It was a brief experience of the big game that gave me a taste of how quickly things happened at that level – and how hard were the hits (especially when you play Fiji!).

A week later I copped a really bad 'cork' playing club football and was knocked out of the running for the match against the All Blacks. It was a lucky break! I honestly wasn't ready for that. As a kid you can play up to a certain level – but the next step up can be a long way. At international level the blokes are massive and the intensity is enormous. As a spectator, I remember that match clearly (New Zealand v New South Wales): a wet one down at Concord, and the sight of Marty Roebuck getting absolutely smashed from a quick lineout. 'Mmm. It might be a little fortunate that I'm not out there today,' I thought.

I was still no more than a kid in 1992 – and acceptance of that hit home hard after I played fullback for the Australian Under 21s against New Zealand Colts in a curtain-raiser to the Second Test Australia v All Blacks. The call-up for the game had come in the wake of my playing for the Emerging Wallabies v Scotland in Hobart – a game that ended in a 24-all draw – and then for the national 21 side against the Barbarians. In Brisbane the prospect of facing the Junior 'Blacks', 61–9 victors over the Aussies the previous year, was daunting enough in its own right. I was nineteen and still growing – and to get an up-close and personal view of what was virtually the Junior All Blacks was, to say the least, challenging. We lost a spiteful game 20–10. My memory of that entire night is more general than specific – although I recall getting into clear ground at one point when I took a pass from our outside-centre. I ran about 30 metres while sizing up what to do, and finally looped a moderate pass over to one of our wingers – who dropped it.

The incident was thrown back at me when I was down at the AIS the following year. At a get-together, head coach David Clark, in discussing that game, virtually declared that we would have beaten New Zealand that night if I had chipped and chased. It was the first time I had really been put on the spot – blamed for something that had happened (or didn't happen) in a football match. I remember thinking, 'Hang on a sec. There were plenty of other times in that game when other blokes could have lifted *their* games . . . taken different options.' I wasn't over the moon at being singled out.

The main memory of that night is of later, of watching the Test match from the sideline – an awesome experience. Viewing a top-level match from that close is pretty remarkable. Even television, with its up-close cameras, tends to sanitise the experience a bit. Up close you hear every grunt, every smack of big bodies at full charge and the whooof of air being knocked out of blokes. It was a tough Test in which Australia's Paul Carozza had his nose badly broken. As a teenager looking on that night, I asked myself the inevitable question: 'How would I go if I was thrown into this?'

That season was a valuable taste of the 'big time' before my career settled back on to a more even keel of weekly appearances with Eastwood. We won our last six games, but failed to make the semis by a whisker. I missed making the Wallaby squad to the UK, turned down an offer to go to Queensland and play fullback for the Reds, and in October was added to the 1993 national squad – an indication that a year of real possibilities lay just ahead. In December there was a flurry of media support for me to be flown to the UK to replace Wallaby skipper Michael Lynagh, who had been injured on tour. Randwick's veteran back Lloyd Walker got the nod instead, and in one of my early declarations to the media I said: 'I wasn't pinning my hopes on it, but if I had been chosen I would have been over the moon.' To be very honest, I didn't ever think I was going to be picked. I had played some relatively good football in the club competition, but we missed the semifinals that year and when it comes to representative teams it can sometimes be a case of 'out of sight, out of mind'. I had had a taste of rep stuff in 1992, though, and I was happy just to get a mention and to get a game at that level. Things were good – I was happy to be a young adult and pretty content with the point I had reached in my life.

Formal summer training was non-existent back then. These were carefree and happy-go-lucky amateur days in rugby, and it wasn't until early February that there was any sort of collective training. I used to do bits and pieces with some mates – go to Palm Beach on a Sunday morning and run up some sandhills and then have a game of touch footy. But basically all of that was an excuse to get on the drink at night. Did I watch my diet? Well, no. Everyone just lived their lives and got by on their natural ability.

Chapter 3

LUCKY SEVENS

Sevens football, the racy, pacy cut-down version of the real thing, came into my life in a big way in early 1993. I played in a series of tournaments, culminating in the Rugby World Cup tournament in Scotland in April.

That year I was picked in the NSW team for the Western Samoan Sevens – in a side coached by Glen Ella. The star of the tournament was a bloke named Lolani Koko, a 110-kilogram winger who either ran around the opposition or trampled straight over the top of them. He wasn't fussed either way – and he was devastating. We got bundled out along the way, and I got a taste of what to expect any time we lined up against the Samoans, Tongans or Fijians. The crowd roared with laughter each time one of them came up with a massive hit, which was often enough.

The next time I played Sevens at a serious level – just after the Samoan trip – I finished up in the forwards, at hooker! It was a match in Terrigal (with the Sydney team) and I did all those things that hookers do. I packed in scrums, and threw the ball into line-outs. It was great fun, actually. I can't imagine what hookers make such a fuss about. It was one of those Sevens days when you played a lot of football and ran yourself into the ground, but enjoyed yourself along the way. Sevens were big that year – and by the time the next tournament came around, the Canberra Festival Tournament, I was in the Australian team for the first time, along with the likes of Sam Payne, Illie Tabua and Jim Williams. Western Samoa bumped us out in the semis, with Koko scoring two of the tries.

My keenest memory of the Hong Kong Invitation Sevens that followed is of Jason Little, one of the premier centres in Australian rugby, doing a war dance – with the Fijian side! Fiji needed an extra player and, under the rules of the competition, were allowed to pick someone from one of the beaten sides, which included Australia. Jason was the first white man I saw do the Fijian version of the haka. The other thing I'll never forget about the Hong Kong Sevens experience is the noise that greets any Australian side. Tim Horan had warned me about it. Apparently, there had been an incident some years before when an Aussie had decked an opposing Taiwanese player during a match in which the Aussies whipped Taiwan by 50 or so points. This incident had ensured that subsequent Australian teams always met with a hot reception. And so it was – a venomous reception. This was the lead-up tournament to the World Sevens in Scotland, albeit minus big guns such as Michael Lynagh and David Campese.

The inaugural World Sevens of 1993 in Edinburgh was the hardest tournament I have ever played in. By the time the dust had settled we had played ten games (I had played nine out of ten matches) and we had gone awfully close to winning it. England beat our young side 21–17 in the final after we had pipped Ireland 21–19 in the semi. A major memory of the decider is that our 1991

World Cup heroes, David Campese and Michael Lynagh, were below par as the Poms sent their big blokes charging at us. The six foot eight backrower, Tim Rodber, broke through at halfway and picked up pace. I was running alongside Campo and I looked at him, thinking: 'Mate, are you going to make this tackle?' The look I got at about the 22 line answered my question. 'Nah, he's all yours.' And I thought, 'You're kidding!' Footage of the match shows me diving at the big bloke near the line and us sliding over together. It was my first experience of Campo and his tackling technique. One of the big standouts on that tour was Tonga's Semi Taupeaafe, a fantastic Sevens player, who went on to play for New South Wales in 1993–98.

I came back from the Scottish Sevens experience in May to a run-on debut for New South Wales, at outside-centre against Transvaal in a Super 10 match at Waratah Stadium. In that game I got absolutely drilled by their No. 7, a bloke named Ian McDonald. We pulled a move called 'Oi', in which the outside-centre runs inside and takes a pass from the five-eighth, bidding to beat the sliding defence. Suffice to say that McDonald didn't fall for the lie – and crunched me. Welcome to the big time! I remember the moment: I slipped past François Pienaar, but the angle I was running at coincided exactly with the waiting McDonald – and he absolutely snapped me. I kept the ball, though, and managed to place it back for the forwards. But I was shaky all right, and when I managed to get up without the stumble-and-fall-down thing I was pretty happy. Marty Roebuck was at fullback that day and calling the plays. He reckoned later that my eyes were going around like poker machine reels! 'Mate, we mightn't call that move next time. What do you reckon?' he said. 'Probably a good idea,' I mumbled. We got beaten 10–3 – and I got the '3' via a penalty goal – being thrown the ball after Marty had missed four from four and I'd missed three from four. I was nervous, and even though it was successful my kick showed it.

Calling the match for Channel 10 that day was David Fordham, brother of the man who was later to become my manager, John Fordham. My strike on the ball was a lot less than great, and as I learned later David's call went something along the lines of: 'Well, that's probably one of the worst kicks I've seen in international rugby . . . But . . . oh, it's gone over . . . *Great work* from Matt Burke!' I shared the joke with David when I met up with him a couple of years later. 'The first time I kicked for New South Wales you gave it to me,' I reminded him. We both laughed. David recalled it well.

The day after the Transvaal match I was sore, but I was keen to play the club game against Easts and was happy I did when we beat them 25–21 with a late try. I think being able to back up after a tough game is an important quality for any footballer of serious intent – an important step along the track in the learning process, adding a layer, both physically and mentally.

Five-eighth Tim Wallace was knocked out early in the match against Transvaal – bringing Scott Bowen into the game for 60 minutes or so. Scott had already played 80 minutes for NSW Under 21s in a curtain-raiser that day. Tim fronted up for his club, Gordon, the following day – and I suspect that NSW coach Greg Smith would have been quietly posing the question: 'Where do your allegiances lie, your state or your club?' Anyhow, both Scott and I played the next Super 10 game, against Wellington, the following week – and I finished up with a hat trick of tries (we won 56–11) and revelled in the opportunity to play outside Scott. It was the beginning of a good partnership in rugby. He was without doubt one of the best five-eighths I played with, a guy who could run the backline like no one I had seen before. He had a great passing game and a great kicking game – and at No. 10 he could tackle, which was becoming increasingly important the way the game was evolving. That game against Wellington was a big confidence builder for us both.

As my career moved into this different orbit I suddenly found myself playing with the big boys – the likes of Phil Kearns, Tony Daly, Tim Gavin, Warwick Waugh, Campo in bits and pieces – blokes I had watched winning the World Cup only a couple of years before when I was a teenager sitting in the lounge room at home and wondering how the hell Campese had passed that ball to Tim Horan.

I guess I was a kid who never really thought he'd go that far. Now I was edging up, and getting a close-up view and an understanding of the intensity with which these sort of men played. I came into their company with a mixture of awe and respect. I found there was quite a big segregation thing between the senior blokes and the up-and-comers. It sure is different today! The young blokes coming in at senior level today give the older blokes all the stick in the world. It's unbelievable. There is respect, sure – but they certainly throw it out there, too. There is no shortage of confidence – and that's good. But as the song says, the fundamental things still apply. For all their confidence, today's young blokes are footballers of limited experience, working out who they are and what they have to offer – and there is still the need for them to rely on the older players to provide direction.

A decade ago I guess I had confidence within myself. But there was no way I would hand out stick to the older blokes! These days the likes of Kearns, Richard Harry, Michael Brial, Jason Little and John Eales are close personal friends. But when I started in senior football they were so high up in the pecking order they were just about out of reach. The senior blokes stuck with the senior blokes, and the juniors with the juniors – and we just didn't talk with the others much. Maybe it was just the way it had always been: do the hard yards, prove yourself, build your own reputation, then eventually you would be 'in'.

At the time of my arrival in the NSW team the coach was Greg Smith; his assistant was the Randwick legend, Jeff Sayle. Greg was a strange bloke with a dry, sarcastic sense of humour who really took some figuring out. Phil Kearns was interviewed for a questionnaire once and in answer to the question: 'Who is the funniest person you have met in world rugby?' he replied: 'Greg Smith.' The rest of us were all scratching our heads about that, trying to work it out. Maybe there was a comedian called Greg Smith we hadn't heard of? Surely he didn't mean *our* Greg Smith, the coach whom we considered to be quite bizarre? But Kearnsie *did* mean him, all right. And as we all got to know him more, there was at least *some* sense in it. Smith did have a certain humour about him, but in the early days I don't think anyone knew how to take him. We were all bamboozled.

One day he sat us all down in the dressing room for a talk. 'Do you know,' he declared, 'that one in twenty blokes is gay?' He then said that because there were twenty of us sitting in the room, the likelihood was that, on the law of averages, one of us was gay. Everyone had a bit of a chuckle. 'And I think it's Matt Burke,' he said. 'Look at his hairstyle!' Then he turned on his heel and walked out. Talk about strange.

On another occasion he came up to Andrew Blades just as Bladesie was taking off his shirt before having a shower. 'Mate,' said the coach. 'If I was you, I wouldn't let the selectors see you with your shirt off!' It was often that way: Greg would make some comment, and half an hour later we'd still be thinking, 'What the hell was *that* about?'

Greg's early death was a tragedy, and I'm happy to say that in the latter part of our association we had a good friendship. But he was an odd bloke at times, and loved playing mind games. Season 1994 was an example. When I had a good opportunity of being picked for the Australian Sevens side in 1994, he said to me: 'Go away with the Sevens – and you don't get chosen for New South Wales.' Suddenly I was confronted with a big decision. My main aim was to play high-level XV rugby for New South Wales and, on the spot, that was the course I chose – at which point the obvious thing to do was to wear Australian Sevens rugby gear at NSW training the next day, just to make a point. Which I did.

Greg was always talking about mental and physical toughness and being better prepared than the opposition. Coming into the return game against Queensland he called me over at training one day. 'Mate, how do you think you're going?' he asked. Before I had a chance to say much, he was into me. 'This isn't schoolboy rugby anymore. You just don't run around blokes like Jason Little and Tim Horan.' Greg was playing his mind games . . .

One cold training night at North Sydney Oval No. 2 he pulled me aside during the warm-up. 'Mate, can I have a quick word?' We walked together across that wintry ground, Greg with his arms folded across his chest and saying nothing. I was thinking, 'What's this all about?' Eventually he got to it: 'Mate, big game this week.' I was thinking, 'Yes, well, it is . . .' and so I agreed with him. 'Yeah, nah, *big* game.' There was another silence, then he said: 'Yes, a big game.' That was it. 'Burkey, send your mate over,' he said, meaning our five-eighth Scott Bowen. I heard later that Greg had said the same thing to Scott. Greg was funny like that – sometimes he didn't say much at all, and other times the smart and articulate former schoolteacher could take you apart verbally.

There was another day in 1994 when he really gave it to me. We were at a recovery session in the pool at Riverview College. 'Matt, can I see you afterwards?' he said quietly. But it was more a direction than a question. So, after I showered, I went to see him and he asked me in a very laid-back, laconic sort of way: 'How do you think you're playing this year?' I thought I was playing okay. I mentioned a few of my performances and told him that I thought I had increased some of my skills. He just looked at me and said, 'Mate, you're playing like a ——, a ——. He said it five times. I was a bit shocked. After I had gathered my thoughts, I said, 'Well, thanks for your honesty.' And he just walked away.

This was on the eve of the game against Queensland when I switched from outside-centre to fullback. I ended up playing a pretty good game against the Reds. Maybe the coach's verbal attack had provided me with some sort of spur. Even today, I don't really know.

Assistant Coach Sayle, one of the great characters of the game, was just the opposite of Smith – a fantastic bloke who talked in jokes and riddles and seemed to enjoy every moment of what he was doing. Sayley, was the forwards' coach, so I didn't have all that much to do with him, but he was good to be around – he kept you entertained *all* the time. His favourite saying was 'What a beauteeeee!', and that got a big workover. A truly passionate rugby man, he helped to balance the ledger in those sometimes strange days under Greg Smith. Sayley was one of those blokes who, if there happened to be a 21st birthday or engagement party at a hotel or motel where we were staying, would inevitably end up with the microphone, telling jokes and entertaining total strangers.

Greg Smith the football coach was ahead of his time. He came up with a concept of sequence plays, which would be along the lines of: 'A scrum here, work to a point *here* after putting on a move, then get the forwards to take it on a bit, then we'll head further the same way with the forwards taking it on again, and then we'll sweep it back the other way, via the backs.' This was a pretty regimented approach, and a lot of people in the game had problems with it – in line with a more traditional belief that the way to play rugby was to let it flow, to play what was in front of you. Smith started his strictly ordered methods with New South Wales and tried to implement it as Australian coach from 1996 – sequence one, sequence two, etc. Two years later it became the norm in rugby – but I think that with New South Wales, in particular, Greg Smith hammered a good thing too much, and too early.

In 1996, when I was working for a time at Eastwood Rugby Club, Greg rang me seeking a reference. He was going for the Australian job. Bob Dwyer was leaving the position after the 1995 World Cup and Greg, after all, was a relatively successful NSW coach. 'I would like to use you as a referee,' he said. And I thought to myself, 'Holy shit!' At the time I certainly had some reservations about whether he could take the step up to the Australian job. This was tricky. If I knocked him back (which was probably my inclination) and he got the job, what would that then mean for me? In the end, I wrote a very carefully worded piece. His final words to me on the phone were these: 'Mate, just make sure it's a good one. Otherwise I'll rip it up.' Regrettably, I didn't keep a copy of the reference, but it was 'diplomatic' – along the lines of: 'Greg is a very honest man. He works hard, calls a spade a spade and I'm sure that any job he does will be up to the standard he set with New South Wales – and that hopefully his coaching record will continue.' I ended up playing fullback for him that year – so I can only assume the reference was okay!

Chapter 4
GOLDEN DAYS

In mid-1993 the rugby media was starting to speculate about me as a possible Test player – a winger. It was the start of something that followed me through my career. I never thought of myself as a jack-of-all-trades in the game, yet down the years that's pretty much the way it turned out. And maybe it developed that way because I was always pretty easygoing and didn't stick up for myself enough. Being the 'nice guy' no doubt saw me shifted around more than should have happened. I think too often it was a case of 'Okay, then, let's ask Burkey. He's pretty low-key and there won't be any dramas.' So it was that I pirouetted around from fullback to centre to wing (occasionally). Probably I should have stayed at fullback the whole time and just contested that position, but having played a fair bit at 13 I found that pretty easy as well.

In those early days, as my career was growing, I wasn't

position-specific. Even with the club side I'd play fullback or centre. I think I saw myself then as a centre – I liked being up there in the action, as you are at 13. At fullback it's more a matter of choice – sit back and be a goal-kicker-fullback, or get in there and do the attacking work as well. I think a player's greatest handicap can lie in being too versatile. It's fantastic for a coach to have people he can juggle around from position to position, but it can be the worst thing for a player. For a back like me, not only did I have to learn all the moves – at times I had to learn them from three different positions (wing, centre, fullback). It can be unsettling and arduous. It's got to be easier, I reckon, to be a one-position player, learning all the intricacies and nuances of that one job.

The representative season to the point where I was being touted for Test duty had been something of a rollercoaster ride. In the New South Wales v Wellington game I benefited from the wonderful service provided by Scott Bowen, scored three tries and was voted 'Man of the Match'. This match, a week before we played our 'old enemy', Queensland, was a great confidence booster – producing eight tries and a thumping 57–11 win. But wouldn't you know it, on the big night at Ballymore the Reds hit top gear and thrashed us 37–15. I'll have more to say about the much-discussed matter of New South Wales' problems with Queensland over that season. The only bright note of the trip north was my back nine at The Palms, Sanctuary Cove on a golf day. I shot a one under par 34. Maybe we all should have stuck to golf on that particular trip.

My selection in the NSW team to play South Africa in July 1993 was something special. This was a team coming back on to the international scene after years of isolation – a team with a great rugby tradition, and one undoubtedly on the rise. The South Africans' cockiness was apparent the day we faced them. But we played very well before a crowd of 16,000 at Concord, squeaking home 29–28 against an international opponent to keep the flag flying, considering that Australia were the current world champions.

The thing I remember most from the game was winger Alistair Murdoch's 50 metres try down the left side. It came from a mistake. Playing the centres, I was supposed to pass the ball to David Campese. I've got to say that Campo didn't show a whole lot of interest in the play and so the ball went loose. David Fordham, calling the game on television, nominated the pass as about the worst he had seen in his life. But my centre partner, Richard Tombs, snared the ball, passed over the top, and Murdoch raced away and scored in the corner. Beauty! To me it was an early example of how a genius player like Campese, always unpredictable, could make life difficult even for his own team. But we scored anyway in a game that I have always remembered as a pretty special one.

A few days later, I played fullback in the Australian 21s side that thumped New Zealand Colts 31–8 at Eden Park. I got smashed in that game – hurt a couple of ribs and was on the deck for a while. In really tough conditions in Auckland, with a strong wind sending rain squalls sweeping over the ground, we played very well. But there was no sense that day of playing the All Blacks. They were just a junior team, albeit a good one. The only time you play the All Blacks is . . . when you play the All Blacks.

When I was overlooked for the Bledisloe Cup match in New Zealand in July, the respected rugby writer Phil Wilkins generously described me in the Sydney press as 'one of the three most mercurial players in Australian rugby union'. But he added the sting in the tail: '. . . the interpretation of Burke's absence from the team is undoubtedly the selectors' desire for the gifted back to offer evidence of a harder, more consistently tenacious attitude in performance.' Phew! I don't know that my career had ever been analysed to such a degree before. The layman's interpretation of that seemed to be something along the lines that I needed a red-hot poker put up my backside! Bob Dwyer was the Australian coach at the time, and at that stage of my career he used to say that to me all the time. He reckoned that I had the 'Eastwood lope', and that I had probably caught the complaint from Marty Roebuck and a few others. Bob's message really was about 'getting involved' in matches, not sitting back and just letting the game flow, but being proactive and *making* things happen. It was a strong and true message – then and now. The more involved a footballer gets in a match, the better he plays, although there's a greater risk of making mistakes, too.

Looking back, I think I had a couple of problems at that time as I made the transition from 'schoolboy' footballer to something approaching a 'professional' player. One of them was the jack-of-all-trades factor I have already mentioned. What was I? A fullback? A winger? A centre? The other problem was my fairly relaxed attitude to playing rugby. Fundamentally, I was just happy to play some footy and have a beer and enjoy myself on a Saturday night. If there was the occasional bonus of some free gear – well, all the better. I was just happy to be a part of it.

But on 14 August 1993 I took my next step – maybe you could call it a giant leap – as a footballer. I was picked on the reserves bench for the Australian team to play South Africa in the second Test at Ballymore. It was hard to believe that I was suddenly to be in a gold jersey and among these blokes who were legends of Australian rugby. I remember introducing myself to Tim Horan.

'Ah, g'day, Tim. How're you going? I'm Matt Burke.' 'Yeah, g'day,' he said. 'I'm Tim Horan.' Well, I *knew* that.

It's very hard to describe what it was like to be handed my first Wallaby jersey. I became Wallaby No. 710 – the 710th Wallaby ever to pull on the jersey. So, considering the 100-plus years of Wallaby football it's a pretty rare and special club. As I write these words the count is still only up to about 790. So, in my time, fewer than 1000 have been part of that amazing little group. For me the feeling never changed from that first time back in 1993. I thought about it years later as I neared the end of my career, with 81 Tests on the register – and it was still, and always, the jersey that I played for.

I didn't actually get on to the paddock on the day of my first Test, although things got quite exciting towards the end. Marty Roebuck played fullback, and with a couple of minutes to go he hurt a shoulder. I was warming up and thinking, here's a chance to get on and win a cheap Test cap, put my name in the annals of Australian rugby . . . all that kind of stuff. But Marty battled on to fulltime and so I didn't quite get there. It was an exciting time; we won the game after they had taken the first Test in Sydney, and that made it even better.

In retrospect, maybe it was a good thing I didn't get into the action that day. For a newcomer, there were new moves to be learned in a fairly short time. I remember one called 'Ballymore' and another called 'Queensland' that were quite intricate – and as a reserve I had to learn them from the perspective of wing, centre and fullback. The moves were similar, but with subtle differences, and I spent most of one night learning them. I was quite proud of myself. The next morning, I rattled them off to Scott Bowen (our playmaker at No. 10) with great confidence. 'Mate, how about this? Ballymore: A, B, C, D; Queensland: W, X, Y, Z.' There was a bit of a pause and Scott just looked at me. 'No, mate,' he said. 'It's the other way around.' Back to the drawing board . . .

Playing for Sydney against the South Africans before the third Test, I survived what was probably one of the most dangerous moments of my career. In those days you weren't protected when you were in the air, and when I went up for a high ball a bloke took my legs out from under me and I came crashing down on my neck. It was a pretty horrible moment and it's amazing, really, that I didn't hurt myself more than I did, although I've had something of a dodgy neck ever since. Then, in the lead-up to the third Test in Sydney, for which I was again picked on the reserves bench, I suffered a bad cramp in my right calf, couldn't straighten it out properly and wasn't able to train for the next three days. So I shaped up for the Test with a crook neck, a dodgy leg and with virtually no training under my belt!

To make it worse, on Test day at Sydney Football Stadium, Saturday, 21 August, I almost brought myself undone before a ball had been kicked in anger. Those were the days when teams used to run out with souvenir footballs and boot them into the crowd. I trotted out and a bloke hollering and waving from the top tier of the stand caught my attention. 'Up here! Up here!' he called to me. 'I can do that,' I thought. Well, we had warmed up, but I wasn't warmed up enough to boot a ball 60 metres. I reefed the ball and went within a millimetre or so of ripping my right hamstring. I walked back clutching my leg and muttering to myself, 'Stupid bloody idiot! You'll never do *that* again!'

This day I made it on to the field as a left winger when Damian Smith took a knock after 34 minutes and came off concussed. And what do I remember of my Test match debut? Well, not very much of those few minutes before halftime. I got a good shot on their hooker Uli Schmidt, who used to hang around on the outside . . . or did he get a good shot on me? What I *do* know is that we both hit the ground hard and I was winded. But I bounced straight up, saying to myself: 'Don't show anyone you're hurt. Just get on with it.' Almost on the stroke of halftime I cleaned up a kick through, put it on my left foot, and it rolled and rolled and finally went dead. The hooter sounded, and I was happy enough about that.

Early in the second half there came a moment that I won't ever be allowed to forget. At my farewell lunch many years later, in August 2004, the film clip was trotted out (again!) and shown with some glee. Several times. I had positioned myself to field a high kick, out near the left touchline. With the ball in the air, Marty Roebuck was on my inside. 'Let's go, mate,' he called. 'We'll run it, we'll run it.' And I just forgot the basic thing that you tell all school kids: you've got to *catch* the ball first before you do anything with it. My mind was just galloping too fast . . .

I dropped the ball cold. It squirted through my hands, bounced once and went into touch. And 40,000 voices groaned: '*Oh, my God*' – a truly terrible sound. Maybe the worst thing was that I had goofed *right* in front of the Australian bench, in full view of the coaching staff and my peers. I looked across and there was Dan Crowley with his hands around his throat, making a choking noise. Welcome to international rugby union!

I gathered myself together and attempted to refocus, and thankfully things improved. We ended up winning the game 19–12 – and I was probably only one pass short of scoring a debut Test match try. David Campese put a pass over to Tim Horan, who carried it on and scored in the corner. I was there, one pass away, if needed. We had won the game – and the series – and I had survived my first Test match.

That night, at the traditional post-Test dinner, I was mindful of the fact that I had to play for Eastwood the next day (against Parramatta). Sometime after the dinner, with some reluctance, I was about to hop in a taxi outside Jackson's on George and take myself home, in view of the fact that there was some football to be played the next day, when a bunch of my mates turned up. 'C'mon, Burkey. You've got to have a drink. You've just played your first Test match!' So I ditched the cab and went out, and got home extremely late, and significantly the worse for wear. Never before had I done that before a game. The next day I knew why: it's the hardest thing in the world to play football when you feel like I did that day.

The match was played at T.G. Millner Field. After I kicked off, they booted it straight back to me and we went pass . . . pass . . . pass, and scored in the corner. As the try was scored I was standing back on the halfway line. It was as close as I could get. I took the shot at goal and it missed by about twenty metres. About then I was thinking that it wasn't such a great idea to get on the squirt the night before a game, but that maybe I would be shown a bit of leniency because of the circumstances. Fortunately, we won.

Eastwood's steady progress that year helped me to stay an Australian player, I'm sure. It was a semifinal season for us – and could have been even better. In the minor semifinal against Warringah we led 12–3 with five minutes to go – and got beaten 13–12! But playing finals football at least means you stay in the selectors' minds. And so when the team was read out for the tour of Canada and France, the name 'M. Burke (Eastwood)' was among the chosen. I was picked as one of four centres, along with Tim Horan, Jason Little and Pat Howard. However, when we were in camp, Tim Kelaher dropped out with an injury and the selectors brought in Queenslander Ryan Constable and shifted me to fullback.

A big part of every rugby season then (and now) was the end-of-season medal – back then, the Rothman's Medal; these days, it's the Catchpole Medal. It's traditionally a let-your-hair-down night. I went along, of course, and managed to be among the five or six players and stayers at the end of the night, at the Fishbowl at the top of Kings Cross having a drink which somehow dragged on until sunrise. I was then an Australian player, soon bound for a major overseas tour.

At seven o'clock or so on that Friday morning, someone had the bright idea of running out into Darlinghurst Road and scaring the early morning commuters. It seemed like a hilarious thing to do at the time. We took it in turns. When it was my turn to sprint like an idiot out in front of a car, I looked up to catch the look of surprise/terror on the face of the driver. Bad choice. The driver of my selected vehicle happened to be Bob Dwyer, the Australian coach with whom I was soon to tour the world. This was my introduction to touring life: seven o'clock on a weekday morning, dressed in a dinner suit and trying to scare the Australian coach as he headed off to work. Thankfully, Bob saw the humour in it – and smiled. We have since had a chuckle about it.

Chapter 5

THE WIDE, WONDERFUL WORLD OF RUGBY

My first tour with a senior Australian team started in Long Beach, California – and it was a fantastic kickoff. I was twenty, just a fresh-faced kid in that senior team, and my boyish appearance had me in real trouble if it should happen that I fancied a beer. The legal drinking age in the United States was 21, and I looked about seventeen. The team was sponsored by XXXX beer, but I was actually barred from attending a rugby function one night because I was under age. It was one way of getting out of a promotional obligation, I suppose.

The place was hot and friendly. We trained at the University of California, and one morning after a run a few of us went to the 'varsity shop to pick up some souvenir gear. The bus back to our hotel was due to leave at eleven o'clock, and by the time we got through the checkout it was ten past. 'No problems,' we thought. 'They'll wait.' But there was no bus. A little way on was another bunch of Wallabies, sitting on the kerb. All of us were victims of the SS Rule – the Stiff Shit Rule – the basic message of which is: if you're not there on time – well, stiff shit. Via a succession of lifts from some friendly locals – a maintenance bloke with a 'ute, some Tongan guys with a van, and a young girl who was sweet-talked to the extent that she drove us all the way back to the hotel – we made it 'home'. The girl only had a five-seater, though, so Tim Horan had to make his own way back. The SS Rule applied.

We played an American XV in blistering conditions, the temperature topping 38 degrees Celsius, at a place called Riverside. My most vivid memory of the game is of halftime, which we spent sitting in front of big fans called 'Cool Zones' that blew a beautiful chill mist over the players as we gulped down our water. It was one of those days when the heat made it almost dangerous to play. Anywhere else the game may have been called off. We won the match narrowly (26–22), but I think it took all of us who played two or three days to recover fully.

Canada quickly provided a serious contrast. That part of the tour started with a match against Canada B. On match morning, my roommate, Rod McCall, came back from early breakfast laughing. 'What's so funny?' I asked him. Rod just opened up the curtains – and it was sleeting. I played that day, and it was a new experience – so cold in the second half that our mouths and cheeks froze and we couldn't talk, so it became increasingly difficult to make the game 'calls'. We won 40–3, and the papers talked of us going from 'fire to ice'.

Despite the cold, we had a mighty time in Canada. The hospitality was great, and the memories are all good ones. There were some hilarious moments, too. One day, Coach Dwyer blew up at training, as used to happen now and then. Bob is a bloke who could certainly get animated on a football field, and if he had a go at you and you came back at him he would just keep blowing up, even stronger. Afterwards he was always happy to discuss things and take on board an alternative point of view. With Bob, there were no grudges.

On the Canadian tour, Damian Smith, Scott Bowen, Barry Lea and myself were the four young blokes. Bob would crack the whip on us at training, trying to bring out the potential he believed we had. There were plenty of blow-ups from the coach, and we kept score. We would walk back during a backline session, ready for the next move, and I'd look up at Barry and hold up three fingers; Barry would look at Scott and hold up two fingers – and so it went. We all kept score on the number of times we were blown up. Each time we made a blue, we knew it was going to be a little worse for the next bloke who made a mistake. On one particular afternoon before the Test match against Canada (a game I wasn't selected for), things weren't going too well and the coach had been giving us a rev-up. I was running at outside-centre at the time (I had been picked at that position for the tour) and the next move was a 'double cut'; in which 10 misses 12 and passes to 13, and 13 misses 15 and passes to 14. I caught my ball okay and threw the pass to Barry Lea on the wing. It was a fair pass but a bit out in front, and he was going to have to do well to catch it. He juggled the ball once, twice, three times . . . and finally put it on the deck. His head went down and so did mine and in a flash the coach was alongside, screaming: 'Barry! What the *hell* are you doing? With the skills you have, you black blokes are supposed to *catch* those balls – not bloody well *drop* them!' There was nothing racist in this. Bob had been around some wonderful indigenous players in his time and was just making a point in the heat of (training) bat-tle. There was a pause, and then Barry, an Aboriginal player of real talent, held out his hand. 'Well, mate,' he said. 'I'm black on the top . . .' – and then turned his hand over – '. . . and white here! That's the problem.' It was a rejoinder that broke the ice and, I suspect, put us on a smoother path to not being blown up quite as much.

We moved on from Canada to France – and to a whole new experience. Our hotel rooms were so small that we had to remove some of the furniture to make room for our bags. It was that senior–junior thing again. The senior players got the good rooms . . . and the new blokes got what was left.

We arrived in some style amid a Parisian transport strike. With no taxis, buses or trains for commuters, we eventually found ourselves aboard the team bus – and with a police escort guiding us down a jam-packed highway to our hotel. Using batons and their feet to bang on car doors, they found gaps for us on the three-lane road, turned it into four lanes here and there, and guided us through – leaving behind, I suspect, some dented Renaults and Peugeots.

The French tour has traditionally been a very tough experience on the rugby calendar, posing challenges to players in surroundings that are new and very different. There is the language problem, French food, the travelling, the weather, and the French style of playing, which can be a mixture of the cavalier and the boots 'n' all. We toured widely, campaigning through the south at places such as Perpignan, Nimes, Avignon and Bordeaux before trekking back up to Paris. I was very much the rookie in the midst of it all, needing the older blokes to show me the ropes. We played some tough football – and took in the sights and sounds. In Paris we strolled down the Champs Élysées, headed up the Eiffel Tower, experienced the traffic chaos around the Arc de Triomphe – and went to the Lido, where we sat in the front stalls. Afterwards we were invited backstage and met some of the girls – including a couple of Aussies who were dancing there at the time. That was fantastic – and so was the whole experience of France for a young bloke from Carlingford.

Playing fullback at places like Agen, where I was judged 'Man of the Match' on a wet track, and Narbonne, I enjoyed my first taste of footy against the French. It was football with an edge, though. After a spiteful game against Languedoc-Roussilon, Test No. 8 Tim Gavin needed fourteen stitches when he was booted in the head. I was quickly into the swing of it and playing good football, and I knew it, although I was careful not to get too cocky. I was breaking the line, catching the high balls easily and generally in the 'zone'. Coming into the game at Narbonne I was starting to think, 'If I go well here, I'm a chance for the Test team.' But football can bring you to a dead stop in a single second, of course – and in the second half of that game at Narbonne, with things going well, I got a clearing kick away just as a tackler hit me in the air. I came down hard, flush on my right knee. God, it hurt! I got up and tried to get the knee working as physio Greg Craig ran out. Greg quickly did the various tests for ligaments. At first everything seemed okay. Then he did one for the posterior cruciate and it dropped about three-quarters of an inch. 'Have you ever hurt your knee before?' he asked. 'No,' I told him. Meanwhile, the French referee was in on the action. 'You play? You play?' he asked. '*Oui, oui*. I play. I'm ready,' I replied. Craigie just looked at me. 'Mate, you're dead. You can't go any further on that,' he said.

It was the start of an injury struggle that was to last through the tour. Craigie was a bit of a guru regarding injury management and I did all the right things in the days that followed – and ended up getting picked for the Test in Bordeaux, taking the fullback spot away from Marty Roebuck, on the proviso that my fitness was okay. Well, it *wasn't* okay, really, but there were people around me saying, 'Now, if we do this and that and strap it up right, you'll be okay.' And hell, I wanted to play for Australia! When I think about the circumstances of that Test and my selection, I do so with a little discomfort. Probably I shouldn't have played. And I'd like to think that it was probably the only time in my career that I was selfish in shaping up for a match. People do play with injuries – but at 90 per cent, or whatever I was, was it the right call to take the jumper from a bloke who was 100 per cent fit?

In Bordeaux on that 1993 tour when I was named fullback ahead of Marty for the first Test, I honestly felt a bit awkward. After all, I was the young upstart, stealing a Test jumper from a World Cup-winning player and a good friend. The team announcement was made in a room in our hotel. As I walked down the stairs afterwards to head off to training, Marty was the first to congratulate me. Marty Roebuck is one of the world's nicest blokes.

In the end, in Bordeaux I had a painkilling needle in the knee and played – taking Marty's fullback spot. Almost certainly I shouldn't have. I still have among my souvenirs a note Marty wrote me before the game – enduring evidence of the sort of guy he is. He wrote:

Dear Matt
Congratulations on what has been a great tour so far. I know you will absolutely dominate today's match. I know you understand that what will seem easy for you looks inspirational for all who watch – so relax . . .
Take 'em apart.
Marty

As I was to learn later, Marty had also left a celebratory cigar at my dad's hotel door, to mark the occasion of my selection.

Marty's words and the gesture of the little gift were beautiful sentiments from the bloke I had beaten to the Australian fullback spot. Sadly, things didn't work out quite as well as either of us had hoped. My leg wasn't great, and the French, understandably, made me, the rookie, something of a target. Some of our moves went badly wrong that day, and at times it was like I had a big cross on my chest. I was bashed by Philippe Sella every time I got the ball. I was definitely below my best and they hammered me. Apart from the physical caning I took, I was peppered with 'high balls' (or 'Garryowens') as part of their strategy. Catching the high ball was always something I was pretty good at – but the rule for defenders was more relaxed then than it is now. Players today are protected by the rules from being smashed while they are in the air. But not then. You could get really crunched in the air and it was just 'play on'. When it happened to a fullback, a melee would often follow, with the forwards running in to dish out some rough justice. And so it was that day. France won the Test 16–13. Thierry Lacroix's goal from 54 metres out got them across the line in the end.

But something happened in that match that irks me to this day. The French scored their only try in the Test from a blindside move, and it should never have been scored. Being an Eastwood boy, I was a product of the Marty Roebuck school of defence (for full-backs). Once, in a club game, I had failed to stand in defence on the short side of a scrum, and the other mob took play that way, and scored. It was pointed out to me in pretty direct terms that it should never happen again.

In the Test, with the French having a scrum feed twenty metres out from our line and with a 'blind' of about twenty metres I headed across to take up my defensive position there. But our captain that day, Michael Lynagh, playing at No. 10, screamed at me: 'Burkey, what are you doing?' 'This is where I've got to be,' I told him. 'Mate,' he shouted. 'Get across there. Get outside Jason [Little, out-side-centre]!' I tried to argue, but he was the captain – and so I went. Up in the grandstand that day, Marty Roebuck was urging me to stay where I was. 'How come you didn't stay?' he asked me later. And I told him I had just followed the captain's orders.

Anyhow, the French raided down the blind side, with the lock Marc Cecillon and the halfback Aubin Heuber putting on a move – from which Heuber scored in the corner. To this day, it's the defensive lapse that plays on my mind more than any other. It was something that was easy to cover, but all I could do was obey the captain's call – and then watch from across the other side of the paddock. I made a pledge that it would never happen again. Anytime I get the chance to coach fullback to young blokes, I emphasise where they should position themselves in such a situation.

Sitting in the dressing room after the game, I thought: 'That was so close, yet so far.'

That afternoon I suffered a bad cork to my right leg, the one with the knee problem, and the combined problem was serious enough to prevent me playing again on the tour. Marty won back the fullback spot for the second Test at Parc de Princes in Paris and absolutely killed it. We won the game and he got 'Man of the Match' in what was an outstanding finale to his international career. By that time I had gone from being Test fullback to what was known as a Double D – a 'dirty, dirty' – a reserve for the reserves. The only bonus was that I got to see a bit more of Paris than I would have if I'd been in the team!

For me it was back to intensive injury management to try to get ready for the 1994 season for New South Wales.

I guess it's timely here to talk about coach Bob Dwyer, who guided us through that unusual campaign – all the way from California's heat wave to a brilliant second Test triumph in Paris (24–3). I played a lot of football under Bob's guidance, from when I was a twenty-year-old at the start of my career in senior football, and then later when I was NSW captain under his coaching. Coach Dwyer was there or thereabouts for a major proportion of my playing days. And I enjoyed and valued the experience and got on very well with him – although I know that some others didn't, and that there are mixed views on him. You had to know how to handle Bob. He had very strong views about the things that needed to be done on a football field – and any change required a certain amount of subtle persuasion so that it seemed the idea had come from him. There was give and take with Bob – and I always thought of it as a sort of 'joint venture'.

He was a vastly successful coach who orchestrated many victories for Australia, including the 1991 World Cup. Apart from the team thing, he coached 'the player', too – which not all coaches do. I have spoken earlier of a tendency by some coaches to take talent, skill, and so on, for granted. They have the attitude that if a player has reached a certain level in the game, he doesn't need further honing or individual work. Bob never believed that.

He had his own style. He loved repetition as a basis for excellence, and under his coaching you would do things over and over again on the training field. I've already mentioned his monumental blow-ups. Bob could see the potential in blokes and would become angry when he saw that it wasn't being reached.

Great coach though he was, we probably saw the best of Bob Dwyer *away* from the football field. He wanted his players to learn about rugby, but just as much on the tours – and maybe more – he wanted us to learn about the world, too. He certainly didn't want players sitting in their rooms watching TV. So, if we happened to be in Paris, we'd be out strolling down the Champs, having coffee at a café, watching the world go by and being Parisians for the day. In Edinburgh he'd have us out and about on Princes Street, or looking at the 27 pubs or whatever it is on Rowe Street – then taking a right turn and heading up to the castle.

Bob was big on the food experience, too. On the French leg, when we crossed the border into Spain on one excursion, we lunched out under the coach's direction on the local paella. It was never just rugby. We tried the food and the wine – and learned, or in my case remembered from school, enough of the language to get by on. The French serve their steaks very 'blue', and two words that became very popular on tour were '*bien cuit*' meaning 'well cooked' – and especially so for Timmy Horan, who prefers steak of the charcoal variety.

The coach wanted his players to take in the wider experience that any tour offered. He understood that for some, the chance might only come once – and that even for the enduring players, careers are over remarkably quickly and ordinary life resumes soon enough. Bob Dwyer taught a lot of footballers to be part of the wider world – and to take it all in. It was a great message.

I came home from France to a job at Eastwood Rugby Club in 1994, as fulltime development officer. I think it was one of the first of those kinds of jobs on offer in rugby – where a club employs a player in order to ensure that he stays put. But to me it wasn't a token job. Like everything I have done so far in my life, I wanted to do it to the very best of my ability. I saw the job as a chance to grow the game of rugby. And so I started the program virtually from scratch – and the coaching and advice I gave the kids was very much based on what I had learned, and was learning, as a member of the Australian team. And I emphasised the basics – just as they had been emphasised to me during my own school days; there was a lot of work on catching and passing and doing the little things right. I enjoyed that – and the thought was always in my head that the youngsters I taught, whatever level of rugby they might go on to play, would perhaps benefit from some of the things we talked about and worked on.

I took it all very seriously. My 'office' was a tiny room next to the club gym, which would have ranked fairly highly among the world's worst gymnasiums at that time. I got myself a table and a chair and a filing cabinet, and cleaned the room up and did my best to kid myself that I was actually doing a real job. For a while the sole office phone was pretty much open go for the players – until the bill came in, recording one long call to Fiji on what was a longish list. There were swift moves to get locks put on the doors and windows and to have a key phone put in. Now and then the club would stage coaching camps for young players, and they would roll up in great numbers. After one Easter when I had hosted a three-day camp for kids at about ten bucks a day (from 9 am to 4 pm) I realised that we were providing close to the best babysitting service in town. But overall, it was terrific. I enjoyed working with kids and teaching them the game I played – and the job enabled me to push on with my university studies.

The demands of professional rugby, which lay not so far ahead, made it increasingly hard for players to pursue life and skills away from football. As I progressively had some success and became better known at the elite level, I found myself in demand now and then to step up as a guest speaker at functions. I did a public speaking course through Tony Dempsey, the Rugby Union Players Association boss at that time, and that helped me on the path. In the new world of professional sport, players had to be able to hold their own out there by acquiring media skills and developing confidence at public speaking. Since the early days when I would do a nervous Q & A thing as a guest speaker, I have become better at it – through practice – and I now enjoy the chance to share a few yarns and hopefully provide a little enlightenment about rugby when I give a talk. The funny thing about guest speaking, though, is that when you agree to a gig, it always seems a long way off – then suddenly, at ferocious speed, the event is upon you and you're thinking, 'Geez, it'd be nice to have a quiet night at home with the family tonight.' But it's good fun when you get there, and it's good for rugby – and it's good for you too, nudging you out of your comfort zone.

The main task in 1994 was getting back to football on my wonky knee. I had to get it sorted so that I could run again, the problem with posterior cruciate damage being that stopping and starting are made more difficult because the knee tends to slide forward rather disconcertingly. But I worked hard on the knee and was back in form in time for the early days of the Super 10 series, making it into the 'biggest hits of the year' lineup in the match against Western Samoa, which we won 25–23. Unhappily, I was on the *receiving* end – of a real bell-ringer from Samoan centre Too Vaega. The ball came across the backline, and David Campese took off too early on the wing, leaving me posted.

The Super 10 Series of 1994 is remembered for the Waratahs making the difficult decision to call off the scheduled match against Natal because the region was then in a state of emergency. We took on board advice from the Department of Foreign Affairs warning against travel to the republic until at least after the country's first multiracial elections to be held in April. The warning followed factional violence in central Johannesburg and the city's environs that left 51 people dead and more than 300 injured. The final call on the trip, ten days before the elections, was ours – and we decided not to go. We received no competition points and subsequently protested to the Super 10 committee, at which point coach Greg Smith commented: 'Charles Manson could be released before Super 10 gives us anything!' Natal got the four points, and we missed the final because of it.

For the first Test against Ireland, under Bob Dwyer – a match that arrived early in the season – it seemed that Timmy Horan and Jason Little had the centre spots all wrapped up. But both suffered serious knee injuries – in a horrible coincidence, in the Super 10 final against Natal – ruling them out of the internationals against both Ireland and Italy and, on indications, perhaps for the whole season. Up to that point I had been thinking 'fullback'. I was seriously contemplating the possibilities that might exist one day and reached a conclusion: 'If there is any position I can make my own, it's going to be fullback.' But circumstances being what they were for the Test against Ireland in Brisbane, I was in the centres, with Matt Pini at fullback.

The day at Ballymore was a considerable thrill. For the first time I was selected in the Australian starting lineup, one of those milestones that any footballer of ambition dreams about. I played outside-centre, alongside the Australian Capital Territory's Matthew O'Connor – and it was fantastic to score a try in a winning Test. It was my first try for Australia, so it sticks in my mind: the moment of chasing a Michael Lynagh kick and snapping it up about five yards out from the line to dive over. The Ballymore crowd, some no doubt well fuelled as is the tradition, gave the Aussie try a typically enthusiastic reception, and so too the match result – a clear-cut 33–13 to Australia.

For the second Test in Sydney, with Pini injured, I was picked at fullback. My appearances in my first three encounters with Test football now read: winger, fullback, outside-centre. And if it hadn't been for Pini doing his hamstring I would have played inside-centre in that game, my *fourth* Test. We won the second Test 32–18. Afterwards I thought to myself, 'I'm enjoying this!'

Life was good, and even edging towards the glamorous. For the Sydney Test we stayed at the Park Royal in Darling Harbour, just down from the city's heart – and this was all right: strolling around the city, being waited on hand and foot back at the hotel. I figured I could get to like such a lifestyle.

With the Irish despatched, we played Italy in Brisbane and probably were lucky to beat them 23–20 in a Test that would rank as one of the worst of my career. 'Australia were no world champions last night,' wrote the *Herald*'s Greg Growden. He was being kind. It was an ugly game. Our vice captain, Phil Kearns, likened the lineouts to a 'dockside brawl'. A highlight was replacement Tim Wallace's mighty conversion from the touchline after I had scored a try from fullback – Tim's kick edging us away to 20–17.

In the second Test, which we won 20–7, David Campese scored one of the dodgiest tries I've ever seen. Thank God they didn't have video referee that day – because Campo was at least three feet over the sideline when he plonked the ball down. He had gone hard for the corner but hadn't mustered enough pace to flank the fullback who cut him down with a low tackle. The referee was about 25 metres back up the paddock and the touch judge a good fifteen metres away. In the absence of certain knowledge they awarded the try. But it wasn't one. Tim Wallace, a fantastic goal-kicker, getting a rare chance at five-eighth that day in the absence of Michael Lynagh and David Knox, kicked five goals. For the second Test I was back in the centres.

The first match against Queensland up there that season (which we lost 22–20) provided a good example of how simple it is for a footballer's chance to come . . . and then be gone. A player from Gordon, Brett O'Neill, was chosen at fullback – and I was picked in the centres. O'Neill played a reasonable game, but there were a couple of mistakes along the way and as quickly as he was in the team, he was out. I was moved back to fullback, had a good game in the second match in which a couple of NSW tries came from countering runs I made – and we won the series. The move back to No. 15 was a lucky break for me. Marty Roebuck had retired, and the other contestant for the Australian fullback job was Queensland's Matt Pini, a good fullback in his own right – more of a defensive-style player than I was. The media had a field day wrestling with the question of where I 'should' be playing. *Sports Weekly* posed the question, 'Where's Burke's Backyard?'

When I thought it over, fullback was just fine . . .

Not for the last time in my career, I found myself under pressure from the media during that midpoint of the season. As we shaped up for the series decider against Queensland, there was talk about my having been in a 'lengthy form slump'. Aussie coach Bob Dwyer had applied a little needle through the press. 'He's definitely coasting,' Dwyer was quoted as saying. 'He's only playing at 50 per cent capacity. I think he can play a lot better.' I was aware by then that when it comes to sport, sometimes the pen is mightier than the sword. My attitude throughout my career was always to discount by 50 per cent whatever was written about me – whether good or bad. And so it was back then. I felt that my form was reasonably solid, and on the night we played Queensland and beat them for the first time in three years, 38–8, the biggest win since 1975, I had a strong game that I was well satisfied with.

This was a huge thrill – to beat the Reds, the Super 10 champions, and take the State of the Union series. The hiding we gave them, added to the Natal situation that season and our loss of points that could have seen us as the champs, produced a cutting comment after the match from NSW Rugby Union (NSWRU) chairman Peter Crittle that really put the cat among the pigeons. In his speech, Crittle made a reference to the Reds being the 'Super

Nines' champions (they *had* gone to South Africa), which apparently pissed the Queenslanders off to a considerable extent, as they walked off the ground and didn't join in the post-game socialising.

The journey of a rugby career is a learning experience all the way, and it was certainly so for me in 1994. I was left out of the Australian team to play Western Samoa because of the arrival of Joe Roff, an up-and-comer. 'Who is this bloke, this upstart?' I wondered. To rub it in, I was then called in as a squad member, as the team used the Western Samoan game (a 73–3 near-walkover) to get ready for the Test against the All Blacks. As a squad member, your job is to do everything in training that the selected team members do. The only difference is that they're in the team – and you're not. I was with blokes like Scott Bowen and Tim Wallace. The squad members were basically out every night, then rolling up for training the next day. It wasn't the happiest time.

For what is now in the history books as a famous Test match – against the All Blacks at Sydney Football Stadium – I was on standby for Matt Pini, who was carrying an injury. The game has its place among the special ones because it's the one in which George Gregan (who had hair in those days) made his famous tackle on the All Blacks' Jeff Wilson. It was to be a defining moment in George's career, standing alongside such achievements as his 100th Test, and then his record-breaking 102nd in 2004. It was an amazing tackle in an amazing situation – and was thankfully recorded for posterity in a brilliant still photo. It's easy to recall: a couple of unsuccessful lunges from Australian defenders, one of them Campo, who, having missed and finished on the deck, had one of those 'we've lost the game' looks on his face – and then Wilson racing for the line. Suddenly, the head-geared Gregan came into frame and launched himself horizontally, knocking Wilson over with a super shot and thus saved the Test match – carving himself a niche forever in the annals of Australian rugby.

Oh, yes, I certainly remember *that* moment – everyone does – but I remember the Test in pretty sharp focus too because of my own bizarre preparation. As a 'standby' player, I was asked to represent the team at a pre-game function held at Rosehill Racecourse. While my gear headed to the stadium with one of the management team, I made my way through the traffic to Rosehill, not knowing whether or not I would be in the team. It was a weird experience being out there pressing the flesh at a very relaxed social function – having no idea if within a couple of hours I'd be playing a Bledisloe Cup match. I even had a beer – forced on me by one of the guests. As a young fella, I thought I'd better be polite and accept it. I finally broke away from the function and made slow progress back towards the Moore Park area – and to Victoria Barracks, where parking arrangements had been made. There, it took me ten minutes to convince the bloke on the gate that I was one of the team, and that possibly I would be required to run on against the All Blacks that night. I had no car pass or identification, so I suppose his caution was understandable. Eventually I made it to the dressing room. 'No, he's okay,' they told me of Pini. But he wasn't. He played about half a game, then came off. And was I filthy about that? Well, yes.

Not long after that disappointment I was named in the Emerging Wallabies tour to South Africa. I withdrew. I used the excuse of my studies, but my reasons probably had more to do with ego. I thought that I had already arrived as a Test player, and so to step back to the 'Emerging Wallabies' was – well – a step back. Maybe I was wrong, and I certainly had pangs of regret later when the guys who *did* tour told me of the good football and the fun times they had enjoyed.

I stayed home and played some club rugby for Eastwood, and

found a goal-kicking groove that we kickers tend to find now and then. As the Woodies headed into the semis, I strung together 25 goals from 27 shots at one stage. I had started to do some work with the English kicking guru Dave Aldred. As a result, I had slowed down the pace and rhythm of my approach to the ball. Instead of trying to kick it as hard and high as possible, it was now a case of being nice and controlled – same rhythm, same approach to the ball every time. In a semi against Northern Suburbs, I landed a 53-metre penalty goal. A Kiwi journo quoted figures subsequently that I was 'batting' the highest percentage of shots at goal over 40 metres in international rugby – a bizarre statistic that had never crossed my mind.

Chapter 6

PUTTING IN THE BOOT

I was a goal-kicker from the time I started playing rugby with the Beecroft–Pennant Hills Under 11s. Crossing over from soccer, it was always a certainty that my style would be round-the-corner, soccer-style. For me it was the natural way. By that time, around 1984 or so, the kicking revolution that was to change the face of both rugby games was well under way – although blokes like Mick Cronin and Mal Meninga, old-style toe-kickers, were still booting plenty of goals in rugby league.

The fact that I was thrown the ball for goal-kicking duties from my very early days gave me the chance to work constantly at the fine points. I could always kick the ball quite a long way, and I believed that it should go over the crossbar as hard and high as possible. And very often it did – my kicking record at school was pretty good. But when I look at footage of my early days as a kicker, I was all over the place. My style was far removed from the more refined and constant thing it became, and my technique looked lazy. My arms and legs were everywhere; I was lucky to get away with it. But from the start, I was a good *natural* kicker. I believe that kickers are born, not made, although a 'made' kicker can make good progress over time with hard work and good coaching.

The only time I didn't get to kick in those formative years was 1989, when I was in Year 11 at school and chosen for the first time in Joey's first grade. Tim Kelaher was the kicker that year, and went on to play – and kick – for Australia.

I think Matt Burke was born a goal-kicker. People are either born to it or they're not, and then it's your application to the task. His application to goal-kicking has been first-class.

Eddie Jones

Goal-kicking has been called an 'art form' by some. I'm not so sure about that. The fluency, and a style that was uniquely mine, came later, the result of a great deal of practice. Even at school I would do a lot of work on my kicking away from the formal training sessions. There is absolutely no doubt that this investment in time has paid off for me over the years – that my ability as a kicker got me across the line on a few occasions in terms of selection in teams. It was a skill that I always worked at – and will continue to work at for as long as I'm a football player.

He has just got a beautiful approach to the ball – very fluent. He's got great rhythm when he kicks the ball. And the big thing with Burkey is that he kicks the big goals, the ones that count.

Rugby league's Andrew Johns

As early as 1992 I conducted a goal-kicking clinic at Sydney's Knox College – and got paid a couple of hundred dollars for my trouble. 'How good is *this*?' I thought. I even had one of the parents that day asking me to take their son on board as a private student for weekly lessons. I said 'no'. Fact was, the kid couldn't kick.

In late 1994, I did a lot of work with Dave Aldred, an expert in the business, who over the seasons has worked with a number of the European kickers – most notably, England's Jonny Wilkinson. He didn't *change* my style, but I would say he enhanced and refined it to an extent. I discovered when I joined the Newcastle Falcons in the UK in 2004 that most of the current Aldred-taught kickers are an absolute mirror-image of his style. I was a little different, having taken bits and pieces of what he taught and adapting them to my own style – and practising, practising.

Dave Aldred's model for goal-kicking was basically . . . himself, and in the Australian context Scott Bowen and I were his guinea pigs. Dave could really kick the ball – punt it a mile – and knock over a place kick from wherever on the field to show how it was done. Excellence in technique and repetitions are still the keystones of what he preaches and teaches. Essentially, he wanted his students to be able to produce exactly the same kick, whatever the pressure situation in a match. The search was for perfection – to be able to produce the flawless kick over and over again.

He used split-screen video technology, superimposing a 'perfect' stick-figure kicker over your own style to point out any discrepancies. Goal-kicking, which once produced all manner of methods and styles, has grown to become a science under Dave's tutelage. He has written a thesis on the whole business of kicking, in which he compares it with a golf swing. He talks about 'leg shape' and 'swing path' and the 'moment of contact'. And he talks of the 'hard foot', and of how the sound is different when you hit it just right. It's true – you know when you have hit the ball well. You don't even have to look up to see the outcome: the ball sailing true and high between the posts. Such a thump means there has been the right 'shape', that the plant foot is right, your kicking leg going through is in the right arc, the contact on the ball is perfect, the follow-through is as it should be. When it all comes together and you hit it right, everything flows. It's a special feeling.

Dave Aldred is still the England kicking coach. He coached Rob Andrew in Rob's time, and endures to this current era through masters of the art like Wilkinson. Precision is a big part of what he teaches. When I first started kicking goals, I would stand the ball straight up and muck around with my angle into the ball and the number of steps – and then go in as hard as I could and give it a mighty old reef.

Nowadays, I lean the ball forward a bit, which opens up the bottom of the ball; I'm trying to hit the bottom one-third. I have it pointed directly between the goal-posts. I take four steps diagonally back from the ball, set myself and think about watching a spot on the ball and then hitting it. It's always the same spot – down at the bottom. Kicking is a timing thing. Just because you hit it hard doesn't mean it's going to go a long way.

It's important not to look up too early after you've kicked it. I take a step through, and then have a look after that. But I know whether I've hit it well or not without looking up. Your movements have to be constant every time. If you haven't got the same routine each time, you're dead to start with. It's a case of you've done it so often it should come naturally to you. Outside of all that, you've got to block out all of the extra stuff that's going on in your head and out there in the crowd.

It was pointed out to me a few years ago that I shared a practical trait with a great league goal-kicker of earlier times – Balmain's Keith 'Golden Boot' Barnes. Some of Barnes's practice work would always be up and down the sideline in the search for precision and accuracy. Some of my practice over the seasons has included shots from the corner post, the bullseye being a hit on the goal-post. My aim was to be able to shoot dead straight with the round-the-corner style, rather than curve the ball as some kickers do.

When it comes to goal-kicking, there are up to fourteen other people in the team who have the opportunity to take it on, but I can tell you most of the other fourteen don't want the opportunity. It's the guy who has the talent and the belief in his ability and the courage to stay composed under pressure who can score those points for you and become a singularly important member of the side.

Bob Dwyer

It wasn't until around 1996, when I kicked just about every day for hours on end, that I finally started to get the rewards from what I had learned. My method of practice was repetition. When we were training at Concord I'd go there before training and do an hour's work on my kicking – and then I'd stay back afterwards and do another hour. I got to the stage where I'd do 100 kicks a day, five days a week.

For a time I did a *huge* amount of kicking. Dave Aldred's sessions lasted three hours or so and at the end of it I'd limp to the sheds, my leg just about kicked off. There came a point in the 1997 season when I hit the wall. One afternoon I went for a kick with Scott Bowen before training at Concord Oval and was doing some punt kicking on my right leg. (My left leg was sore and I couldn't run.) And in the course of it I pretty much ripped the tendon off the bone in my groin. I have no doubt that what happened that day was the result of over-kicking. The pain was unbelievable and I knew I was in big trouble.

During the period of my rehabilitation, eight long months, I could barely lift my left leg off the bed when I was lying flat. I lost all flexibility. I had fallen victim to the youthful fallacy that I was indestructible. I wasn't. I'm wiser now – and in my kicking work, quality ranks well ahead of quantity. In recent years I have also worn a groin strap. It's a reality for any footballer: you have to maintain your body. If you don't – well, you're not going to be playing a lot of footy.

As a kicker I guess you could say I always toted an idiosyncrasy or two. My left foot is bigger than my right, so I wear a size nine-and-a-half on the right and a ten on the left. In earlier days I used to wear two pairs of socks on the right foot to take up the slack for a boot that was too big. I like to have a tight boot on the right side, and I've played that way for years, my foot crammed into a smaller boot that leaves my toes callused and bruised and not pretty to look at. But for goal-kicking, and for me, it's right. By jamming my foot in, I have the feeling of *actual contact* when I kick the ball. My boots are essentially the tools of my trade. My tip to any young aspiring kicker is to be particular about your footwear – make sure you get the right boots.

Funnily enough, Burkey can kick just as well left-footed as blokes usually do with their right foot. Hardly anyone gets to see it, but I've seen plenty of it at training when we were both having a shot – and we'd both be kicking with our left foot. The thing is, I'm left-footed and he kicks better with his left – and he's right-footed! The talent he possesses is pretty great.

Mat Rogers

With goal-kicking, I have paid my dues. Very likely the kicking has got me into teams I wouldn't have been in otherwise. But I've worked bloody hard at it. People just see what happens on a Saturday, and if you've had a good day it'll be: 'How good is *that*?

How good a goal-kicker is *he*?' But what it's really about is all the work you've done during the week and what you might have had to put up with to get there.

Chapter 7

BLUES FOR BILL

Season 1995 dawned hot and early, with a February kickoff and momentous events ahead. It was World Cup year and South Africa awaited. The challenge of retaining the Cup ('Bill') was the overwhelming focus for everyone in rugby, and most of us in the game played on blissfully unaware of the other huge earthquake that was building in football, the turbulent undercurrents of which would change both rugby codes forever. Forces way beyond the reach of mere sport were gathering.

For the Waratahs, it all started far from home – in Perth, the beginning of a brief tour which it was hoped would shape the team, knock off the rough edges and ready us for the Super 10 competition, and beyond. The game there produced the expected result: a big victory over Western Australia (65–10). Coach Greg Smith had managed, however, to make life uncomfortable for one of the Waratahs. Jason Madz was a player with the potential to be great, but he had his mind badly messed with by coach Smith before he ran on in that game. Every time you run on to a football field you live with the pressure of expectation. Everyone is going out there to play well, and it's pressure enough. But on this day, Jason was about three or four metres from the sideline when the coach said: 'Mate, if you miss a tackle today you won't be playing for us anymore. If it happens, I'll take you off.' Imagine having *that* hanging over your head! Jason struggled in that game but came on tour – and did well.

From Perth we headed away to another world, to Zimbabwe. For all of us, it was an intriguing and eye-opening venture on to the African continent, where the World Cup would be held a little later in the season. In Harare we won 76–10 against Zimbabwe. Campo captained us in that match – and earned rave reviews from the local press.

Owing to the policies of President Mugabe and his government, there has been a considerable slow-down in international sport in Zimbabwe in recent years. There have been cancellations and inevitably a great deal of soul-searching whenever a tour there is under consideration. The road where the president had his mansion was closed to the public between 6 pm and 6 am. If anyone happened to stray down there – well, chances were they'd be shot. I'm pleased, though, that I had the chance to visit the country. It was a very sobering experience to see how things were there – the shanty towns, the poor standard of living, the repressive regime, the realisation of the HIV epidemic in Africa. Australia seemed an especially fine place when viewed from such a troubled perspective. When, after the game, we handed out some gear to fans I think we did so in the hope that even that small gesture might bring a little happiness and light into lives that must have been more difficult than any of us could comprehend.

* * *

It was soon afterwards, on our return to Australia, that the magazine *Sports Weekly* posed the question: 'Where's Burke's Backyard?' – another reference to the debate that pursued me through my career. 'Was I a centre, a winger or a fullback?' they asked. Well, for the Waratahs that season, I was at fullback, where I was very happy to be. And there was much talk of the forthcoming tussle for the Australian spot – me against Queensland's Matthew Pini. From this distance in my career I can stress that wing was certainly *not* where I wanted to be. I have never wanted to be a winger, even though my career took me down that track a few times and I had no option but to run with it. Frankly, I don't like playing wing; it doesn't do it for me.

By then I was pretty much immune to newspaper talk classifying me as one thing or another – or damning me or praising me, for that matter. There has never been any chance that I'd crumble under the pressure of things said in the papers. The media has crushed more than a few players over the years, but I was determined it wouldn't happen to me. I would take everything that was said with a grain of salt – the good *and* the bad equally – in line with what I came to understand: that there is an awful lot of crap written and spoken about sport. Having said that, I'm appreciative of those who have supported me over the years and unconcerned about those who haven't. One day I'll go through the scrapbooks that my father kept meticulously throughout my career and get a better idea of who thought what about M. Burke. But none of it matters too much. Everyone is thoroughly entitled to an opinion and, as they say, today's newspaper stories are used to wrap fish 'n' chips tomorrow. From fairly early on in my career I made the decision that I would just get on with business, knowing that the media would get on with theirs. For me, the vast bulk of what was said or written would be no more than water off a duck's back.

* * *

There really was only one game in town in 1995: the World Cup –
especially so as it was to be played in a newly proud South Africa,
back in rugby's fold with the ending of apartheid. For Australia
the load was heavy and the expectations high. We were, after all,
the defending world champions.

Through all the prelims of that season, the Cup shone like a full
moon in the minds of the leading players in all the rugby nations
of the world. At home, the Super 10 tournament was like a four-
rounder before a fifteen-round title fight, albeit keenly contested
and an obvious testing ground for what lay ahead.

Our NSW Super 10 season, under coach Greg Smith, was
limited to just four games – a 21–18 loss to Transvaal, a draw
with North Harbour (6-all) and wins over Otago (31–16) and
Western Province (23–21). It was a brief season of erratic form.
My best game came at the end, when we pipped Western Province
after one of their blokes had bombed a try in the last few
seconds. Like other World Cup hopefuls, I kept my hand in with
spasmodic appearances in club football. From the previous September
I had been a member of the train-on squad, the first step along the
track.

The 1995 World Cup campaign in South Africa was tagged
'Mission REPEAT' – the 'REPEAT' an acronym for 'Return to Ellis
Park and Ensure Another Twickenham'. And on a day in May
when Steve Waugh was making his brave and famous Test 200
against the West Indies in the Caribbean, thousands of kilometres
away, I became part of it.

The word was that candidates for the team would be informed
by courier at around 7 am. Unable to sleep I was up well before
that – glued to the cricket – well, with half my mind, anyway. Seven
o'clock came and went and then eight o'clock – and no courier.
Around then I was thinking, 'Maybe if you don't make it, you
don't get a letter.' My next thought was, 'Well, you'd think they'd

at least send a bloody note to let you know that you're *not* in the squad!'

Could someone *please* knock on my door? But no one did, and eventually I rang Scott Bowen. 'Mate, are you in?' I asked. 'Yeah, sweet. The courier's been,' he replied, sounding excited. 'How about you?' I told him there had been nothing. 'Mate, I don't think I'm going,' I said.

It was Scott who settled it for me – by ringing Glen Ella, who was the backs coach at the time. Yeah, I was certainly in the side, Glen told him. Scott rang me back with the news. That courier never did arrive, although the later letter of confirmation from the Australian Rugby Union (ARU) chairman Leo Williams did. It wasn't untypical of the way things could work with the ARU back then – that it was only through a mate, third hand, that I learned I had made the World Cup side! Later, on another occasion, I learned of my selection in a Wallaby team via *Sports Tonight*. In 1995 I was just delighted to be there – in a team of 26 to be captained by Michael Lynagh, with Phil Kearns as his vice captain and Bob Dwyer as coach.

For the first gathering of the team a few days later, we were told to bring along just socks and jocks. We were to be given everything else – a first step down the track of this looming 'new professionalism' in rugby. And so it turned out – so much gear was dished out, we didn't have to bring any street clothes at all if we chose not to. Nowadays if you wore team kit everywhere on tours away, you'd be ridiculed out the door. But back then, it was really something to be handed all this gear.

We flew South African Airways, big sponsors of the game at the time, sharing the flight with the All Blacks. I found myself sitting next to Josh Kronfeld, an open side flanker who developed into something special, and just down the aisle from Jonah Lomu, who became one of the most formidable rugby players of all time. Our base for the campaign was the Holiday Inn Cape Town, not far from Newlands Ground. We were welcomed with a colourful fanfare of tribal dancers and musicians, which created a fantastic atmosphere for this historic first Cup on African soil.

I was one of two chosen fullbacks in the Australian squad – effectively No. 2 behind the more experienced Queenslander and Test incumbent, Matthew Pini. We had ten or eleven days before the first game, and so had a real chance to familiarise ourselves with Cape Town. The important extra members of the team met us at the hotel – our appointed security men, Willem and Yanni. As it turned out, Yanni, a good young bloke who went on to play some provincial rugby in South Africa, would be the security guard for the team. Willem pretty much became the security guard for David Campese, the fact being that Campo with his stature and reputation in rugby was tackling a particularly busy campaign.

In the room allocation I drew Tim Horan – the theory being to put a young bloke with an older bloke. Timmy, the perennial prankster, was a guaranteed lively roommate for a greenhorn like me, and kept me right on my toes. Next door were established half, Peter Slattery, and another rookie – Scott Bowen.

It seemed a reasonable game plan on arrival night to go and see the town and have a beer or two. Scott had a cold, so he bowed out – but when Peter Slattery knocked on the door and asked: 'Young pup – do you want to come out and have a beer?' I figured it would be impolite to refuse. To cut a long story short, I got to bed at 5 am – and Timmy Horan, being a good roomie, had to go and fetch me some breakfast, owing to my fragile state.

Coach Dwyer had called the first meeting of the tour for nine o'clock that morning. I managed to get there, although very likely still the worse for wear. I survived training – and went back to the hotel and slept through the afternoon. During my career I only ever had one Big Night Out before a game, but there has been a training session or three over the years at which I have been hung-over. Back then, we all did it. At those sessions the trick was just to go quietly about your work, hang in there and make sure you didn't do anything that was going to make you look too conspicuous.

Not long after I woke from my afternoon sleep that first day in Cape Town there was a knock on the door. It was Slatts. 'Mate, do you feel like a beer?' he asked. 'It'd be wrong if I didn't,' I replied.

I got home at four the next morning.

Tim again got me my breakfast. I struggled down to the team meeting, made it through training and once more slept right through the afternoon.

The pattern was pretty much repeated for the first seven days, at which point I decided that if I was going to be a chance of getting into the side, I'd better change my ways. So there was an evening about a week into the tour when Slatts knocked on the door and I told him I was going to ease up on the socialising for a bit. 'Yeah, I'm going to do the same,' he said. Peter was in pretty much the same situation as me, the reserve halfback and a tour understudy – to George Gregan.

Everywhere we went in those early days of the tour, people gave us the same advice: 'You have a fantastic team, but watch out. We are a united country now and we have the potential to do very well. Don't count us out.' The passion that existed for the home side really showed through in the lead-up to the first game – when we played them at Newlands. I had got my act together then after the early flurry and was named on the bench. As the crow flies we had no more than about 500 metres to travel from our hotel to the ground, but the streets were absolutely crammed with people. Throughout that slow crawl our bus was belted by hands, plastic bottles, flags, banners and anything else the fans could get hold of. The hostility was extreme – and bizarre. We had the feeling that we would risk being lynched if we got out of the bus.

The mood continued at the game, where the noise of the crowd was amazing. There being no spots for reserves on the field, we were up in the stand with the fans. Anyone required to take the field would have to fight their way through the crowd on the stairs. As it turned out the call didn't come for me that afternoon.

I have no doubt that the fact we were defending World Cup champions and early favourites for the tournament increased the pressure on the team. But I was just thrilled to be there with the chance of playing for my country, and my own enthusiasm and expectation levels were sky-high. I honestly didn't feel the pressure until our premature exit . . .

The Springboks outplayed us that first night, confirming the warnings that we had been given just about everywhere we had been over the past ten days. They smashed us from pillar to post with a characteristically physical and aggressive approach. Nothing much went right for the Aussies – and to be honest, we didn't show a lot. I remember us pulling a familiar move where the ball goes from the five-eighth behind the centres to the blind-side winger – and David Campese, who took the pass, was nailed twenty metres behind the advantage line. It was that sort of day. A couple of late tries made the score reasonably respectable (27–18) – but we had been decisively beaten. It was a big wake-up call.

For our second game we lined up against Canada – who had opened their campaign with a spiteful game against the Springboks. This time, I made the side – one of nine changes from the first game, replacing Pini at fullback, and rapt at being given the opportunity to play my first World Cup game. We won 27–11 in a fairly scratchy display. I played okay, taking some high balls and making a few runs. The critics were kind, but more importantly I was quietly satisfied that my form had been solid. I knew that the goal-kicking, although not part of my duties that night, was an added string to my bow.

For the third game, against Romania, I was both fullback and goal-kicker. I don't have too many happy memories of playing Romania – although chance had it that we were drawn against them in all three World Cups in which I was to play (1995, 1999, 2003). The three games are pretty close to the three most spiteful games in which I have ever been involved. In Stellenbosch in 1995 the blood flowed and our team doctor, John Best, declared it one of the most physical and damaging games of his experience with the team. We beat them 42–3, which looks easy when you write it on paper – but afterwards the doc was kept busy inserting stitches and stemming the blood flow.

I scored a couple of tries, and played with confidence at fullback, despite some of the ugly stuff that was going on up front. But when I was batting only two out of five with the boot (although I reckoned my first, disallowed kick was actually a goal), our skipper that day, Rod McCall, threw the ball to John Eales after we had scored a try in the corner. Typically the camera was on me (the goal-kicker!) when Ealsie lined up – and landed – the first kick. They always do that. Having me on screen was no doubt a spur to Ealsie, who couldn't possibly have steered it any straighter over the black dot. Meanwhile the camera lingered on me. Maybe they were hoping I'd spit the dummy and mouth, 'You bastard!' Ealsie went on to kick four sideline conversions that day, one of a number of shining lights in what was a brilliant campaign by the big bloke.

The victory took us to a quarter-final showdown with England, and with the All Blacks to come after that (we hoped). When the team was announced, I was there at fullback, ahead of Pini. The match turned out to be an epic struggle that ended in absolute emptiness for us, the defending champions. At 22-all three minutes into injury time, England stand-off Rob Andrew thumped a field goal shot from way up the park, 45 metres or so. 'My God, that's a good kick . . . I just hope I'm not standing under the black dot,' was my first thought as it left his boot. But I was – and the ball seemed to sail higher and higher and dead straight between the posts. A single brilliant kick, and we were gone.

It was hard to believe. I had relished the game, surviving under a barrage of high kicks from the Poms. There's no doubt they set out to give me – the new chum – a good test. But I had done my job and defused them all day as the scores had crept along – just one try each, but plenty of goals. Near the end we had fought back to lead 22–19 before England levelled up.

Then Andrew kicked one of the great World Cup goals. And that was it. Nine years and a whole football career later, the same Rob Andrew, then a coach, was to recruit me to join him in the UK at the Newcastle Falcons, and he reminds me of it to this day.

It didn't sink in for some time that we were really out of the Cup and had just three days to get out of town, just like in the old Western movies – that being the World Cup rule. We spent those three days drowning our sorrows and wondering what might have been. Only then did I really feel the pressure of this, my first World Cup. The recriminations began. Were some of our players not up to scratch in their fitness? Were there some who had hung around too long? That second question is always a tough one regarding football teams, as it gets to the heart of the need for a balance between new blood and old heads. I suspect I lived through a version of that syndrome late in my own career. Maybe there were young blokes saying then that it was time for the old bloke to go. One commentator in South Africa observed tersely: 'The fact was that the 1995 Wallabies, with nine players from 1991 plus Tim

Gavin [who would have played in 1991 except for a broken leg], were too old, too injured, and not fast enough and fit enough to mount a serious challenge.' That was a big call.

The ending to it all was very abrupt. There had been so much expectation – combined with enjoyment of the long build-up, when we were able to do the tourist bit and visit Table Mountain and Robin Island and those sorts of places. Now it was over in the second or two that it took Rob Andrew to shift a football from 45 metres away on a grassy field and over a distant crossbar.

The disappointment hit home with a great jolt when we flew into Perth Airport to resume our normal lives. There, waiting to fly out the other way, was a group of fans heading to South Africa on a tour booked in the hope that we would be in the semis . . . and beyond. And we were back home before they had even left.

In one way I was happy to be back – but there was a big ache, too. And especially so when I settled down to watch the New Zealand v South Africa final, a game drenched in subsequent controversy, due to allegations that a number of the All Blacks had gone down with food poisoning the night before the match. 'Had it been a level playing field over there?' I wondered – remembering the angry crowds who had confronted us en route to our first game.

But the chance to beat England had been in our own hands – and we hadn't managed it. A line had been drawn, and all the positions in the next Australian team would now be up for grabs. The critics talked of me 'coming of age' as Test fullback, and I guess I could take some solace from that.

The season's ending after the World Cup experience provided at least a first hint of a new dawn, and fresh hope that next time – 1999 – things would be different. New South Wales took on and defeated our old enemy Queensland in successive games to take the State of the Union series. And for me it was a bumper time – 23 points in the first game, 20 in the second, thirteen goals from sixteen shots and a 'Man of the Series' award.

At the very end came the experience of playing Bledisloe Cup football for the first time. A hamstring injury forced me off the paddock early in the first Test, played in a vicious, swirling wind at Auckland's Eden Park, a game we lost 28–16. But I made it back for the second game in Sydney – against a New Zealand team that was hell-bent on taking revenge against everyone within cooee after the sour experience of their World Cup final loss. They beat us again, 34–23. But with some new faces on board, we played pretty well and had some fun – and were united in our pride at being part of that most famous of all local derbies.

The Australian team had been significantly revamped in the wake of what was rated a disappointing World Cup campaign. Man of the moment then was big Jonah Lomu, back from the Cup, but in an All Black side disappointed that they, too, had come home without the Cup. There was a moment in the Sydney match, in which I was handed the kicking duties for the first time, when I had an up-close and personal taste of Lomu's power. The All Blacks had a move in which the No. 10 dummied to the No. 12 – and then switched the ball to Lomu, charging through on the inside. The move had threatened all game, and finally arrived – with Tim Horan at inside-centre and Scott Bowen at five-eighth being unable to stop the big bloke. He came through the line hard, and I went for the tackle that I *had* to make and was pretty chuffed with the outcome – until I realised there were about four other blokes involved! Jonah was just devastating, the real killer among the game's ball-runners at that time. The only chance of stopping a man of his power is to take him low – and it was in that Test that David Campese, a player not renowned for his tackling prowess, chopped Lomu down with a bootlace tackle. It was a dead-set one in a million event. Other times, Lomu ran around or over his rival winger. But on this occasion Campo felled him first time, later making the point coolly that it wasn't so difficult to stop the big fella.

By the time that old and traditional game was played, rugby's world was in the midst of huge change. The Rupert Murdoch-backed Super League onslaught on rugby league in early 1995 had almost torn that game apart – and similar forces were abroad in rugby. The game swirled with rumours, and it seemed that unstoppable forces had been unleashed that would change rugby forever. All of us just got on and played our footy, but in quiet times alone, and over post-game beers, we wondered what the new direction might be.

Chapter 8

WHEN WORLDS COLLIDE

The separate worlds of the two rugbies – union and league –
were in turmoil in 1995, the centenary of the original
breakaway in the north of England that had led to there being two
distinct games. The Super League raids, which divided league for
years and changed the game forever, hit early in 1995. Rugby
union looked on nervously as league went through its agonies –
the game breaking into two camps: the Super Leaguers (backed
by Rupert Murdoch) and the Australian Rugby League (ARL)
traditionalists (backed by Kerry Packer). There was talk of mass
signings of union players as part of the power struggle, and the
unease experienced by the blokes running the still 'amateur' game
was thoroughly understandable.

There was much talk from early in the season of rugby league
'hit lists' – and mention was made that I was certainly on one of
those lists, along with the likes of Tim Horan, Willie Ofahengaue,

Ilie Tabua and Jason Little. But much of it was just paper talk. I had World Cup (rugby!) in mind, so playing rugby league wasn't on my agenda. The thing was, I didn't play league . . . and I never really *wanted* to play league. And that's nothing whatsoever against the game; I just didn't see it being for me. Yet rugby league, and its players, had been among my influences. I grew up watching the game, and idolising players like the quicksilver Manly (and other clubs) backline star, Phil Blake. A try he scored one day, a double chip 'n' chase, still rates highly for me among football's great individual moments. And I had huge admiration for the likes of the gifted Parramatta duo, Bretty Kenny and Steve 'Zip Zip' Ella. I respected the game and its players back then, and still do so today. It doesn't matter which football code you might come from, you would have to admire the skills of men like Andrew Johns and Darren Lockyer, and the strength and aggression of the likes of Shane Webcke and Gorden Tallis. For all that, if it was true that I was on rugby league's list back in the tumultuous season of 1995, it was just as true that the thirteen-a-side game wasn't on mine.

Rugby's initial response to the gathering storm in the season heading up to the 1995 World Cup campaign had been to come up with offers of 'A', 'B' and 'C' contracts to current and fringe Australian players – to secure them for the game's future. There was a big difference between the three contracts. The 'A' contract, aimed at the senior blokes, was worth about $80,000; the 'B', geared for blokes with a dozen or so Tests on the board, about $50,000; and the 'C', for the remaining new chums and fringe dwellers, around $14,000. The difference was such that the theory circulated that the 'C' group were probably seen as blokes who were going to jump the fence to Super League money. I imagine that every single player in both games wondered where they stood and what the future might hold.

With the sort of money that was being talked of in league, it was a test for everyone. Within rugby the loyalty factor seemed strong when we players were together – loyalty to both the game and the team. But away from the group it could be very different, notwithstanding the genuine nature of that loyalty. After all, football careers can be short and all of us – now, and back then – have, and had, obligations to self and family and future. I'm sure that very many rugby union players quietly asked themselves the question: 'What will I do if an offer comes along that is simply too good to refuse?'

On a particular morning around that time I headed in to ARU headquarters in North Sydney. On the way in I passed David Knox. 'How're you going?' I asked. His answer consisted largely of expletives. I quite clearly got the drift that he wasn't over the moon at the offer they had made him.

My turn came. A bloke whose name now escapes me and who had the look of a pen-pusher opened a manila folder that lay on his desk. It contained an official ARU spiel which he read out – about how I was important to their plans and how they were prepared to make me an offer. I felt like I was going for a job interview. When he finished, he spun the manila folder around and sort of pushed it in my direction. 'Matt, we are happy to offer you a "C" contract,' he said.

'You're *what*?' I replied. 'Aren't you happy with that?' he asked, stating the bleeding obvious. 'Mate . . . you're kidding!' I said.

I had gone into that room knowing I wasn't going to be offered the top contract. But I honestly thought I'd be in the middle and that a 'B' contract offer was a chance, and arguably fair for a player at my stage in the game. All they had given me was a kick in the teeth. The dispute ended up going to an appeals committee of sorts and eventually they bumped their offer up to about $20,000.

But the first message was roughly this: 'Thanks for coming. We'll dangle just enough extra money in front of you to stop you going to rugby league.' It was my first encounter with 'professionalism' in Australian rugby union.

To be honest, a fair bit of the stuff that went on prior to the 1995 World Cup – which added up to the most tumultuous times for the two rugby codes in Australia since the 'split' here of 1907/08 – had gone straight over my head. It may just have been that I was either too young, too dumb, too naïve or, occasionally, too drunk – or maybe a combination of all four. While the two codes had wrestled with their individual agonies – in rugby, it was the establishment versus the breakaway World Rugby Corporation (WRC) – I had sailed blithely on.

It was on our return from the Cup campaign that the whispers became a roar. Word was that the breakaway group needed 100 signatures from around the rugby world before they could make it legitimate. Secret meetings were held at an office in Alexandria, Sydney, and I went to a couple of them – driving my dad's car. My own car had 'Eastwood Rugby Development' written all over the side – and no way was I going to take that and get spotted! The press had more than a whiff of it and for sure the story was going to break in a big way. New rumours were circulating every day, it seemed.

The rugby establishment, understandably, were worried and there was meeting after meeting as they tried to secure 'their' game and 'their' players. Eventually it sunk in with all of us that we were living in momentous times, experiencing the inevitability of what had once been the most amateur of all sports becoming professional – because it *had* to happen. There was a great deal of campaigning and pulling and pushing, and there's no doubt that some of the senior blokes saw the breakaway group as their 'retirement fund'. There was a belief within that group that if the game continued on its traditional establishment path, there was no way they could do anywhere near as well as if they took WRC's 'new money'.

For my own part, as a player who had gained some recognition and who perhaps was starting to build a bit of a profile, I found myself under heavy pressure to sign with the establishment. 'You'll never play for Australia again if you don't sign with us,' I was told. Questions were quietly asked of the senior players: 'Under the WRC will we still get to play for Australia?' 'Yes,' we were told.

Were we getting sold down the garden path?

It was a thoroughly stressful time. There was a good deal of pressure being applied by the WRC true believers. It's well known now that Phil Kearns was a big part of the operation. Ewen McKenzie came to me with the message: 'Mate, everyone else has signed and you're going to be left out if you don't.' It wasn't an easy call; my background, after all, had been through a very traditional rugby path – along a track taken by so many players in the game's history. I wasn't sure that I wanted to break away to some new 'World Series Cricket' type of organisation.

It was cloak-and-dagger stuff. 'Don't tell your parents, don't tell your girlfriend . . . don't tell *anyone*,' I was told. And I didn't . . . and I joined. I put my signature on a WRC contract late one afternoon in the car park adjoining North Sydney Oval No. 2. I signed for a six-figure sum that was healthy for a young player of my status – but in the deep shadows compared with the sort of money names like John Eales and Jonah Lomu were whispered to have been offered. They were at the peak of the pyramid. I was somewhat lower down the slope, but on a good wicket for someone just coming on board in international rugby.

Every day around that time it seemed as though the world of rugby union held its breath. The deal was the 100 signatures had to be in and lodged with a solicitor by a certain date in 1995 – November, from memory. If everything was okay at that stage, the details would be revealed and the backer(s) would step forward. On signing we were given no clue as to who that might be, although the name 'Kerry Packer' was always up there when the blokes involved met for a quiet beer or talked on the phone – and the rumours, of course, were proven correct.

In the other corner was the ARU, drawing the support of Rupert Murdoch and his pay-TV interests. The lineup, therefore, was exactly as it had shaped in rugby league: Packer v Murdoch – the two corporate giants, head-to-head. The pressure was intense.

The second Test against the All Blacks that year was held right in the middle of all the drama. After a thrilling game in which we went down 34–23, Kearnsie addressed the huge crowd, hinting at the turmoil that was plaguing the sport. 'Thank you very much for your support,' he said to the fans. 'And whatever happens, please keep giving us that support.'

Members of the team were called to a crisis meeting the morning after the Test. Leading ARU administrator Phil Harry fronted the meeting and essentially put everyone in the room on the spot. The theme was WRC contracts – and who had or hadn't signed them. The message was blunt: 'If you have signed, get out of the room. We don't want you.' Harry took a paternal stance, using his son Richard (who was in the team) as an example. 'If my son was in the position of being chased for his signature I would hope he would come and talk to me.' That was a bit harsh on Dick, I thought. We were all under the pump that morning. 'If anyone has signed, leave the room right now.' It was a stand-and-deliver message. The thing was that about three-quarters of the team had signed the provisional contracts, although I was aware that

Tim Gavin hadn't signed – and neither had Jason Little, who was being pursued by rugby league as that game fought its own battle.

There was an awkward silence in the room for a moment and then Tim Horan, the practical joker, stood up. Everyone looked at him, aghast: *Timmy, what are you DOING?* And Tim just cleared his throat: 'God, I've got to get a glass of water – I'm parched!' We had come to the meeting off the back of a big night out and were all feeling a bit like that. When Tim got to his feet, it broke the ice. Bob Dwyer eased the tension with a few words and the gathering just sort of broke up. No decision was made that day on which 'side' we should support as a group. In the *Sydney Morning Herald*, Greg Growden reported: 'Although several players including centres Pat Howard and Jason Little have already signed with the ARFU, a high percentage of Wallaby squad members is contracted to WRC.'

Like a lot of the other players, I had a WRC contract, but no deal – and as a result found myself one morning again at the office of Ian Ferrier, of chartered accountants Ferrier Hodgson. A contract was pushed my way, together with an accompanying message that could be paraphrased as: 'Sign this. The situation effectively is that if you don't sign now, you won't play for Australia.' I took the contract away with me, perused it closely, thought the whole thing over and eventually, some time later, I signed – for less money than had been offered by the other side. I now held contracts from both sides. 'It's very hard at the moment,' I told the media. 'Both of them [the contracts] are pretty good.'

At that point, I was back in the fold. I had pretty much kept my head down and made no fuss throughout the turmoil, so for me there were no recriminations. Some others, though, ended up paying a price. The talk has always been that Phil Kearns lost his Australian captaincy over the episode.

* * *

Rugby union's future direction was settled soon afterwards. The establishment, backed by Murdoch, won the day and the WRC contracts were despatched to various waste bins. The decision had been made for us.

What happened was that South Africa declined to come on board. This meant that the breakaway group didn't include the current world champions. This represented a monumental stumbling block to the venture going forward. The Springboks plonked for cash as their decision-maker, and the rugby establishment over there offered the players more of it than did the WRC. The settling finally came in the form of a huge ten-year contract, backed by Rupert Murdoch, which locked up TV rights in the Southern Hemisphere. Kerry Packer, perhaps an equal mix of sports fan and businessman – faded back into the shadows.

Professionalism had arrived in the 'amateur' game. Well, 'amateur' if you didn't take into account the back-door deals that France and Italy had been doing for years. By 1996 the published figures were that the cream of NSW players were being paid more than $3 million in total to turn out for the Waratahs and Australia that season.

So, this was it: a brave new world of professional rugby, with the game heading towards an annual Super 12s tournament now embracing teams from South Africa, New Zealand and Australia.

Like the players, the coaches had to adjust to being committed fulltime to the game. I suspect that the first thought that crossed their minds was the opportunity the new regime offered for *much* more training. When the Waratahs' campaign started out in early 1996, the day began at six o'clock with an hour of deep-water running in the pool at the St Joseph's College complex. So the first change was the step up in training; the second change, close behind, was the fining system. Lateness incurred an automatic fine, as did wearing the wrong gear . . . and so on. After brekkie there might be the chance of a quick snooze, but by ten o'clock or so we'd be on the training paddock for a solid session. After lunch there'd be a fitness session, then weights in the late afternoon or evening.

It got to the stage where every joint in your body was sore, and you'd walk into door-frames because you were so tired. I was lucky – young and relatively healthy – when the game went professional. It must have been tough for the senior blokes – and especially if they were dealing with niggling injuries.

Despite the downsides of rugby's new world order, it brought together all my dreams. I could now pursue as a career the game that had been so much a part of my life. The fact that I had declined approaches from rugby league in order to stay with the game I preferred made it so much more legitimate. The prospect was a golden one: to be paid to travel the world playing the game I loved.

At that point I made a decision that could be considered 'professional': I would do whatever I could, in terms of the way I looked after myself and conducted my life, to ensure a long career. I would maximise the opportunity that had been handed to me, along with all the players of that era. I understood what was at stake. I would continue to be mature about the playing side of the sport, but I also knew that I needed to be mature about the other aspects of my life, too. Playing rugby for money gave me a golden opportunity in my twenties to provide a solid foundation for the rest of my life. I don't think my motivation for playing the game changed once money came into it. Contrary to what some people have suggested in the media, I was always motivated by the wish to play for my country – the highest pinnacle a player can reach. The thought of seeing the world, playing in front of fantastic crowds in great stadiums, and testing myself against the best in the world was what inspired me to play the game.

Having made my decision to opt for a legitimate 'career' in rugby, I set out to get the right advice. I took direction from my management group and from my father, whose advice was always conservative, but solid, along the lines of: 'Make sure you put some of your wages away.' New money certainly brought the opportunity for some new pleasures as well. I love cars, and went from a Sigma GL, to a clapped-out Corolla, to a BMW 318IS. Now, *this* was professionalism! For some players in both codes it was a time of fast cars, wine and women, and good times. And I must say I enjoyed myself, too. But the thought that I could build something good in my life through this unexpected opportunity was never far from my mind.

All of us have different skills and different potential for achievement. My potential just happened to be on the sporting field. To be able to earn my living from that, while also travelling and, hopefully, growing as a human being, is a special privilege. The training is hard, and sometimes a grind, and the game by its nature inevitably extracts a physical toll on the men who play it at a high level. But it became a great environment for me – and especially in my more mature years when I had a family, and was able to spend a lot of time with them and to experience my daughters growing up. It beats the hell out of a 7 am to 7 pm job, I reckon – although I know I'm going to have to do that one day! The new professionalism of 1995/96 offered blokes like me a privileged lifestyle. I was one of the lucky ones. All these years later, I'm still grateful for the lifestyle and quality of life the sport of rugby has provided for my family and me.

Chapter 9

THE CHALLENGE
OF THE SUPER 12s

In this brave new world of professional rugby, the Waratah pathway towards the first Super 12 tournament came via a trip to the British Isles on which, according to the blueprint, the team would sort itself out for the challenge ahead. It was over there that Scott Bowen and I continued the schooling that began in late 1994 under the direction of kicking guru Dave Aldred, with its vast amounts of kick-training designed to get you into an automatic groove.

In the first match of the campaign, at Bristol, I broke a couple of ribs. When we headed on to Ireland the next day, I was in considerable discomfort. I battled on with the pain for a couple of weeks, trying to train and to play. But it was no good. I just got more and more sore. When I asked the new doctor on tour for some pain relief help, he gave me half a Panadol! In agony at 2.30 the following morning I knocked on his door. 'Do you know what time it is?' he stormed. 'Mate, I'm sure I've got broken ribs. I need more than half a Panadol,' I told him. He made to give me a Panadeine Forte and I grabbed the whole packet from him and headed back to my room.

We were in Belfast then for the match against Ulster, and next day I trekked down to the hospital for X-rays, which revealed that I did in fact have broken ribs. When I got back to the hotel, the concierge, who knew where I was heading that morning, said: 'Gee, you were quick. Which way did you go?' I told him I had gone down Falls Road. 'Falls Road!' the bloke said. 'God! And you made it!' On learning that I had ventured along one of the most dangerous thoroughfares in the world, I was relieved I had made the trek in civvies and hadn't been sporting anything that looked vaguely like a Union Jack.

On this first step down the path of professional rugby, a number of the players decided to make it a 'dry' tour. The feeling was that with all the extra training and the changing lifestyle, it made sense to maximise the physical side. Giving up the grog for a while was a sacrifice made in the interests of taking a more professional approach. But the choice created its own problems. The guys didn't seem to know how to relax and take it easy, and as a result the tour became tense . . . and intense. 'Uptight' might be the right word. It got to the point that, after one of the games in Ireland, coach Chris Hawkins virtually *ordered* us to go out and have a drink. We finished the night sitting in the team room, singing songs and in a good mood. All we needed was a campfire. It was an early message about 'balance' – the need for 'escape' time amid the hard work. We played eight games on tour (we lost one match to snow, in Pontyprid) won six, and lost two.

They were weighty times in the game, and we were in the middle of it – fulltime professionals all of a sudden, earning our livelihood from playing a game that we had all started playing simply because we enjoyed it, but these days having to be very accountable for the performances we turned in. Preparing and playing as well as we possibly could was now a very serious business indeed. There was an understanding among all the sections of the rugby community that the world had turned – and players knew that they had to perform, or very likely they'd be out of a job. But the game settled into its new era, and today's top-level players, earning good money from the game, still play rugby because they love it. The only thing that changed back then was that money came into a game where previously there had been none at all for the blokes who provided the entertainment.

That was a breakthrough tour. The players came to terms with the realisation of what had happened in the game, and of what they needed to do to be part of it in the long term. Wallaby pride is a very special thing – but I can report that there was genuine Waratah pride, too, on the campaign of 1996.

Chris Hawkins had taken over as Waratah coach in 1996, having the distinction of being the first coach to inherit a team that was virtually fully professional, in a newly professional game. For Chris the job was a juggling act. He was general manager at Gordon club at that time, with duties and obligations there, so he had to split his time. It wasn't the ideal arrangement at a time when the NSW players were coming to grips with the new requirements – the fulltime commitment and intensity – of being professionals. Chris's obligations elsewhere meant that he had to delegate some of his duties as NSW coach, leaving the rest of the coaching staff to run things at times. It wasn't perfect, and there was some unease among the players about the situation. We were looking for direction in these challenging and changed times. Our days were now committed fulltime to rugby – yet sometimes the coach would arrive only just before a training session to kick it off.

Like most things in life, I think good coaching is about getting the balance right. With some coaches of my experience their preparation has been right over the top. They do so much analysis and percentage work in the preparation phase that the actual playing of the 'game' is forgotten. Percentages and stats go only so far. You can't count on the percentages: they might tell you that your opposite number goes off his right foot 62 per cent of the time. If you put too much weight on that probability, the chance is there that he'll take the 38 per cent option – and leave you grasping at nothing. I have always believed that you have to play what is out there on the field. I think it's an imbalance in the game at the moment: there's too much whiteboard time, and not enough work being done out there on the training paddock.

An early triumph for Coach Hawkins in 1996 came in the preparation for and deliverance of our win over Transvaal in the opening round of the Super 12s competition. The coach predicted a 34–11 result – and, remarkably, we won 32–11 against a team that contained members of the World Cup-winning side. I had a ball that night playing fullback. I picked up a couple of tries and generally enjoyed myself thoroughly. My goal-kicking sharpened by the Aldred methods, I picked up 20 points against Western Province (30–22), 19 against North Transvaal (29–32) and 20 against the Brumbies (44–10). I was getting thoroughly involved in matches, and relishing my football. Brilliant at times, New South Wales didn't finish the season off as strongly as we would have liked. But when I look back, I think of it as one of the best seasons of my career. I was 23 years old and full of confidence. In terms of my point scoring and playing, it just seemed to come easily to me. I had moments that others have written and spoken of: match days when I felt I was in the 'zone' – absolutely confident of what I could do, and with the feeling that those around me, and the game itself, were moving in slow motion. The way I felt in 1996 no doubt was part of the story when I was named NSW's 'Best Player' that year – a special accolade, really, considering that the voting was done by my peers. At 23 I had the feeling that I was going to be around rugby for a long time . . .

A big feature of the Super 12s, following on the reintroduction of South Africa to world rugby in 1992, was the opportunity to play in the highly charged football environment over there – or should I say 'environments'? The conditions can differ greatly, from the sea-level games in Cape Town and Durban to the move up to the high veldt and plain – to Johannesburg and Bloemfontein. Loftus Versfeld Stadium in Pretoria, where we played Transvaal in that first year of the Super 12s, is an exciting place, but always a difficult challenge. You're 5000 feet above sea level, where the oxygen is getting thin. An advantage is that you can boot the ball further than usual, no problems. But physically, the place asks very tough questions of you. My experience was always of a burning sensation in the lungs, which I'd get within ten minutes of running on for any match. My throat would become as dry as dust and start to burn. After that initial period I was generally fine, adapting and working my way into the match. Then the last twenty minutes of any game was the real struggle. I'd be gasping to drag in enough air. But it's a magnificent arena to play on, and a place where rugby is taken extremely seriously – probably a little *too* seriously. The passion for the game over there is amazingly high, to the point of being bizarre at times.

My memories of that first season of Super 12s add up to a mixed bag. Against Natal at the Sydney Football Stadium in the first game we just tackled and tackled and tackled in the first half, with almost nil possession, and somehow managed to go in at the break leading 6–3. In the second half we were out on our feet and they ended up running over us 34–6, much to the disappointment of a big home crowd of 30,000. After an up-and-down season, Queensland beat us 15–13 with fourteen men to bring an embarrassing end to our semifinal hopes after Damian Smith had been sent off in the opening minutes following a stink with David Campese. The big punch that Damian threw as they battled on the ground fortunately missed; I hate to think what it would have done to Campo's head if it had landed. Damian Smith in my view was one of the most lethal players of his time. He was a big bloke, 190 centimetres or so and weighing in around 105 kilos, a player with ability and attitude. Once he crossed that white line he was the original angry young man. The return game in 1996 was an especially fiery one – and not long before his send-off there was a stink on the sideline when Damian put a high shot on me. I made the most of it and gave plenty of advice to the referee: 'That's his second offence,' I said. 'Two yellows make a red. Send him off! Send him off!' Smithie was alongside, and I was laughing at him. He wasn't laughing in return. It was bloody disappointing to lose that game – with John Eales kicking five penalty goals. It was the start of the rot. From 1996 to 2004, when I played my last game for New South Wales, we never managed to beat the Reds in a Super 12s game. We beat them on other days – the key State of the Union game that year, for example – but never (so far) at Super 12s level.

The State of the Union tussle in 1996 certainly had its moments. We beat them 29–25 in the second game to take the series on aggregate. It was a fiercely fought match in which Michael Brial (New South Wales) and Dan Crowley (Queensland) decided to have their own two-man war. Part of it was on the field in the first half and it continued in the tunnel as the teams left the field at the break, with coaching staff and referees jumping in to try to restore the peace as the pair went for each other. Winning and losing the series came down to a penalty given our way with one minute and 22 seconds to play, when their breakaway David Wilson jumped a fraction early from a scrum, with New South Wales in front 26–25. Needing to beat the Queenslanders by four to win the series on aggregate, we took the tap kick, bidding to move the ball quickly out along the line. But it was knocked down illegally and the penalty was returned to the spot.

A penalty goal would do the job for us. At that point my old man, sitting in the stand, saw our front row man Richard Harry come over and speak to me. As he told me later, Dad was really taken with that – how Dick had taken the trouble to come over to offer words of encouragement and inspiration. In fact, what he said to me out there was: 'Thank God it's *you* taking the kick, and not me!'

Despite the pressure of the situation, I couldn't hold back a chuckle as I walked to the spot and put the ball down, waiting for the tee to be brought out by one of a couple of young Eastwood kids who were handling the ball boy duties that night. The young fellow with the tee, a boy of about nine, trotted out and then about fifteen metres away slowed to a dawdle. 'C'mon, mate. Hurry up,' I urged him. I was keen to get it over with. He finally arrived, saying: 'Tough kick.' I could only agree with him. 'Absolutely . . . yes,' I said. This was getting tougher – what with Dick Harry and the kid. He stood behind me as I lined up the ball, showing no great inclination to leave. 'Mate, you have to go now,' I told him. 'Good luck,' he said, and then added 'Don't miss it!' over his shoulder as he walked off. It was almost an order. I was really under the pump now.

The history books tell that I duly took the ball boy's advice and landed the goal from 25 metres out, enabling us to clinch the State of the Union series. But it's funny – if I ever happen to think of that occasion, I think of the minutes that preceded the kick, rather than of the kick itself. I suppose that successful kick sort of summed up my year with the boot. I was hitting them beautifully most of the time, and my stats in early June were that I had kicked 80 goals from 99 shots – a 'batting average' of 80.8 per cent.

The Waratahs finished seventh in the Super 12s in 1996 – a moderate result, and one that unfortunately was to set the standard for too many Super 12 seasons ahead, all of which had one thing in common: they started out with high hopes and expectations. Over the years we have had some very talented teams, but rather too often there has been a failure to produce the class performance on the day or night it was needed. That failure to nail it on the big days has been the downfall of NSW rugby in this modern, professional era. My comments refer only to my own experience and I live in hope seasons of success lie ahead for the Waratahs.

I have a theory that New South Wales is too big and too crowded a state to run just one team. There should be two, making it more personal and tribal, and enabling people to identify more easily with a team closer to home. In the NSW teams I played in over the years, we had blokes coming from as far as two hours away for training sessions. That's four hours' travel a day, just to get to training. The guys live anywhere from Sutherland to Hornsby, from Coogee to the outer western suburbs – and it works against the Waratahs. The socialising that bonds teams together when you are on tour is great, but it's terribly difficult at home when blokes have to travel long distances. Sydney is such a huge city now. There is no doubt in my mind that with two teams – say North Side and South Side, or Metropolitan and Western – there would eventually be more success, and more support, as people identified with their 'local' Super 12s side.

* * *

In 1996 there were some big score blowouts – indicating a game skewed towards the attacking side. Against Auckland we scored 44 points, but they got 56! That's too many points in an 80-minute game of rugby. Adjusting the rules to arrive at the 'perfect game' has been a major quest and talking point for years. There's no doubt that rugby in the mid-1990s was slanted too much in favour of the attacking team. In my view, from the perspective of some seasons later, there is still a lot of work to be done in the fine-tuning. The thing that really seems to get up the noses of fans is the International Rugby Board (IRB) directive to referees on how to control games. Over the years, more often than not, that advice produced a result that didn't benefit the players *or* the spectators . . . *or* the game. All of us have watched enough of those sorts of games – frustrating matches dominated by the persistent shrill of the referee's whistle.

Frankly, I think that some of the refs are still really struggling. The players are getting bigger, faster and stronger – but the referees have strained to keep up. There remains a lot of fixing to be done, and until it happens it will be no more than the continuing bunfight – same old, same old.

My first experience of playing for Australia against the men of Wales in their famous red jumpers came that season of 1996 – and it was something short of memorable, even though we won 56–25 and I managed to pick up a haul of 21 points. I played fullback in the match, in Brisbane, and my expectations were certainly a lot higher than the reality of a game that seemed flat and which only generated the usual sort of local crowd enthusiasm late in the proceedings. With no one really 'getting into it', I commented to Tim Horan at one point: 'Mate, this feels like a *club* game!' There was a funny moment, though, featuring Alistair Murdoch in his second Test appearance after a long break. (He had made his debut back in 1993.) With the new professionalism in rugby, shoulder pads were in vogue, along with anything else that might turn a good footballer into a better one. The rules on shoulder pads were strict – you weren't allowed to wear anything that wasn't actually part of the jersey (for reasons that escape me) – and in the Wales–Australia Test the referee made it quite clear that he wasn't going to take any messing about in the shoulders department. He checked a couple of blokes early – 'Show me your shoulder pads' – and then grabbed Alistair on the shoulder. 'C'mon, show me your shoulder pads,' said the ref. Alistair, who spent a *lot* of time hanging around the gym, just looked at him before ripping off his jersey to reveal a body not unlike Arnold Schwarzenegger's. And no shoulder pads. 'Oh!' said the ref, with a smile . . .

It's funny how sometimes it's the little things that you remember through the blur of all the matches that make up a long career. The second Test against Wales that year went pretty much the same as the first – a 42–3 victory against a team that just couldn't match it with us. My game was pretty solid, highlighted perhaps by a 'bomb' I put up from 35 metres out. I kept my eye on the pill and dodged the traffic as I headed downfield – and took a clean catch adjacent to their fullback, close to the line. I was dragged down, but popped the ball inside – to none other than prop Dan Crowley, who I don't think had ever scored a Test try. He was going to be the happiest man in the world! But the ball slipped away from Dan about three metres from the line, and it was Owen Finegan who slinked in and scored the try.

The moment was a real buzz, one of those instances that everyone enjoys – players, fans, the media. The real kick for me at those times was in the quiet realisation that I had managed to do something a little out of the ordinary – and that it had brought a try. To be able to perform strongly and consistently is the basis of being a good rugby player, but the great thrill comes if now and then you can add value and do something special. With no hubris, I will just say how fortunate I have been to have been blessed with the skills to be able to do that now and then.

A further memory of the second Wales Test is of a small irritation. I had somehow misplaced my special kicking tee and had to use a different one. Whatever the reason, I was shanking the ball all over the place, missing left and right. I missed five of the nine shots I took.

Fortunately, it all came back the following week at Ballymore when I found the missing tee and rediscovered my kicking form. We crushed Canada 74–9 in a mismatch of a Test. My 39 points (three tries, two penalty goals, nine conversions) was an individual Test scoring record and brought up my 100 points (in fourteen Tests), but the gut feeling was that this was an example of poor programming, sacrificing one of the minnows of the international game. We were in the groove by the time we played Canada, readied by the hit-outs against Wales. We should have played the Canadians first up, as a warm-up game to the season. I had no problem with the fixture itself – teams like Canada need to be exposed to the whole spectrum of world rugby if they are to raise their standards. It was just the timing. Sometimes, though, such games can be cruel and embarrassing as, years later, when Australia crushed Namibia 142–0 in the 2003 World Cup. The 39 points I scored against the Canadians beat a record established by Michael Lynagh (28 v Argentina in 1995) – and stood until the Namibia game eight years later, when Mat Rogers scored 42. For me, there is a natural satisfaction in records I may have achieved over the years, but also a feeling that they are not in any way to be trumpeted. Yes, I have been happy with some of the things I have achieved, but the opportunity to do that comes every time from what my team-mates have managed to build in the game. I much prefer to think of it that way. After the Canada game I told the media, 'I'm just there to kick the goals; it was a team effort.' And that's honestly the way I always felt about it.

Rugby is a game that can bring you back to earth on a single after-noon or evening. And so it was when we played the All Blacks in windy Wellington in that season of 1996. We got smashed 43–6 – and I remember it most for being one of those games in which the pre-match workload played a part in the way things turned out. Greg Smith was the coach – and, despite early season successes, he had been copping some flak for the very programmed style of play he had introduced. As I have mentioned, Greg, offbeat char-acter that he was, was probably ahead of his time in his theory on 'sequence play'. He wanted our team then to be playing the way the game is played now – plays upon plays upon plays, with a series of calls designed to get you to the tryline. It was intricate stuff, with variations possible at any point. Greg, no doubt, had a Grand Vision – the idea of controlling the match to the exact point he wanted it to go. It's never easy.

Against Wales in Brisbane, our first try came from a perfect sequence play. Sequence number 2 it was, involving us hitting it up at outside-centre, the forwards taking it on, a change of direction, then . . . pass, pass, pass and Joe Roff scored next to the posts. This was in the first 50 seconds of the match. Happy days!

But it was just one play that worked out. The fact was a lot of the players didn't like the Smith philosophy at all – they thought it was far too regimented. But he was a new coach, bringing in new methods and ideas, whatever their worth – just as Rod Macqueen, his successor as Australian coach, did. It's what coaches do.

The week in New Zealand stays in my mind. We arrived at our

hotel at 7.30 pm on the Wednesday before the game – and were told we were heading straight out to train. Everyone was a bit tired and lethargic. We'd been up the back in economy for the three-and-a-half-hour flight, and without sounding too precious, economy-class seats are a tight squeeze for some of the big guys. We were on Sydney time, had had little to eat – and then the coach called a training session for 8 pm on a field at Lower Hutt.

We trained in alphabetical order, a back with a forward, and I was with Andrew Blades. We did more than an hour of fitness and then followed up with ball work. It was 10 pm when a halt was finally called. By the time we got back to the hotel, everyone was absolutely stuffed – and famished. By the time we'd had some food and any physio work that needed to be done, it was after midnight before anyone hit the sack. It was pretty shattering, and not a great beginning to the challenge we faced.

All week the prediction had been for wet weather. The All Blacks did most of their preparation indoors, light sessions that kept them fresh. On match day it was a bog. George Gregan, who was on the reserves bench for the game, recalled in conversation sometime later how his legs were just about 'gone' after the warm-up we did. He wondered how the blokes in the starting fifteen must be feeling!

Well, we got smashed, and it was no great surprise. They held the ball in atrocious conditions, scored six tries and beat us 43–6. Pulverised pride and deep embarrassment were our main emotions after the game, and especially when someone in the media declared: 'Sucked in. We don't have the worst scoreline anymore.' I think it was ex-Wallaby (1971–73) now media man Russell Fairfax, and we could have done without it after the night it had been.

The following week's challenge against the world champion Springbok side in Sydney shaped as a true test of character. And it was a source of great pride that we were able to pick ourselves up after the nightmare of Wellington and beat the 'Boks 21–16 in a real war of attrition – a match slogged out on a (thankfully) dry track. Tim Horan scored an opportunist try, Joe Roff scored one in the first half, and I landed a few goals (three penalties and a conversion) and made a try-saving tackle on my fullback rival Andre Joubert that gave me a buzz, even if it became a source of annoyance because of a poor call by the referee. After I had nailed him, Joubert just sat there on his knees, failing to release the ball and waiting for some support. And when the ref finally arrived he merely waved 'Play on'. The Aussie defence that day was outstanding – with Michael Brial really standing up and making his presence felt.

Andre Joubert was a mercurial player – one of the great fullbacks. He never seemed flustered. He had a massive boot on him, and was a tough, hard character who would turn up all the time and be heavily involved in any match. He really could play the game, and I respected and admired him.

Against such opposition, it was a passionate performance by the Wallaby team and a fantastic turnaround. The celebrations that evening at Mansions nightclub reflected how we felt. My standout memory is of Chris 'Buddha' Handy (an ex-front rower) signalling me over to the bar at one point early in the evening. 'Come over and do a tequila shot with me, Burkey,' he said. 'No thanks, mate. I'm not into those,' I replied. I then watched Buddha in action; he had salt lined up on the bar, the shot of tequila and the required lemon. He then proceeded to snort the salt up his nose, smash down the tequila shot – and squeeze the lemon into his eyes! 'Australia 21, South Africa 16 . . . you little beauty!' he roared, before lining up a repeat performance. 'Mate, you've got to join me!' he demanded. But I was very proud of myself that happy night – I declined.

* * *

A fortnight after that game there arrived out of the blue one of those moments in a career that I suspect all of us who aspire to be footballers dream of. We shaped up against the New Zealanders in a return game that was *all* about pride for Australia after what had happened in Wellington, and something very special happened. It left the legacy of the sort of yarn a grandfather might tell his grandkids as he dandles them on knees made wonky by years of football.

Chapter 10
ANATOMY OF A TRY

Just occasionally, on an afternoon or evening when you least expect it, and when the rugby gods choose to smile on you, something amazing can happen on a football field. So it was at Brisbane's Suncorp Stadium on 27 July 1996 with the Bledisloe Cup up for grabs between the two fiercest rivals in world rugby. Thirty-seven minutes into the game, deep down in our own territory, I retrieved a ball at fullback that had bounced loose . . . and it began. The next ten seconds or so added up to one of the truly thrilling moments of my career.

We had headed into that Test hot-wired with our plan to beat the All Blacks, and they with theirs to beat us. But the event that took place just before halftime that night didn't come off any drawing board – it came out of nowhere, from something that went awry. The plan was for the ball to go from our No. 10 (Pat Howard) to Richard Tombs in 12 – and for a long kick downfield into open space, and maybe into touch for a large gain of territory. Instead the pass came short to Richard, who was unable to get a proper grab on it and knocked it sideways and backwards. I was lurking behind the play – having a bit of a rest, it has been suggested – and when the ball went loose I positioned myself so that I could retrieve it and save Richard from being belted, which he surely would have been. In later tellings of the tale, Richard proposes the theory that it was his pass that put me through the gap that eventuated.

From 80 metres out I slipped past Andrew Mehrtens, who charged through, but a bit too quickly. Then, heading into top gear, I got through Josh Kronfeld and Zinzan Brooke. I think Walter Little had a crack at me, too. Meanwhile, I was looking for Ben Tune – he had the legs, the speed and the gas. But suddenly I was over halfway, racing away from the defence and into some clearer space. Ben loomed up on the outside, although still back a bit, and both of us were chased hard by Jonah Lomu. All Black fullback Christian Cullen in the last line had to make his decision quickly – to tackle me or to try to block off Tunie. At the critical moment as I dummied as if to pass to Ben, Cullen did neither – overcommitting himself and sort of jumping in the air in what was a half-tackle and a half-attempt at a knock down, leaving him with no more than handfuls of thin air. Suddenly out on my own, it was at about that moment I thought, 'Well, here it is . . . Just pin back the ears!' And I did, and when the tryline arrived at great speed I was happy to be there just ahead of Jeff Wilson's covering tackle. I finished with a fairly stupid dive, a bit of a hoopla thing, to score what is generally agreed to be one of the best individual tries of my career – and arguably the most famous. In the background, the chasing George Gregan raised an arm in acclamation.

'Burke's try will live forever!' shouted one of the newspaper headlines the next day (even though we had lost the match 32–25).

I'm not so sure about that. But it remains to this day a special memory – and the best thing about it was that it wasn't planned. It was just a bloke playing what was in front of him at a particular moment in a match. It wasn't until I saw the footage later that I had some sense of what all the media fuss was about. At the time, the pleasure of scoring such a try – and against *them* – was quickly dulled by my disappointment at missing the conversion attempt. Again, that's just football – it gives, and it takes away.

> *He just carved up through the middle and nobody touched him between there and the line. To me, it was probably the single most special moment of Bledisloe Cup games that I know – to see that young man score.*
>
> Chris Handy

That day was the first time I used the Dave Aldred goal-kicking technique in a Test match, leaning the ball a little differently to open up the sweet spot. 'Just trust yourself,' I said to myself as I took the first penalty shot of the afternoon from 54 metres out, having convinced Ealsie that it was worth a try. Well, I gave it a nudge – and if the posts had been back another fifteen metres it would still have gone over. I hit it just right, and the fact that it sailed right over the black dot made it even more satisfying. Later, I landed another penalty from 51 metres, proving that 'round the corner' kickers could get the same distance as the old toe-kickers.

None of it, of course, was worth a bean when the All Blacks beat us in the last minute, having rushed on 23 points in the last seventeen minutes from what seemed an impossible position, to steal victory away. We had led 16–9 at halftime, and for two-thirds of the game we had been clearly the better side. In our disappointment in defeat that night, we were *not* joined on the sideline by our coach Greg Smith, whose attitude seemed to be 'Let them stew in it.' I understood his disappointment, but I was disappointed in *him*, too. He knew we were hurting and he was part of the team – yet he chose to stay away.

Some of the praise I received from the media after that game probably went straight over my head to a fair extent. In one newspaper I was called 'a great fullback in the tradition of Dr Alex Ross and Roger Gould', and I knew enough of rugby history to realise they were generous and humbling words. I had heard Peter Fenton talk of Alex Ross, a member of the famous 1927 Waratahs, and I had read of Gould. But I was no historian. In fact, not until I first broke into the Schoolboys team did I have any sense at all of the great progression of rugby players down the years – of that long line of top-line players stretching all the way back to the late nineteenth century. My own early heroes had come from outside rugby, and much to do with taking on board the game's history was still a work in progress for me.

It was always an interesting experience to go from the 'glory' (or near glory, in this case) of a big international game back to the amiable Saturday arvo get-together of club rugby. I took that small step in 1996 and remember clearly the afternoon we knocked over mighty Randwick, a club always rich in stars and an expectation of success. George Gregan, who played for the Greens that day, remembers the match as the one in which the Eastwood players 'all faced Mecca' at the moment of an unexpected victory. Desperately hanging on to a narrow lead (21–17), we won the last scrum of the day and our No. 8 passed the ball back to me – at which point I booted it way into touch, and perhaps right out of the park. It was at that point the Eastwood players sunk to the turf – providing George with an indelible memory of footballers assuming the prayer position. It was Randwick, however, who finished our season later, beating us in the wet at Concord – while I looked on from the stand, nursing a crook shoulder I hoped would be okay for the upcoming Wallaby European tour. Essentially, I had been ruled out of the game by the ARFU, after the Union's doctor had declared me unfit. The decision prompted an outburst from both clubs. 'It smacks of Big Brother,' declared 'Wicks coach John Maxwell, while Eastwood president Bill Papworth said, 'This absolutely disgusts me and has thrown everything into chaos.'

This was the ongoing dilemma of club football. Probably, at a pinch, I could have played that afternoon – but I was a contracted Australian player, and to do so would have put my tour in some jeopardy. And in this new age of professionalism, rugby at the top level was my *business* as well as my game of choice. Leading players face up to that question most years. I think if you gathered together a group of the top blokes and asked them in open forum whether or not they wanted to play club footy, they would say 'yes'. Delve a little deeper, though, in off-the-record conversation, and the answer would be 'no'. Club footy is no walk in the park. The standard is fairly good . . . though certainly not great. But one big risk lies in blokes who set out to cheap-shot a leading player – to try to prove some obscure point to themselves or someone else.

At the end of season 1996 I was named the *Sydney Morning Herald*'s 'Player of the Year' and also the Schweppes Wallabies 'Player of the Year'. I took pride in such recognition, as any player would. As far as the Wallabies were concerned, it was the only time I was to receive that sort of accolade. The success reminded me of something funny that had occurred a couple of years before, when Tim Gavin was named 'Wallaby of the Year' on 264 or so votes, ahead of Jason Little on about 250. The system then was that all players would vote after matches – and as a matter of course, each player would give himself five points – to ensure that at the end of it at least everyone would be 'on the board'. After the award had been announced, the newspapers ran the full list – all the way from the top blokes down to M. Burke on twenty points and M. O'Connor on five. Dad checked out the list and declared: 'Well, at least you've received a few votes, mate.' And I explained: 'Dad, you give *yourself* five points a game . . . and I played four Test matches.' 'Oh, . . . right,' he said. Matt O'Connor played one Test that season.

I went on to win the *Sydney Morning Herald* award the following season (1997), too, but was disappointed at missing out on the 'Waratah Players' Player' award – not because of the award itself, but because of the events surrounding it. The prize was a trip to Fiji, which I would have loved to have won at the tail end of what had been a hard season. But at the big function to celebrate the event, NSW coach Matt Williams came up to my table with some news. 'Mate,' he said. 'I just wanted to let you know that we're not going to give you the award this year. We're going to give it to Pinko [breakaway Stuart Pinkerton].' 'Fair enough,' I said. 'He had a great season.' The coach continued: 'No, no . . . it's not just that. We just thought you'd been winning too many awards, so we decided to give it to someone else.' I was really filthy about that and in my later, more confident and mature, years I probably would have said something. But I didn't. It's not something I have ever talked about publicly before, but I was very upset. I mean, why play? Why try? You get recognised by your peers and then something like that happens. Afterwards, Pinko came up to me and told me of his embarrassment. And when I won the *Herald* award, with him second, he got up and said some kind things about me being the 'rightful winner'.

The situation of the 'Players' Player' award was a sobering lesson for me, reinforced in the last months of my career in Australia when my years of service and loyalty to the cause appeared to count for not much at all. I will talk about it later in this book. But to me the message was the same: for all the talk about the 'team must come first' and all that kind of stuff, the reality in this game we play is that you are there by yourself, you and your family battling the rest of them. I had a glimpse of that back in 1997, but it wasn't until 2004 that it really hit home. Footballers are expendable. People will fawn over you when things are going well, but they might take advantage of you too, and then quickly discard you if there is a perception that your 'use by' date is nearing.

The eight-week European tour that was the icing on the cake at the end of season 1996, taking in Tests against Italy, Scotland, Ireland and Wales, was the usual mix of good fun, good hard footy, a tonne of training, some dud weather – and some strangeness under the Wallabies' new coach, Greg Smith. It was a wonderfully successful campaign – and one that brought down the curtain on the career of David 'Campo' Campese, whose final match was against the Barbarians. For the first time ever, a Wallaby side went through unbeaten, twelve out of twelve.

The opening international against Italy in Padua, Campo's 100th Test, was preceded by an odd decision from Coach Smith, who declared to ace centre Tim Horan, 'You're a winger, not a centre,' and promptly plonked him on the wing for the Test match. Timmy responded by scoring a runaway chip 'n' chase try at great speed – at which point he celebrated by 'doing the train' (getting up, elbows cocked at 90 degrees and launching into an impersonation of an old choo choo steam train), absolutely revelling in the moment. Tim was always a bloke who had fun, on and off the field. There was a moment in a Test against South Africa in 1993 when he scored a try and got up and did the point to the forehead thing, like the ice-cool Swedish tennis players. It was just fun with Tim and he could justify it because he was one of the very best players around.

The lead-up to the match was overwhelmed completely by the attention paid to Campo, who had lived in Italy for several years and was long since part of Italian sporting folklore by then, I suspect. Before the Test there was no space for any normal pre-match rituals – it was all Campo. He was presented with plaques and platters, and it seemed that just about every man and his dog was out there trying to get a photo of him on the big day. And good luck to him. To get to 100 Tests is a fantastic feat, taking him into very rare rugby territory, and testimony both to his longevity in the game and his ability.

We won the Test 40–18, but it was a pretty ordinary performance. Apart from Campo, I remember the Italians putting on a dummy switch play in front of the posts and their fly-half, Diego Dominguez, going straight through David Knox's tackle as if he wasn't there to score under the sticks. Knoxy wasn't much up for contact, loved running with the ball – but would forget every now and then to defend. Just before that moment I had nailed one of their blokes on the corner post to stop a try, and after the game Greg Smith was terse on the subject of the Knox 'miss': 'If I was Matthew Burke I wouldn't have been happy, and if I was the captain I would have gone right off my rocker.' He took no prisoners, the coach!

It was cold at Murrayfield when we beat the Scots (29–19), but they put on a move so hot it broke our defensive line. We subsequently pinched it without shame for our own armament, and called it 'Scotland'. Then it was *really* cold when we shifted across to Ireland. The scheduled mid-week match against Dublin at Leinster was called off, with the ground under ice.

But the weather didn't stop the team training at a local sportsfield. We had conscripted Bart Pilecki, son of Wallaby legend Stan

'The Man' Pilecki, from the local comp because we needed an extra prop for practice sessions. Bart was given some stuff out of the team kit, notably a jersey that was too small for him and a pair of shorts, also too small. He went out to train wearing only those on what was one of the coldest days I have ever experienced – and at the end of the session he was literally purple. For our 'Tongan Mafia' – Fili Finau and Willie O – and a couple of the other boys, it was a nightmare. They had every possible item of gear on, including beanies on their heads and socks on their hands. But it was just too cold, and after fifteen minutes or so they walked.

Coach Smith had given us the rev-up in the dressing room, but when we trained that day, Alec Evans took the session. Meanwhile the coach was back in the clubhouse, his hands clasped around a hot cup of soup. Everyone was filthy about that. The wind cut through you like a knife. When it became so strong that it was blowing the tackle bags off the ground, a mutual decision was made to call it quits. Back in the dressing room we were greeted by cold showers – although the water temperature didn't seem too bad at all after the freezing conditions outside.

We beat the Irish 22–12 in Dublin, then headed on to Wales, where we made very heavy weather of it in the second half before winning 28–19 in extra time on the back of a penalty try. Timmy Horan captained the team for the first time in this Test, and his calls, in line with what he understood to be the coach's philosophy – for us to kick for touch rather than shoot for goal in the second half – nearly proved our downfall. The *Daily Telegraph*'s Bruce Wilson reported it this way: 'The second half was 12 minutes old when this madness started. Four times Horan declined the chance to kick at goal when his side was leading 18–9 in a Test match. Each time kicker Matt Burke walked towards the spot and each time some strange option was taken.' After the games, Greg said to Tim in the dressing room: 'Mate, you made some tough decisions out there. I wouldn't have gone that way – I would have been taking the shots for goal.' It was pretty bizarre. As Tim was quick to point out, Greg was the bloke who had been urging us to play attacking football.

In Wales, I roomed with David Knox, who wasn't in the Test team or on the reserves bench. Knoxie basically just dropped his bags in early in the week and departed. 'See you on Sunday,' he said . . . and was gone. He was a funny roomie – he just did what he wanted to do.

It wasn't a Grand Slam tour – missing the fourth 'leg' – against England. Instead we finished with a rousing win over the Barbarians in front of 70,000 fans at Twickenham, and I certainly enjoyed it with a couple of tries and some goals for 24 points – a record for a match against the Barbarians. Campo got the big reception he deserved in this final game of his international career. Away from the glare of the spotlight, which was focused, rightly, on him, I was able to take quiet satisfaction in my own game. A journo kindly observed the next day: 'It may have been Campo's day, but it was Matthew Burke's game, and for that matter, year.' The tour had brought me 136 points and a lot of good memories. And all of us had a good time in London in the build-up to the Ba-Bas – traditionally a game that is approached with less intensity than others on a Northern Hemisphere campaign.

Afterwards, H.G. Nelson (Greig Pickhaver) was conscripted to join us at a happy hour back at the team pub after coming in for a beer in the dressing room following the game. A big feature of the happy hour (and later) was that everyone had to do a Greg Smithism. Everyone had a favourite phrase or expression. The coach had plenty of sayings, as coaches do – and they were all churned out: 'That's maniacal!' and 'Yeah . . . nah'. Even H.G. joined in. Jason Little got to shave the team doctor's back, having won a bet that we would go through undefeated. Dr John Best being an hirsute sort of bloke, Jason was able to tastefully trace a nice stick figure of a man on the doc's back. For the big dinner that officially ended the campaign, everyone had to buy a present worth no more than five quid for someone else on the tour. Hooker Marco Caputo gave his fierce rival Michael Foley a toy dump truck. 'Here, mate, this is for you – and you can give it to your son after the tour,' said Marco. 'But in the meantime, I thought it would be useful to hold all that shit you've thrown at me after every game.' Everyone laughed. Hookers are regarded as being a little different in rugby's world.

Reflecting on David Campese, and his departure in 1996, I suspect I'm like many others in that I hold some mixed views on Campo. When I first came into contact with him at club level in 1991/92 he was an amazing footballer; and when I first played with him in the Waratahs team of 1993 I became aware that he was a player who could do truly freakish things on a football field. He could do terrible things, too, although without doubt the good outweighed the bad. Oh, yes. Campo could play.

I find myself now writing 'but' – and I imagine for plenty of people there have always been some 'buts' about David Campese. I had him as a roomie a number of times, owing to the rooms being dished out in alphabetical order, and I must say the bloke could be quite bizarre. He was not what you could ever call an understanding roommate. I remember him turning on the TV at 2.30 one morning. 'I can't sleep,' he said. 'Well, *I'm* going okay,' I replied. 'Well, *I* can't . . . and I'm the senior player and you do what I do.' And that was that. 'Inconsiderate' is a word that comes to mind. My experience of being Campo's roomie was that you became pretty much his personal assistant as well. You'd find yourself taking messages for him the whole time. I concluded that he needed to take someone away with him on tour to look after all his personal stuff. Rooming with him, I formed the impression of a bloke entrenched in his own world and one without too much respect for those around him. Whatever Campo did . . . that went.

The biggest gripe from the younger players in teams in which he played was that he never really bothered to get to know them. To be fair, that was pretty much the wider mentality of the team back then. The young blokes came in and they didn't say a word. You spoke when you were spoken to, there was no joking around and it was all pretty regimented. It's a very different scenario today, when there is a warmer reception for the younger players and the chance for them to take more responsibility. Back then it was very much a senior–junior thing – just do what you were told to do.

Campo was such an extraordinary talent that it's a shame how things have gone since he retired. I think as far as the Wallabies go he has lost his way – and the team has lost some respect for him. I vaguely remember his parting words when he left the team all those years ago. They were to the effect that he understood what pressure we were under because he'd been there, and that he wouldn't bag us through the media as some ex-players had. From the next international season Campo was a member of the media – dishing out the criticism and bagging individuals. His words of assurance seemed hollow then.

Chapter 11

WHODUNNIT? THE MYSTERY DOCUMENT OF 1997

Before the Waratahs' 1997 Super 12 match against the Brumbies at Bruce Stadium in Canberra, which turned out to be a shocker, something mysterious and highly suspicious took place. At a training session at Concord, all the NSW players were handed a document bearing an ACT Brumbies letterhead. Basically, it was a run-down on every Waratah player – an analysis similar to the ones that have caused some embarrassment in the cricket world in recent times when inadvertently pushed under the wrong hotel room door. It ran through statistics and opinions on all of us – from fullback through to the front row. I wish I still had it, but I threw my copy away in disgust. Next to my name were comments along these lines: 'Good runner, but doesn't trust himself. Doesn't counterattack. Kicks all the time. Can't tackle. Doesn't get involved enough.' So it went on from player to player – and the general reaction from our team was that it was a little suspicious.

The 'mystery' surrounding the document concerned its source. Was it really something that had leaked out of the Brumbies camp? The general reaction from all of us after reading it was roughly the same, along the lines of: 'That's not how I play the game!' followed by: 'Is this *really* what the coach thinks of me?' Whatever . . . it didn't work as a motivational tool, if that had been the intention. The players went into the game in a resentful mood and we got smashed 56–9, after having beaten them 44–10 the previous year.

Sadly, a couple of our blokes – top players – were virtually never seen again after that game. Richard Tombs, a strong performer week in and week out – a player who could catch and pass and tackle – pretty much disappeared off the radar after the match. And so too Scott Bowen, who was replaced early in the second half after copping a bagging from the coach at halftime. Scott disappeared back into the outer reaches of club football, finally switching clubs to Easts to try to lift his profile.

The whole thing was just a sad episode. I think we all had a pretty fair idea of who was responsible. It was a joke – playing mind games like that with mature adults. It was a sour episode in a season of fluctuating results.

My memories of the 1997 Super 12 season are a mixed bag – just like the performances of the NSW team itself under coach Matt Williams. We were up and down like an elevator in the CBD. In a couple of games I battled a stomach bug that made me feel like I'd rather be anywhere than on a football field, being monstered by 110-kilogram Kiwis or Springboks. In the match against Transvaal at Ellis Park, we badly stuffed up after fighting back from a half-time deficit of 26–6 to hit the lead 27–26, before trailing 29–26 in the late stages. At least a bonus point for a loss of four points or less looked to be in the bag. But a head-phoned runner arrived on the field with instructions from the coach. 'Scott [Bowen, our No. 10], you've got to run it . . . We've got to score a try, we've got to win this,' he said frantically. At the time we were deep in our own half. Scott glanced up in the direction of the grandstand and responded: 'Mate, we're not playing schoolboy footy now . . . You can't just shoot it around on your own tryline and pull a game out of the hat.' But we tried anyway, as instructed, and went belly-up. A ball went to ground amid the desperation, and Transvaal snapped it up and were over the line in the blink of an eye. They kicked the goal and won 36–27 – and that was goodbye to the Waratahs' consolation bonus point.

We lost to Natal 23–28 at Kings Park, Durban. During the match I scored what I reckoned was a fair try in the corner. The referee, Tappe Henning, effectively awarded the try, and as I was lining up the sideline shot that would have given us a booming start, he walked over to one of the TV screens on the sideline to have a look at the replay. Back he came. 'It's no try,' he said. 'You hit the corner post before you got the ball down.' The giant screen at the ground probably confirmed that it *wasn't* a try, but the bloke had awarded it! Under the laws of the game he couldn't alter his decision. Henning went on to cane us 21–7 in the penalty count.

Against Northern Transvaal, whom we beat 43–29, I scored three tries in a personal tally of 33 points. Just before the third one, I was on the deck with a bloody sore hand and wrist after someone had landed heavily on it in a ruck. Maybe a size 12 boot. I thought I had broken something, for sure. Our physio, Ian Collier, came out to attend to me, but as I was lying there I heard the call from Scott Bowen: 'Burkey, we need you!' 'Gotta go, mate . . . Gotta go,' I said to Collier. And suddenly it was catch, pass . . . catch, pass – and the ball was in my hands on the wing and I was over for a try. My hand and wrist ached like buggery (though later X-rays cleared me of any bone damage). Collier came straight back out to resume the treatment, so I couldn't take the kick at goal. Scott was the reserve kicker, but Campo came bustling over and said, 'No mate, I'll take this one.' It was one of those kicks from touch that reserve kickers love. If they happen to land it they are instant heroes; even if they go *moderately* close it's a case of, 'Wow! That was a great kick from a second-stringer!' It's win–win. Campo, who was neither a first- nor second-choice kicker, duly missed by a mile or so.

It was a nothing sort of a year, although I did get to attend the 'Penthouse Pet of the Year' awards lunch. I was in Otago, New Zealand, when one of the marketing people contacted me. Could Scott Bowen and I do a promotion in Sydney the following week? I told her I wasn't too keen, that I hadn't been home for ages and was just looking forward to a few quiet days. 'What's the function, anyway?' I asked. 'Oh, "Penthouse Pet of the Year".' 'Well, maybe I *can* manage it.' I even had my photo taken with the winner, as it turned out – OK, with *all* the finalists, as a matter of fact. Well, *someone*'s got to do it!

The move to fulltime professionalism lifted both the profiles and the demands on footballers like me, creating a regular requirement for expert help and advice. For the past seven or eight years the support I have needed has come from a man who is both a close friend and shrewd adviser – my manager, John Fordham. And it was through one of those occasional strokes of good fortune in life that Fordo and I got together. In an interview with the Sydney *Sun-Herald*, Fordham, who was by then building a strong reputation and a stable of high-profile clients – leading broadcaster John Laws and Australian cricket captain Mark Taylor among them – was asked which rugby union player he would most like to have in his team. Fordo nominated me. His own background was strongly rugby union-linked; one brother, Bob, was a rugby Test referee and another, David, a respected TV rugby broadcaster. Yet Fordo's stable at that stage didn't include a rugby player. Anyhow, to cut a long story short, I rang him when I learned of the story and later, with my father, met him for coffee at Aussie Stadium. We got on fine, and have done so ever since. It's much more than just business – Kate and I have a genuinely close friendship with John and his wife, Veronica, and son, Nick, who work in the Fordham business. John is a genial bloke – but very smart and pragmatic and deeply loyal. There is no doubt in my mind that, with his connections and the introductions he has been able to set up for me, he has helped my career a great deal, as well as helping to guide me through some hard times and tough decisions. The night before I left on the Barbarians trip, Kate, the kids and I were at their house having dinner and doing our best to work out where our future lay. It's still a strong friendship much more than a business partnership, and many thanks must go to the Fordham family as a whole. The danger with Fordo, as those who know him will readily agree, lies on the social side of the equation. Fordham lunches have been known to last until midnight.

Apart from the sports management side of the Fordham business, Fordo is a wine expert and columnist. For a dinner at Fordo's you'll generally arrive with a nice bottle of something, which he'll whisk away with some kind words. 'Mate, that looks good, but why don't we just try *this* one,' he'll say . . . and promptly produce a twenty-year-old red or something similar. Late in the evening you'll head home, inevitably accompanied by the bottle you brought along, plus two or three more. He is a familiar figure at a certain eastern suburbs pub, and can be seen now and then holding court outside. Some people have suggested that the placement of a special Fordham stool on the pavement would be entirely reasonable.

When you are out talking sport with J. Fordham, the hours and the beers fly by. Suddenly it's late, and everyone is the worse for wear and probably in trouble at home. There has been a lot of fun, and real friendship along with the serious stuff, in my business arrangement with John – and that surely is the best way.

Through that struggling 1997 season I had the words 'vice captain' alongside my name in the program for the Super 12s games. But it was something of a token offering by Coach Williams, as proven in a game we played against Waikato in New Zealand. The NSW skipper that day was Michael Brial, who left the field injured with about fifteen minutes to go. It was a tight game, with only a few points in it – and with Brial gone I started to say a few things: that we had to keep the ball in hand, play simple football, and so on. Then out comes the trainer with the news that Tiaan Strauss, the former Springbok and rugby league player, was now the captain! '*What?*' I thought to myself. I heard later that the coach had given Strauss the opportunity to lead because he had already captained his country. No disrespect to Tiaan, but I was dirty on Williams for making a decision like that at my expense.

The NSW season pretty much fizzled out in disappointment, although we beat Otago (27–16) and managed to lead the crack Auckland side 20–13 at halftime – before they got us in the second half (34–20).

As the season dragged towards a close, our physio did the rounds one morning, on a final injury check. Any problems? Well, yeah. As a matter of fact, I had a bit of a groin strain – but it was nothing much to worry about. In fact, the thing was to plague me and provide a huge check to my career over the next six months!

It was all to do with the amount of goal-kicking practice I was doing. As I mentioned earlier, over a period of time I had progressively got near enough to ripping the tendon from the bone on the left side. A day or two before we played Queensland in one of the State of the Union games, I was out early at training at Concord to do some kicking with Scott Bowen. For a bit of variety I decided to try a left-footer – but as I hit the ball the pain was unbelievable and I just fell over, squealing.

We played some touch footy after that, and our physio, Ian Collier, reassured me that I'd work my way through the problem once I warmed up. But when Andrew Heath, a prop, stepped around me and ran 50 metres to score, I was slower to turn than the *Queen Mary*. There was much hilarity, but it was no laughing matter for me. I knew I was in trouble.

I struggled through the match against Queensland, scoring a try near the end that had me in trouble again to the point that I declined to take the kick.

I was selected to play against the French in early June but failed the fitness test, which opened the door for Stephen Larkham to play fullback. By then I was having extensive physio work, with Greg Craig assuring me that I was okay . . . and me assuring him that I wasn't. I got to the stage where, if I lay down, I wouldn't be able to lift my left leg more than an inch or two off the bed. For quite a time it followed the same pattern: at training one day I could complete all the exercises and Greg would be saying, 'You know, you should be playing', and the next day I would barely be able to walk. I think that even when the experts are giving you the thumbs-up, there are sometimes occasions when a footballer has to say, 'Look, this just isn't right. I have to stop.' It was an immensely frustrating injury that forced me to miss most of the Tri-Nations tournament that year. There was no visible hint that anything was wrong, and yet I was in desperate trouble. Needles from the doc helped me get through a couple of games, but obviously they weren't the answer. I needed rest.

I struggled through half a comeback game for Eastwood in deep mud at Woollahra Oval and told the media, 'I'm ready.' I wasn't, really – although I went on to play in a fairly lacklustre Test against England in Sydney. Ealsie kicked, we won 25–6, I scored a try – and pulled up sore. As usual.

I was subsequently part of an amazing experience when we played for the Bledisloe Cup before 90,000 fans at the Melbourne Cricket Ground in late July. About half of the crowd were Kiwis, I reckon. The All Blacks cleaned us up 33–18 in a drab game, and that scoreline probably flattered a disappointing Aussie effort. We missed tries that could have been scored, and generally were fairly unimpressive and well beaten by a side that received near enough to a home-town welcome when they paraded the Cup after the game.

I felt sorry for Michael Brial in that game. A good, tough player, he was pulled out of club football to add some zest and spark to the Australian side – and, no doubt, to play the hard man. Afterwards he copped plenty of the general blame for Australia's failure and was pretty much ostracised by coach Greg Smith, who had invited him into the team. I thought it was pretty tough.

For my own part, the season was as good as over. The groin injury was no better, a constant drain on everything I was trying to do in my football career. I knew that it was time for a rest, and so declared myself unavailable for the Wallaby tour to Argentina at the end of the year. Just before Christmas I was back in training again – knowing it was going to be a long haul, but ready to do what had to be done.

Chapter 12

'BURKE 24, ALL BLACKS 16'

The invisible injury I dragged through season 1997 and into 1998 was one of the worst of my life in football. It took seven months out of my career and, thinking back, there were days when I wondered whether I would ever shake the damned thing. But day by day I gradually got closer to being a footballer again – and on 2 February I played sixteen minutes of a pre-season game against Queensland, at Coolum. It was sixteen minutes of apprehension after all I had been through – living with pain and the endless rehab sessions. The media made much of the fact that Burke was out of the match before the midpoint in the first half ('In a blow to Australia's rugby hopes in the coming season, Matthew Burke lasted only 16 minutes in his comeback game for NSW'), but actually it wasn't so bad – one short, sharp bout of pain which was probably scar tissue releasing itself. At least I had put a toe in the water. I had become a footballer again.

By the second of that year's games in the pre-season Southern Cross tournament I was back on deck, and managed an hour against the Canterbury Crusaders in a match we won 36–19 in Brisbane. At fulltime that night I knew I was on my way, that I would make it back.

We approached the first game of the Super 12s season, against the Brumbies, with a motto: 'Nil by mouth.' This was a big game with more than a little of a grudge about it. Both teams had great home records against the other – and we were out to protect that. In a game like this, with a real edge to it, we knew there would be a lot of talking from the other mob. We decided we wouldn't give any back at all – just smile serenely – although we set out to be more aggressive in what we did on the field. It worked beautifully. We underplayed our hand – and they played 'angry', and had George Gregan and Troy Croker sent to the sin bin. In the end the scoreboard read 32–12 our way. It was a great win, and a great start to the campaign.

In the Round 3 match at Sydney Football Stadium that year against the Golden Cats I got absolutely drilled in a tackle by the giant Os du Randt, described in one report as '130 kilos of prime South African beef'. It came on the tail end of a move when we had hit it up the centre after a lineout and then come back to the short side to try to catch out the defence. Our five-eighth, Manny Edmonds, had the ball and just kept running as he headed back towards the blind. And I was calling on him to pass me the pill, to give me a bit of time. He kept running, and finally drew a defender and passed late to me – with the ball catching me out, to an extent, going to my left hand instead of my right and causing me to juggle and prop, and then take a step back inside.

Meanwhile, lurking in the general vicinity was du Randt, who had been fiddling with a boot that had come off in the lineout. He arose from the deck like a behemoth as I was fumbling around

145

with the ball and just about snapped me in half with the impact of his tackle.

As I went down like a sack of potatoes under the crunch of the hit, I did the medial ligament in my right knee – an injury that was subsequently to keep me out for three weeks. Somehow – instinct, I suspect – as I hit the deck under his 130 kilos I managed to pop the ball up and we kept the momentum going. Michael Brial came up to me afterwards. 'Mate, great ball control . . .,' he said. I just looked at him. 'Brially, do me a favour, will you?' I asked. 'Pick my knee up . . . it's back up the field there somewhere.' This wasn't a happy moment. Running into 130-kilo props is a significant health risk on a football field. At least we won the game, coming from 10-nil down to take it 25–10.

I was sidelined for three weeks, but was back for Auckland (25–47) and Queensland (17-all) – a typically rough physical game against the old 'enemy'. Then we faced Otago in a match that we needed to win if we were to stay alive in the competition. My knee was about 70 per cent right, and fly-half Manny Edmonds had been looking after the goal-kicking because of my problem. Because of the groin injury I had suffered I had drastically altered my training routine anyway when it came to goal-kicking. The workload that had helped cause the problem could be as many as 500 kicks per session. Now, and in the future, I was down to about 100. From now on it was quality, not quantity.

Against Otago, when our skipper Michael Brial scored a try out wide in the 72nd minute to get us back to 21–22 and open up a chance, I took the kick. As I took my first step in, my left calf cramped. On the next step I got a cramp in my *right* calf. Unable to get up on my toes I hit the ball with what I later described as a 'dirt rotten scuff' and it bent back left to right – and scrambled over the crossbar! My team-mates called the kick 'a wobbly one wood'.

The next day the guys from *Fox Sports* rang me and wanted to do a piece about the 'miracle' goal. In one camera shot, it looked for all the world as if my ball had collided with a ball that had been kicked at the same instant by a ball boy for the re-start – and been diverted between the posts. The papers fell for it in their match reports, with the *Daily Telegraph* reporting how the ball had struck another as it went over the crossbar. The *Herald* followed suit. It was a great million-to-one chance – if it had been true. In fact, it was a matter of misleading perspective, just like when you see two planes approaching each other in the sky, looking as if they are going to collide – when they are actually miles apart. It caused a nice little media flurry. There was talk of a 'balls-up' and 'the great rugby ball hoax'. Still photos taken from the TV footage clearly showed that the balls had missed each other by three to four metres. Despite the great escape against Otago, we were to miss the Super 12 cut again that season – the Waratahs' 5–1–2 record leaving us just short of the semis.

It was in 1998 that I was invited to play a role in a series of newspaper and TV advertisements for the ARU. There were to be three ads – me as a bird of prey, George Gregan as a cheetah and the NSW front row as charging water buffalo, complete with horns and tattered manes. The ads, brilliantly conceived and highly dramatic, and presented under a Wallabies marketing campaign entitled 'Laws of Nature', are still talked about today.

At Concord Oval one long day, makeup and special effects people turned me into a bird of prey crouched on the crossbar. It was one hell of an operation. When I turned up they gave me my 'outfit', which consisted in its entirety of a ballet-dancer's G-string. Donning it with some misgivings, I then lay on the table for close to eight hours while they applied the makeup. It must have taken four or five hours to do the 'talons' alone. They painted me from head to toe – but just on the front. The backside of Burke was naked and white. We waited for a time until the heat went out of the day, for fear that the paint would run, and then I was despatched up a ladder to sit on a sort of unicycle seat on the crossbar. Behind me, giant eagle wings were put in place in such a way that it looked like I was wearing them. The message that accompanied the vision of me perched on the crossbar was: 'So you've cracked the defensive line. Now meet the fullback.'

Unbeknown to me, the ARU had okayed Channel 9's *A Current Affair* to come out and do a story on the big shoot. There was a heap of people to meet – art directors, creative people, photographers, makeup girls – and me all the while in a G-string, getting ready to impersonate a large bird. But all was going reasonably comfortably until Channel 9 turned up. The shot *they* wanted of me was one from behind – with my bare white butt sticking out. It was then that I put my foot (or talons) down. 'Mate, if they shoot me from behind, it's all over,' I told the director. It all turned out fine. I thought the concept was terrific, and I was very happy to have been involved . . . despite all the discomfort.

Through that early season, as I made steady progress on my return after all the problems of the previous year, there was a lot of talk about Burke v Larkham for the Australian fullback spot. Steve 'Bernie' Larkham had come in to No. 15 at the end of 1997 and had played very well, and continued to do that for the Brumbies. But my goal never wavered – I wanted to reclaim my fullback jumper. I had been the incumbent until injury kayoed me, and I was going to do what I could to get back there. As it turned out, the situation was win–win: I came back as fullback, as I had hoped; and when there was a hole in the side at five-eighth,

Stephen was thrown in there, despite having only ever played a few games as a fly-half – and he's been there ever since! So, maybe I can say I had a hand in Bernie's good fortune.

He was an outstanding player then, and still is today – a bloke with some unique qualities and skills and a great person to play rugby with. Bernie always had a deceptive gait; at times he looked like he was doing things in slow motion. But in fact he has a genuine turn of pace – and, above everything, the priceless quality of field vision that enables him to pick up runners with those characteristic passes of his. People think of him as a 'creator' on the football field – but just as much I remember moments of individual brilliance, such as a try he scored against Scotland in 1997 from a counter-attack situation when he must have beaten fifteen or so would-be tacklers. A great No. 10 and exactly the sort of intelligent bloke you need at stand-off these days when the call sheet of moves is as extensive as it is.

In the Test match against England in 1998, under a new coach, Rod Macqueen, we lined up against a team that bore little resemblance to what they would build in the seasons ahead – although they did have a young fella named Jonny Wilkinson at No. 10. The quality of the side they picked copped some flak – notably from one of our administrators, Dick McGruther, the ARU chairman, I think, who declared the team 'the biggest sellout since Gallipoli'. That was *just* what we needed – someone revving up the other side! But in the end it made no difference. Their side was probably about a third-stringer, inexperienced and injury-ravaged – and it did neither England's rugby nor traditional pride much good when we thrashed them 76–0, a scoreline that broke a whole heap of records. We took a while to get rolling but picked up 33 points in the first half and 43 in the second for a handy 76-blot that's there as a reminder if the Poms ever get too cocky.

My roommate during the internationals in 1998 was Tom

Bowman. Tom was a big, enthusiastic bloke with a whole lot of raw talent, and a very powerful player at the break-down. I don't really know why he didn't go on and play more Test matches. As a team member he certainly brought some positives – and he was fun to be around, as long as you treated him with caution. Tom's nickname, you see, was 'Disaster'. He was 203 centimetres tall, with flying feet and elbows. If you were within a few feet of Tom at training there was a fair chance you'd get stomped on by a size 16 foot or cop a stray elbow or knee. Tom would just laugh heartily and apologise. I remember us all watching a video of a recent match one day and seeing one of the opposition forwards come reeling out from a lineout. 'What the hell happened there?' someone asked. 'Oh, yeah, that's right . . . I landed on his foot,' said Tom. No one was too surprised.

Season 1998 was a good time to be a member of the Australian rugby team. We were on the rise, and we could feel it. Against Scotland in the first Test I picked up 25 points and a 'Man of the Match' award, and that was encouraging for a bloke making his way back after the injury jolt of the previous season. We beat them 45–3 in Sydney and then 33–11 at Ballymore.

Then it was on to Melbourne, the All Blacks, 75,000 fans – and to one of those games that football players dream about . . . the match when everything seems to go just right. It was the night we beat the Blacks 24–16 – our first victory over them in four years – and I managed to come up with all the points, and a record to boot. It was one of my most memorable games, I guess you could say.

The first of three Bledisloe Cup matches that year, it was a frenetic, frantic football match right from the kickoff. The game was barely under way when Walter Little made a clean break. I managed to get there with a side-on tackle, and the ball flew to

Steve Larkham, who went nearly all the way up to the other end. That sequence pretty much summed up the way Australia v New Zealand matches are, with the pace of the game right up there. They scored first that night, an Ian Jones try that covered 80 metres or so, and I found myself thinking, 'Is it going to be one of *those* (i.e losing) games again?' But it wasn't, though it was fast and furious throughout, and in the end we were able to turn that early 8–0 deficit into a famous victory.

For me, my 27th Test match was one in which the cards fell perfectly and I chanced to be in the right spot at the right time. The final tally was two tries, one conversion and four penalties. The goals, obviously, were just part of what I do. But the tries certainly were the icing on the cake. The first in the 29th minute came when Tom Bowman cleaned out in a ruck after Daniel Herbert had taken play deep into New Zealand territory and then George Gregan created a gap. It was a bit of a mix-up, actually. Bernie Larkham was supposed to put me back on the inside, but he went right as I went left and the fortunate outcome was that I was suddenly at the right place at the right time – and over for a try.

The second try five minutes later came from a new style of play we were trying to achieve, something that is a regular feature around the rugby world today. Tim Horan ran a great line and then Daniel Herbert took a pass from Larkham, drew the fullback and gave me a twenty-metre coast to the tryline.

By then my philosophy about playing against New Zealand was well in place. In a newspaper interview before the Melbourne game, I said: 'People tend to put the All Blacks on a pedestal, but they're only human – they bleed red blood like the rest of us. And they're very beatable. The keys are not to be intimidated, to play your own game as planned and not to be sucked into theirs . . . and to play for every last one of the 80 minutes.'

The crowd in 1998 seemed more rugby-educated and more

pro-Australian than the first time we played in Melbourne – the 1997 game which one scribe described as having 'bored a 90,000 crowd witless'. This time they knew exactly when to cheer, and when to boo.

I managed a couple of long touch-finding kicks, too – which led to an interesting moment at the media conference after the game. Someone raised the issue of the kicks and asked me whether I thought the All Blacks were vulnerable at the back. And I just set out to answer the question as honestly as I could: 'Look, if someone isn't there and there is space . . . well, you kick to that spot and put in a big chase. Christian Cullen wasn't there, so I kicked . . .' Suddenly there was a big whack on my knee from coach Rod Macqueen, who was sitting next to me at the table. He gave me a look that said: 'You're giving away too much information. This is secret men's business.' I remember stopping mid-sentence, no doubt looking like a bit of an idiot. There is this thing under Rod's coaching, you see, that we used to call Agenda A and Agenda B. One of them was for the players to know, and one was for the media and the public.

As a bloke who has always worked hard at keeping his feet on the ground, knowing well enough that if sport occasionally elevates you to a special level, it can crash-tackle you just an unexpectedly too, I still allowed myself a little time on cloud nine after that game. The newspapers jumped it out at me, with lines such as: 'Burke 24, All Blacks 16!'

I rang Burkey early on the morning after the Melbourne match to congratulate him on what he had achieved. I was up on the [NSW] Central Coast, having a break with the family. The conversation was a typical one with Matt Burke, always such a modest man, who is genuinely uncomfortable about talking of his own achievements. Some sportsmen of my experience downplay their achievements publicly – but Matt does it both publicly and privately. That morning after what had been a really brilliant and famous performance, I almost had to force him to talk about the football. All he wanted to know was how I was going . . . how the family were . . . and what we were up to.

John Fordham

One of the great things about playing team sports is that even after a special game like that, you still find yourself brought back to earth pretty quickly. In rugby no one is allowed to fly too high – and that's exactly the way it should be.

Seven days is a long time in football (as, it is said, in politics), and by the next week the swings and roundabouts that generally rule the games we play were much in evidence. Against South Africa at Perth's Subiaco Oval we went from the penthouse to the shithouse in 80 minutes that ended in frustration – and lost 13–14. That night I was leaning off the ball a little and missed four out of five kicks, including a sitter seventeen minutes from the end. One kick hit an upright, and the final, critical kick, from 35 metres out just off-centre, sailed straight over the top of one post. From my perspective, I had no doubt it was a goal – and that was no biased opinion. After all, the kicker gets the best 'straight-on' look at the kick – being directly behind the ball.

In rugby, the referee is generally posted five metres or so off-centre, experiencing a slightly different angle that can make all the difference on close kicks like that one. If I could make one small rule change in the game it would be *that* one: to post the ref *directly* behind the kick.

Inevitably when a kicker misses with a shot at the money end of a game, he wears some of the blame for defeat. So it was that night. But we also messed up in not getting set for a field goal in that last quarter of an hour when the match was up for grabs – and it was something we worked hard on at training in the wake of the loss. We pressed hard for the try that would have won the game – and neglected the kick that would have achieved the same outcome.

Subiaco, an open, windy sort of place, hasn't been a happy hunting ground for Wallaby teams. But I couldn't really blame the venue for any shortfall in my kicking in that game. I just didn't hit the ball too well. Some days you can do that and get away with it – with fluffed kicks struggling over. And some days you hit the ball well and bat below your normal average because of some post-shots and fractional misses.

On the positive side of the ledger, the night added something special to a career that had grown almost without my noticing it at times. It was my 26th Test match at fullback for Australia – and so I broke the previous record of 25, set by the much-admired Roger Gould.

Taking lessons from the disappointment of the loss to South Africa, we beat the All Blacks the following weekend. We met them in an afternoon game at Lancaster Park in Christchurch and out-generalled them for most of the way, until the final few minutes when they came from 27–11 down to 27–23 – at which point the final hooter was sweet music to our ears. Day football is always a bonus in New Zealand, considering the (a) cold and (b) rain that seems inevitably to accompany any night fixture. Again that day, a year out from the World Cup, which was now on everyone's mind, there were signs that we were a football team very much on the 'up'.

Best of all was a try that came at the end of eighteen phases of play in which just about everyone in the team handled the ball at some stage or other. (George Gregan handled it fourteen times!) There were switches of play, strong forward charges, rolling mauls – and, throughout a long, intense build-up, the ability to retain possession, even on occasions when we weren't going forward. Again and again we were able to recycle the ball. Usually after such a long phase, something will intervene . . . a dropped ball . . . a kick. But not this time. We worked and worked from 40 metres out from our own line to the eventual killing blow of a try in the corner. Such a sequence provided evidence of a talented side with very good potential indeed. And I was fortunate enough to be on the end of it and to score the try.

But it was still a work in progress and again we couldn't beat the 'Boks at Ellis Park in Johannesburg the following week to get the win we needed to take the Tri-Nations Tournament. They had been twice beaten by the All Blacks, but their 29–15 win over us, following the 14–13 photo-finish of a fortnight before, was enough to get them home.

To this day (or at least, the time of writing these words), Australia finds it very, very hard to win in South Africa. Playing at home, the Springboks *always* rise to the occasion, and visiting teams have to be right on their games to be in the hunt. The South Africans don't play spectacular football and are not seen as the most skilful team in the business – but their enthusiasm, size, pace and power make them awfully hard to beat.

It was another flight home of heavy hearts and sore heads.

More pain awaited me in Sydney.

Chapter 13

A SHOULDER TO CRY ON

A week after the Springboks had cleaned us up to take the Tri-Nations Tournament, I found myself sitting in the in-goal area at Sydney Football Stadium, at the Randwick end, screaming. Blood was seeping from a cut on my forehead, and pain as bad as I had ever experienced was shooting in great waves through my right shoulder and arm.

It was the evening of 28 August 1998, and against the proud All Blacks I had just scored a try that had the Wallabies on the verge of the first series clean sweep against New Zealand since 1929.

I was buggered. Christian Cullen's desperate tackle on the line as I dived across and strained to get the ball down seven minutes from fulltime had done me no good at all.

To our physio, Greg Craig, one of a small, concerned army that had gathered in the vicinity, I offered an opinion: 'Mate, I think I've dislocated my shoulder.' Craigie felt my shoulder and replied:

'Good assessment!' 'Can I play golf next week?' I asked him. He just laughed, but I was serious. We had a week off following this match, and I had lined up six games of golf!

Cameron Lillicrap, our second physio at the time, joined the group to find out what all the fuss was about. He, too, felt my shoulder, which dipped at 45 degrees instead of the regulation 90 degrees. 'Oooo!' he said. 'That one's going to hurt!' Well, he wasn't wrong.

Both physios at least were proving a little kinder than Tom 'The Walking Disaster' Bowman who, in the instant after I had scored the try, arrived on the scene, grabbed my jersey in a giant mitt – and was pulling me up and down in joyful celebration. In his defence, Tom had no idea in those first seconds that I was in a spot of bother.

I guess this has to go down as one of the 'standout' moments in my entire career – despite the pain, the time lost from football and the tedious marathon of the recovery months. Of all the footage taken during my career, that try has probably been shown the most.

It was, I think it's fair to say, a big moment in a very big match. The Bledisloe Cup was won and safely tucked away in a cabinet after our two earlier victories, and the talk before that night was all of history, and the chance of a rare clean sweep. It was incentive enough. Never was there a thought that this was a dead-rubber game and that the team could relax and just go through the motions. This was an Australian team that was bonding brilliantly, and the enthusiasm and drive to go right on with the job and beat the All Blacks for the third time straight in a single season was palpable. We knew that if we played well, we could win again.

The Test was a great struggle, as these games almost always are. They led early, but we clawed back and my try levelled it up at 14-all. I missed three shots at goal, and Ealsie took over as he had in the previous match in Christchurch two weeks before. He converted the try as I wrestled with the agony of my dislocated shoulder, and then added a penalty to wrap it all up. On reflection, 1998 wasn't such a great year for me with the boot. But at least it was a chance for me to focus on just one thing – playing well at fullback and making my 100 per cent contribution that way.

I started, and I guess you could say, finished the critical moment in the match . . .

In the 73rd minute I fielded an All Black kick, put up an attacking bomb that turned out to be weighted about right and chased hard. When one of their guys spilt the kick, I was able to dive on it and retrieve possession. Our forwards, mauling fiercely, cleared it from the ruck and we started a raid down the short side. George Gregan made a break and I switched back inside him on the left side of the field, took the pass, hurdled a fallen player and set my sights on the goal-line.

Cullen, fractionally wrong-footed, turned and chased. A quick, strong player, he got to me a metre and a half before the line, obviously with the idea of trying to turn me in the tackle. The first impact of the tackle split my forehead and knocked out my mouthguard. He then went around my chest, desperately trying to roll me over on my right shoulder. As a result my left side opened up, and we went over the line together, the shoulder vulnerable as I struggled to get the ball down. I just made it – well, I *think* I did. When you look at the video footage, the conclusion is that I must have got it down right on the line. As I put the ball down I landed on it, and Cullen landed on top of me and created a force on my shoulder that it couldn't withstand. In the instant I hit the ground in the Cullen tackle, I was gone . . .

I watched as Matt Burke scored the try. He did all he could to get to the line, reached out with the ball under his arm and as

he hit the ground, the tackler flipped him over and just com-
pletely inverted his shoulder the wrong way . . . and the agony
on his face in that moment. Then they turned to a replay, in
slow motion, and the whole stadium just groaned. They knew
that this unique talent was going to be lost to us for a while.

Chris Handy

I was still sitting on the deck, surrounded by the Aussie medical team, when John Eales booted the conversion and kicked us to what turned out to be a winning lead.

The medi-cab came put-putting out, but I wasn't going to leave a Test match that way, and began the long walk back to the dressing room and the beginning of all the many things that were going to have to happen.

It's funny how clearly I remember all the little details of what went on, as if time slowed down to an extent. As Burke and support group made our slow progress down the field, parallel to the touchline, I watched ahead of me as George Gregan put a little kick over the top of Jonah Lomu's head. The ball bounced into touch. And I remember willing it to do just that, the thought having crossed my mind that Lomu would retrieve the ball, knock blokes out of the way as he used to do, come straight down the line, and I'd have to struggle on there and try to stop him. Even in my dazed and slightly shocked state, I knew clearly enough that medically that wouldn't have been such a great option.

We walked on, Craigie watching me closely. I must have been pretty pale around the gills at one point because suddenly he declared: 'We're losing him, we're losing him!' 'Mate, we're not losing anything,' I told him. 'We're two-nil up in the series . . . We're leading 22–16, and we're going to be three-nil up by fulltime.'

In the dressing room the medicos gave me two shots of morphine, one intramuscularly and one intravenously. But the shoulder was in spasm to such an extent it took them half an hour to get it back into its socket. In my drugged and traumatised state I was laughing and swearing at them as they struggled with it. At the same time I was engaged in a war of words with Louise, one of our medical staff – trying to get her to give me a drink of water, which she wouldn't do. My brother Troy then came into the room, by which time I was very mellow indeed, well under the influence of the morphine. I did the social thing of introducing my brother to all the boys as they filed in. It probably hadn't really sunk in (a) what the team had achieved, and (b) the extent of my injury.

A tough night followed at the Prince of Wales Hospital in Randwick – tough both because of the pain, and because I couldn't be out with the guys to celebrate our famous achievement.

Foolishly, or courageously – whichever way you look at it – I was there the next day, though, when the team met for a celebration lunch and some beers at the Centennial Hotel. I sat there, arm in a sling and gritting my teeth as I swilled a beer or two. Memory tells me that I was even a designated driver for a few of the crew. But after that, there began the very long and uncomfortable road to recovery.

The path that it very quickly became apparent I had to follow was a familiar one – to have a full right shoulder reconstruction. Eight years earlier, Dr Des Bokor had done the same operation on my other shoulder; when I saw him again in that late August of 1998 his first words to me were: 'I knew you would be back sometime.'

I had already done the maths in my head. I knew that the shoulder procedure I faced usually meant six months out of football. So, I could expect to be back in late February or early March

1999, at about the time of the kickoff of the Super 12s. It was a World Cup year, after all, and I figured that would give me *plenty* of time to regain full fitness and health.

Life, of course, is never that easy.

When I revisited Dr Bokor, his advice wasn't what I had hoped to hear. For starters, he estimated that we needed five weeks or so to get some stability back into the shoulder before he could operate. He explained that to go in and operate straight away would be akin to operating on rope that had been soaked in water all day and then left out in the sun to dry. The rope would be dry on the outside, but the inside would still be mushy, lacking tension. So it would be with my shoulder. That was the first setback. There was five weeks gone, even if everything went perfectly. Suddenly March was looking like April . . . or May.

When the operation was finally performed, at The San (Sydney Adventist Hospital) in Wahroonga, the damage I had done, courtesy of the Cullen tackle, was discovered to be pretty bad. At the end of it, as the rehab process began, I only had fifteen degrees of external rotation. What that means essentially is that when I had my arms by my side and attempted to splay them out from my body, I could only manage fifteen degrees on the right side. Most people can make it to around 45 degrees. In a single tackle I had gone from having a perfect shoulder to having a virtually useless one. Along with that problem went the additional drama of wasting, of losing muscle mass. It was very quickly apparent that the physio process would have to be long and intense if I was going to get anywhere close to full fitness back on that side of my body.

At least I had learned something from my first bout of shoulder surgery. Back then I was eating and drinking as if I was still playing – and through the relative inactivity I put on ten kilos in weight and looked pretty ordinary. Bloody terrible, in fact. This time, sick from the operation and the trauma that had been part of the whole thing, I went the other way – and *lost* about ten kilos. On that first occasion, I had been positively bursting out of clothes as I piled on the kilos. Now I was pasty white and thin, and I had blokes asking me whether I had HIV! I was just staying indoors, taking the medication and going to the endless physio sessions. For many weeks, that was my life. It's what happens to footballers now and then – the price that playing a hard game extracts.

Greg Craig, physio at the Narrabeen Academy of Sport, became a big part of my life. One day, early in my treatment, I was lying on my back and unable to lift my left arm towards the ceiling. I just couldn't do it. As a professional athlete, used to pumping out the weights, I felt pretty helpless. Craigy was a tower of strength throughout the long haul, advising and encouraging me. A lot of the credit for getting me successfully back on to the field in 1999 must go to him. But I had some bad times along the way.

Some days I walked out of there crying after three hours of physio. It's the side of professional sport that most people never see. Athletes disappear from the scene, injured – and then reappear six months later, with few people knowing what they have really been through.

He was living at home at the time of the shoulder injury. He was a good patient – his total focus was on getting himself right. When it came to things that were happening out on the field he would simply say, 'There's nothing I can do about that.' His approach to his situation was totally realistic.

Bob Burke

But, of course, good things can come out of adversity. So it was back then in the depths of my discomfort and with me having no chance of being able to drive my (manual) car, that a friend, Alan Crouch, introduced me to the Audi company for what has been – and continues to be – a very happy association. That early intro to Graham Hardy and Anna Burgdorf of Audi led to me becoming an ambassador for the company, an arrangement which has lasted more than six years and which has now been extended to England. The company's friendship and loyalty to me has been unswerving. Even when the ARU had Ford as a sponsor and NSW Rugby had Mazda, the people at Audi never wavered. These sort of arrangements have been among the genuine personal pleasures of my time in football. John Fordham's friendship with the boss of Sony Music, Denis Handlin, led to another friendship-partnership that I value greatly. A professional arrangement with Sony Music came in the wake of the DVD the company had produced on Andrew Johns' career in rugby league. It was to lead to the production of a similar DVD on my life in rugby – and a great friendship with Denis. On the occasion of the farewell lunch before Kate and I flew to England, Denis arranged for everyone in the room (1000 people!) to have a copy of the DVD as a parting gift.

When Matt Williams, NSW coach, put it on me in season 1999 to play, I knew I was nowhere near ready. I went back to Craigie and expressed my concerns and we made some video footage of the shoulder, the lack of mobility and range as a sort of indemnity – so that if I was pressured into playing prematurely and snapped my shoulder again, there was evidence to support where the liability lay. Craigie was very much my minder and mentor throughout the whole rehabilitation time, understanding better than anyone the extent of the trouble.

Matt Williams was a schoolteacher of mine in earlier days and I always thought of him back then as a good bloke, but I came to see things in him that I didn't agree with – and we don't talk at all these days. I will probably make the point more than once in these pages that football coaches are a strange and disparate breed. Ego and ambition certainly feature strongly in the mix with most of them. He had his own agendas – and being a fairly ingenuous sort of bloke myself, I didn't spot some things about him until later. He was a coach who played mind games with his players.

In 1999, when I was working my guts out on my rehabilitation program and was still five or six weeks off my comeback game, Williams got me in for a 'heart to heart' with him and the NSW manager, Peter Rowles. My shoulder then was still very dicey, and I was being guided by the medical experts. At the time I could barely lift my left arm above shoulder height. Williams said to me: 'I spoke to the surgeon and he told me that you are right to go. You should get out there and push it, and even if you fall awkwardly and something snaps, you'll be okay. He says you can just play through it.' I was really filthy about that. He shouldn't even have been talking to the surgeon about something that was private medical information. Although I wasn't that far off playing, I just thought his attitude wasn't right. I wasn't going to have him telling me what to do. There was no way I was going to rush back on a coach's wish or whim when I knew I wasn't all right.

It got worse. By the end of the season I was being pretty much blamed for the Waratahs missing out on the semifinals. (We finished fifth.) I was accused of dogging it by claiming that my shoulder wasn't up to scratch while I marked time for the international season to come around. It was outrageous. With me sweating it out in the stand – desperate to get back, but not ready – the team struggled in the goal-kicking department. The dilemma persisted for a fair bit of the season, with blokes like Duncan McRae, Christian Warner and Manny Edmonds all having a crack at the kicking job. We lost a couple of games that we could have won. (Though it's very hard to blame a kicker for losing a football match. The team must always wear that, in my view.) The bottom line was that I became something of a scapegoat for missing the games I missed. Jason Little, our skipper that year, found himself in the same boat. He suffered a collarbone injury in the first match that was bad enough to keep him out of football for the rest of the season. The way it turned out, the blame was largely placed on my shoulders for a perceived NSW failure that year. I'm still angry about that. I think that most people who know me would agree that I have been a good team man throughout my career. Anyone who knew me in 1998/99 knew how much of my heart and soul I put into trying to get myself fit to play football. I didn't need the allegations that were coming from people such as the coach. I'm not a confrontational type of person, but when stuff gets said about me – well, it's not good, and my natural inclination is to go and find other people to befriend. And that's pretty much how it was between Matt Williams and me. I am aware of other people who had the same sort of experiences with him. He had a three-year tenure as NSW coach and when his third year failed to produce the goods, he departed the scene.

One morning long before Williams first asked me to resume playing I had trekked down to NSW training for the first time in some months, toting a jersey that I wanted to get signed. I had lost so much weight, the jeans I wore were like a pair of baggies on me and my T-shirt looked far too big. I had on a hat and sunglasses, and the guys in the team simply didn't recognise me. Michael Brial gave me a look as I approached a group of them that said: 'Oh-oh, here comes some bloke chasing signatures.' Then, when I removed the hat and sunnies, someone said: 'Holy shit! What's going on with you, Burkey?'

I was still a mess then. I could barely lift my arm above shoulder height. (All these years later I still can't serve over-arm at tennis or bowl at cricket.) I was thin and run-down – and a promotional trip I had undertaken to the Northern Territory had really knocked the stuffing out of me. I'd had my arm in a sling and a thousand commitments to fulfil, including signing endless footballs and shirts – and the whole exercise nearly shattered me. I was just so tired then that virtually anything I attempted completely drained me. Back in Sydney at the tail end of that trek I had a mate's wedding to attend. I made it to the ceremony, but I was so crook I couldn't carry on to the reception.

Day by day, Craigie provided unswerving support. There were endless mornings of training and working to get me back, sessions of three and four hours, over a period of at least six months. And there were days when I just didn't want to do it. At the same time I was trying to complete my university degree, and the painful grind at Narrabeen would generally be followed by a study session. For sure I couldn't go and hit a golf ball!

He'd have probably an hour or an hour and a half of physio, sometimes two hours ... We would come out to the park and do shoulder-oriented exercise, which could be just chin-ups. Or, trying to vary it a little bit, we tried some gymnastics – which neither of us is good at. It was a lot of fun doing it and we set little goals for him to reach – and then go on to the next goals. Burkey would attack every one of them with gusto. Sometimes we didn't quite make them, and then we had to pick ourselves back up again, but on the whole he just set a goal and he would reach it and then head on to the next one.

Greg Craig

The signs of progress seemed infinitesimally small, but very, very gradually I edged back closer to being a footballer again. Throughout it all, the World Cup burned brightly in my mind. I remember another of Craigie's patients visiting Dr Boker not long after being at a training session where Greg and I were kicking and catching high balls. 'How did he go?' the doc asked, interested in my progress. 'Oh, *Craigie* was catching them really well,' said the bloke. But as for me . . . well, *I* wasn't. Because of my limited movement on the right side I just couldn't get my elbows together properly to catch the bloody thing.

Through the summer of 1998/99 and into spring, the work continued – endless passing, tackling, catching, working to get my confidence, strength and movement back. When you're out injured the game goes on without you; the only thing you have control over is yourself and the decisions you make about how hard you're going to work to get back. You are in the shadows, quietly reading the stories of how your replacement is going. The wet Sydney summer of 1998 was a help to me. Part of the rehab involved diving again and again on to the ground, building my confidence and testing my shoulder to make sure it could take the weight. I needed to get used to the uncontrolled movement again, since a football match provides a lot of that. There were good days and bad, breakthroughs and setbacks.

The mental side was a big part of my rehab – the need to keep pushing when my body was telling me otherwise. I remember the breakthrough morning when I lifted a bar holding twenty kilos.

Slowly I edged up – to 60 kilos – and I thought that was great. I gradually moved on and up from there.

Centimetre by centimetre, kilogram by kilogram, I crept back towards being fit enough to play football again – in what was to be a huge season for Australian rugby.

Eventually I was ready.

Chapter 14

TOWARDS THE WORLD CUP: CHASING THE DREAM

The old standby of friends and family eased me through the long twilight of that gruelling rehabilitation program of 1998, and on into World Cup year, 1999. Badly winged, I felt like something of an outsider in the game I played, but the encouragement and enthusiasm of those around me, backing the hard work that I was doing, provided a cushion of support which helped get me through. Now and then I would step back into the rugby community – despatched to fly the flag at this or that promotional event. And that was good, too, reminding me – and others – that I was still around and getting closer to making a return.

Matt had some bad injuries through his career and was always very good at dealing with them. He was a player who put his body on the line, and never spared himself. At times of injury, such as 1998, he accepted that there was nothing he could do about what was happening out on the paddock – and that there was no use worrying himself about that. His energies and 100 per cent full focus were put into getting himself right.

John Fordham

The 1999 season was a major milestone in rugby, being the 125th anniversary of the game's beginning in Australia. Early in the year, I found myself in the company of legends. In succession I was named in three 'best ever' teams, at fullback – for the Waratahs, the Wallabies, and a team covering the span of the 125 years. These events represented a significant honour to all who got the call, I'm sure. I know it was that way for me, and especially so at this time of flickering personal doubts about whether I would come good after the shoulder injury. For my name to be there in the company of Trevor Allan, Ken Catchpole, the late Cyril Towers, Mark Ella and other famous players from across the game's entire spectrum in Australia was very special, although perhaps it will mean even more to me when I am an ex-footballer. They were certainly wonderful honours for any rugby résumé – and something to show the grandkids! The game that those of us in the selected teams had all played (or were still playing) was professional now – but some things remained unchanged. The bond among players of all eras had, I'm sure, always been a uniting force and a foundation of the game. For me to be picked in a team that included someone like the great Trevor Allan was really something. Trevor is a wonderful bloke, always friendly and positive in his dealings with others.

I can't say the same of all the heroes of seasons past. Mark Ella, for example, was a wonderful player, and a giant figure in the game. But he used his column in *The Australian* to regularly get stuck into the players of the modern generation. There was a time when he had a few things to say about me – on both a personal and professional level. But men like Mark have paid their dues and are entitled to their opinions. Maybe some of those players of past generations have chips on their shoulders. They played their football for the love of it at a time when it was an amateur 'game' – and possibly they regret not having had the chance to build rugby as a career, in the way that we have since 1995. In and around the game there are some people I have tended to steer clear of, and others I have been drawn to. I guess that's just life.

But it's often overlooked that today's professionals have their own challenges. The sun sets early on careers in a body contact game like rugby – and today's players can face this dilemma when still only in their late twenties. Then the question becomes: 'What am I going to do now?' The players of past eras at least were able to build parallel careers in rugby and their chosen professions. Today, the money is good when you reach the elite level in the game – but the game consumes your time and your life, leaving not much room for anything else. At the end there is the need to draw a line and virtually start a new life.

As I edged back towards the football field in early 1999, it felt almost like I was starting a second life. Into May, I knew I was just about ready and one night I gave Greg Craig a call. 'Mate,' I said. 'I want to play this weekend.' I told him that I thought the time had come and I just wanted to get out there and have a dig. Craigie had no problems with that. My next call was to Chris Hickey at Eastwood. 'Any chance of a game this weekend?' I asked him. 'Sure. How about in the Twos?' he said. So on 19 May 1999, without fuss or fanfare, I played fullback in reserve grade against Warringah at Millner Field. I wasn't listed in any of the teams. There was a funny moment when I ran out, passing the third-graders as they trooped in after their match. One of the Warringah blokes did a double-take and said, 'Hang on, isn't that Matt Burke?'

I didn't want any fuss about my decision to play that day. It wasn't a comeback to show the world that Burke had returned. It was a comeback for *me* – to confirm to myself that I could still play the game and had the necessary appetite and skills.

I remember some things about that game very clearly. I scored a try at one point – and put the ball down with my left hand, something I had never done in my life. And there was a moment early on when I was called on to make a tackle – and rather than just doing it by instinct, I checked myself as I went to stick my arm out. But I got through it, and we won. It was a classic example of 'one small step', a tiny breakthrough, both physical and mental, in this year that offered so much.

A couple of weeks later I eased back into representative football after a couple more club games, playing fullback in the NSW team that beat Ireland 39–24. My kicking was pretty ordinary (four from nine) and I hit the post with one from bang in front, but the game was just the physical step-up I needed and again I came through well. I scored a try and actually dived for the line when I didn't need to. I was testing myself . . .

'It was just good fun being out there again,' I told the media.

A month later I was back in the Test squad, sitting on the bench in Perth as a reserve, covering centre, fullback and wing, when we played Ireland in the second Test of the series. I got a few minutes on the field and that was more a case of 'welcome back' than anything else. The thing that really struck me was the difference in speed between the club rugby I had played a few weeks before, and this. Chris Latham was playing fullback, as he had done for much of the past year, and scored a couple of tries that night. Afterwards the media's focus on me was entirely related to question of whether I would get my fullback spot back. I responded: 'All I can

Burke's backyard, Barellan Avenue, Carlingford, and I'm in my whites –
11 years old and happy to be in the local Cawsey Shield cricket side.

Family Christmas 1983. Left to right, it's my dad Bob, Troy, Paul, my
mum Maureen, Greg – and in front with the floatie, me.

LEFT Winning the long jump at the annual GPS carnival in 1990. At Joey's, the sequence of my sporting years was locked in tight – cricket, track and field, rugby.

BELOW Early action from Eastwood days – a match against Canberra at Millner Field in 1995 and an attacking moment with a future Australian player, outside centre Graeme Bond in the background (left).

Australia's World Cup campaign of 1995 in South Africa ended far too soon when England pipped us in the quarter-final – thanks to a Rob Andrew field goal. Here, I'm under some pressure – and that's Andrew on the right, moving in for the tackle. Alongside is Phil Kearns, with David Wilson behind.

Byron Bay, summer 1998, and a bunch of Wallabies, friends, partners and kids relaxing, far from thoughts of football.

We had the chance for a 'walk-through' at Millennium before the World Cup Final of 1999. Here I'm with Chris Whitaker and Nathan Grey.

Our 35–12 triumph over the French in 1999 was the biggest winning margin in a World Cup final. My own contribution of 25 points (seven penalties, two conversions) was an obvious source of satisfaction. Here, another three-pointer is just about on its way.

The picture tells the story. Millennium Stadium and a bunch of ecstatic Aussies. The Battle for Bill, World Cup 1999, is over – and rugby's supreme trophy is heading Down Under.

Ben Tune (centre) Owen Finnigan (right) and I shared the points-scoring honours and were happy to pose with the World Cup after the Final of '99.

Just a bunch of blokes mucking around ... a brief, relaxed (well, sort of)
team moment before the official team pic is taken. It's Australia v The
Lions at Brisbane's The Gabba in 2001. Ahead in the first Test, there
unfolded a big win for the Lions (29–13) – but there would be better
days for the Wallabies that season.

Winning the Bledisloe Cup is thirsty work at any time – and especially
when you manage it at the 'House of Pain', Dunedin's Carisbrook. So it
was in season 2001 that I took a large swig, with skipper John Eales in the
background, after we had beaten the All Blacks 23–15 to retain the Cup.

A happy time ... a beautiful day at Bayview ... life is good: the afternoon that Kate and I were married in 2001.

Attacking action against the Bulls in Pretoria in season 2002 – with Duncan McRae (centre) and Scott Staniforth in support. We won the game 51–9 and the newspapers speculated: 'Could this be the year for the Waratahs?' Regrettably, the answer was ... no.

Probably it was the goal of my life. With the Bledisloe Cup at stake and the hooter already sounded, the kick flew true and straight at Stadium Australia on the night of 3 August 2002 – and we had won the match, 16–14, and the Cup. It was one of the best feelings I have ever had in rugby.

The dust has settled to an extent but the euphoria remains as George Gregan and I hold high the coveted Bledisloe Cup, August 2002.

The day I became a father was one of the best of
my life. Harriette and me, September 2002.

Game 1, World Cup 2003 – in action against
Argentina, with Joe Roff in support. We won, 24–8.

This break, clear of Steve Larkham's diving tackle, resulted in a Waratahs try (scored by Lote Tuqiri) in an emphatic Super 12 win over the Brumbies in what was to be my last season in Australia. The 2004 game was a milestone in my career. My 22 points this night took me to 950 overall in Super 12 football, topping Andrew Mehrtens' record of 936.

It's my last game for the Wallabies on Australian soil – against the 'old enemy', New Zealand – and I am trying to get clear of a diving Tana Umaga. An Australian victory and a wonderful reception from the crowd were highlights of a night of deep and mixed emotions.

Skipper George Gregan, a great mate, was standing right alongside when the hooter sounded on my final Test in Australia, 2004 – and then the emotional stuff began.

Kate made her way down from the stand to be at the gate at fulltime of the match against the All Blacks that final night – and it was great to be able to share the moment with her.

Fordo (my manager, John Fordham) and me after the big farewell lunch in 2004.

A new Audi and a new ground to call home, Kingston Park, Newcastle – on arrival in the UK, late 2004.

A 'new' career is underway. Action from our Heineken Cup match against the Newport Gwent Dragons, coached by former Australian rugby league coach Chris Anderson.

In February 2005 a big freeze in England brought a heavy dump of snow, much to the delight of my daughter Harriette, pictured with the snowman we built at home.

Edie and me at home in Gosforth.

My 32nd birthday was celebrated far from home, in England's north – but with the special people in my life, Kate, Harriette and Edie.

So, who'd win a goal-kicking competition out of this group? Take your pick ... but I'm in especially good company here with Jonny Wilkinson (centre) and Newcastle Falcons Director of Rugby, Rob Andrew. Talking footy, I suspect.

JED WEE

Doing what I do, albeit far from where it all began. Goal-kicking for the Falcons, early 2005.

do is look after myself, and if I train well enough and play well enough, hopefully I'll get a start down the track.' The fact was that I had no control over what Chris Latham had done, or would do. I could only ever work on my *own* game. When it came to rivalry for a position, my attitude has never changed over the years. Essentially it is: 'If you are better than me, good luck to you. But I'll certainly give you a run for your money.'

The comeback to football was one of many small steps, as it needed to be. I got three minutes (on the wing) against England when Australia beat them 22–15 in the Centenary Test, and then 80 minutes at fullback for the Australian Barbarians against New Zealand A at Olympic Park, Melbourne. In that match I scored 23 points in a free-and-easy game that showed I could still play full-back, still mix it in the big time and still kick a few goals. Rod Kafer playing at No. 10 was putting blokes through gaps left, right and centre, opening up heaps of scoring chances. He made me look good that night.

The comeback to the game had been as good as I could have hoped. My shoulder was 'tight' but okay, and I was getting my football legs again. I had obviously shown the Australian selectors enough to convince them that I was back in business – and the next week I was picked at fullback in the starting side to play South Africa at Suncorp Stadium, Brisbane. In what turned out to be the biggest win over the Springboks in 66 years (32–15) I scored a try, kicked three conversions and two penalty goals, and was pretty satisfied with my all-round game. It was genuinely a great thrill to be back. After that match I thought of all I had been through, the pain and then the physio sessions beyond counting, and allowed myself to think that it had all been worthwhile.

Victories on the football field last only a week, of course, and when we trekked to New Zealand for the first Bledisloe Cup game of the season the following week, we got absolutely drilled. Andrew Mehrtens kicked nine penalty goals and a conversion from eleven attempts, and they beat us 34–15. A couple of late touchdowns meant that we actually out-scored them in the try-scoring department, but it was small consolation. For much of a very tough night, we had been outplayed.

This was the first 'Blackout' night, and when we ran out the entire ground seemed clothed in black. Fans had been encouraged to wear black and to paint their faces in support of the team. There was even talk that the ground lights would be turned out to make it blacker still, but they were concerned about re-booting the lights so didn't take it quite that far. It was black enough, and quite eerie – and they came out and smashed us. The New Zealand thing really worked for them that night.

The return game in Sydney loomed larger than any rugby match for quite a long time in this World Cup year. Another comprehensive New Zealand win would have dealt a considerable psychological blow to our hopes of beating them in the Cup.

But we kept our nerve.

On a brilliant night for the game, notwithstanding an opening of the heavens that produced thunderous rain for twenty minutes or so, we scored the biggest ever win over an All Black team (28–7) before a world-record rugby crowd (107,042), producing a gate of $7 million at Sydney's brand-new Olympic Stadium. The rain was like nothing I had ever experienced, absolutely torrential and adding to the drama of the night.

I suppose that anyone who had followed my career would think of it as the night I really came back after the long haul with the damaged shoulder. I kicked seven penalty goals (the most by an Australian in a Test) plus a conversion, from eight attempts, for 23 points in all.

At some stages it was like a monsoon and he was just knocking the ball over from everywhere. It was a super night and I think until you play in those matches and experience the pressure and the importance of some of the kicks that he puts over in such circumstances you don't really appreciate it. Again that was just an outstanding performance that allowed us to dominate an All Black team – and that isn't easy to do.

George Gregan

This was a hugely significant win. We were missing some key men – including John Eales, who was out of the side injured – and we had players in there who you could say weren't 'regulars'. But in the building phase towards the World Cup it was perhaps the night when we turned the corner in the maturity stakes. David Wilson led the team, and everyone did their job and had faith in the blokes alongside. It was August, and just the boost we needed as the World Cup crept closer. We were on course, and that was the big newspaper story the next day and a new and positive force for the team to hang on to. The celebration at our Parramatta hotel, at which we were joined by family and friends, was something special. There was a great feeling in the air – and much talk of winning back the Cup we had lost on South African soil four years before.

Chapter 15

KILL BILL II

I was a good deal more relaxed about my selection prospects for the World Cup of 1999 – my second shot at the trophy called 'Bill' – than I had been four years earlier. Whereas in 1995 I was up at six o'clock in the morning on the crucial day, waiting for a courier who never came, this time I was pretty loose and relaxed. My form had been good, and I was comfortable about getting another crack at it. In fact, I can't even remember the exact day when I knew I was officially 'in'. My first memory of what was to be a long and thrilling campaign is some fooling around at a promotional event at North Sydney. Channel 7, the television rights holders, had the team lined up doing a chant of 'Bring back Bill, bring back Bill' – which probably was only partially successful because everyone kept cracking up laughing. They did a big photo shoot with the plan of using the Sydney Harbour Bridge as a backdrop and generally got very excited about the big tournament ahead.

I doubt that the blokes in the team really switched on to it, though, until we lifted off at Mascot, with 30 hours of flying ahead of us. Our mission – under the coaching of Rod Macqueen and captaincy of John Eales, with George Gregan as vice captain – was to complete what had been left uncompleted in South Africa. This chapter on the quest for Bill comes from a very personal perspective. Readers will well know the outcome, and very likely recall some of the specifics, of Australia's steady progress along the track of what many people would regard as rugby's Holy Grail. So the memories here are personal ones, those things that have stayed with me in the years since.

We were based in Ireland, at the Portmarnock Hotel and Golf Links, north of Dublin. A team base with an adjoining golf course – beauty! We were pretty much removed from the heart of the rugby action and there was some feeling among the guys that they'd like to be in the thick of it. But at Portmarnock, a quiet place, there were positives, too. We were away from the fuss and fanfare, with a chance to build clear focus as the days rolled on. Expectations for the team were high, obviously – but there in Ireland we had the feeling that the build-up could be a little quieter and less pressured than it might have been elsewhere.

The quest for the greatest prize in rugby started . . . on the golf course. Arriving after the long trek we played nine holes, basically to keep everyone awake and give us the chance of getting into a good sleep pattern as soon as possible. Tim Lane, whose nickname was Squeak (and maybe should have been Sneak, owing to his ability to cut deals), managed to work out an arrangement with Guinness by which they provided us with a very generous opportunity to become acquainted with the dark brew. With Joe Roff reaching for his guitar, and plenty of Guinness flowing, it turned into one hell of a good night once the nine holes of golf had been got out of the way.

Joe wrote some new words to the tune of 'I was only nineteen', changing the chorus to 'My name is Rod Macqueen'. The song was something of a take off of the coach and the rest of Wallaby life. It was one of the funniest things I have ever heard, although I'm not sure if Rod appreciated it! Throughout the campaign it got a run just about every time we chanced to have a drink.

However, the alcoholic content of the tour was a good deal lighter (well, for *me*, anyway) than it had been back in 1995. I was four years older and somewhat wiser. I understood the momentous nature of the challenge better than I had in South Africa and indulged in far fewer nights 'out' this time around.

I remember the first two weeks of the campaign – until our first game, against Romania – as a difficult time. When you're in game mode, playing week in, week out, you get into a rhythm. But coming halfway across the world under the weight of heavy expectations – with no football for two weeks – wasn't easy. We trained twice a day – sometime three times a day. Without the out-let of playing football the guys were very edgy. The feeling was nervy – blokes were into each other physically and mentally. I guess that's what the coaching staff wanted, to foster that tough edge of competition, to have everyone ready and accountable. We got out and about a little bit – but not too much. In the main it was rugby-oriented. And even in faraway Ireland there was a growing Aussie spirit – in the many supporters, friends and expats who trekked across, typified by a couple of blokes who had bought an old black London cab and painted it with the Aussie flag.

For me it was still a big battle physically, with my shoulder a long way from being right. I spent countless hours in the physio room with Greg Craig, trying not so much to *increase* the mobility of the shoulder, but just to keep it in the range of what we had achieved in the previous six to twelve months.

The challenge of winning a rugby World Cup revolves around six games of football. It's pretty much sudden death – although if you drop one of the first three it doesn't automatically knock you out. But the aim must be to top your group (of four), giving you a path to the quarter-finals. From there, you either win match four . . . or you pack your bags and go home. We had drawn Romania, the United States and Ireland – a useful group, although we knew that Irish pride would bubble to the surface in the third game and it would be a tough one.

Here are my thoughts, match by match, as it unfolded.

Game 1: Romania

We faced the Romanians in Belfast, knowing pretty much what to expect. This was a case of a tough team, and a tough town. As I have mentioned, the Romanians are a physical side *every* time you face them, if still short of the top bracket. On the day before the match I went out and had my usual practice kick, on a ground made heavy by the rain that had been pouring down for days. Wearing fifteen-millimetre studs, I kicked every goal.

But by the time we got to Ravenhill Park, the ground was flooded, and in one of the sillier decisions of my career I switched from fifteen-millimetre studs to eighteen millimetres – seeking more traction in the trying conditions. Every time I went to have a kick for goal in the game, I caught the studs on the ground. Never since have I worn eighteen-millimetre sprigs. But if I were to make such a mistake, it was in the right game. One of those setbacks that can test a team's mettle happened before the kickoff when Mark Cockbain pulled a quad muscle in the warm-up, leading to a last-minute reshuffle, with Mark Connors coming into the team.

Experienced teams handle such unexpected adversity. Even on

the heavy track, which can be a leveller, we were far too good for them, and won 57–9 in a match that is memorable more for the streakers than the football. A girl and a guy out there on some sort of radio promotion discarded their gear in the interests of the company – and earned a huge cheer from the crowd. It was a light moment in a serious football match in which we did what needed to be done. That night, the match won and the campaign under way, we went out, and it was a good release valve after the edginess of the long build-up to the match. The problem came the next day when those of us who had been picked for the second game were required to turn up for morning training while feeling a little the worse for wear.

Game 2: United States

We played the Yanks in Limerick, a great town. A memory I have of that game is of the eerie silence that accompanied any kick for goal. This was requested by the ground-announcer out of respect to the kickers. But in fact it was quite off-putting. Generally at big football matches there is plenty of noise all the time. It was a bit odd to line up a kick with a deathly silence hanging over the place. Nevertheless, we did what everyone expected we would do – and beat the US, 55–19. But the Yanks had the distinction of scoring what turned out to be the only try posted against us in the tournament. I would like to make the point for posterity that the try, by Juan Grobler, was scored on Scott Staniforth's wing, not mine – and that it was scored against us under the captaincy of Jason Little, who I'm sure will thank me with a cheery smile for this reminder when he reads these words. There was a moment in the game 1 section v Romania when Jason came up to me and asked: 'Have I lost my tooth?' His capped front tooth *had* in fact been knocked out, and my response wasn't all that sympathetic. Actually, I laughed, as Jason had always prided himself on being one of the pretty ones.

Afterwards we had three days off. We could get away from the footy thing and just bum around and catch up with some of the sights, like ordinary tourists. It was a smart move by the management.

Game 3: Ireland

We beat the Irish clearly, 23–3, at Landsdowne Road – but it was a tough match, mentally and physically. The wind gusted strongly throughout and, playing fullback, I didn't have one of my best games. Timmy Horan and Ben Tune scored tries, giving us enough leeway to win decisively, although we never got close to subduing their spirit. There was a downside, though, in a foot injury sustained by Phil Kearns – an injury that was bad enough to pretty much kill off the tournament for him. That night we toasted our victory with Guinness. We were in the quarter-finals, and it was mission accomplished . . . so far. But the tough stuff lay ahead – with Wales awaiting us at Millennium Stadium, Cardiff.

Game 4, Quarter-final: Wales

The pre-match debate at the spectacular new stadium was: 'Will they, or won't they, close the roof?' The weather had its say, with the rain tumbling down on the days before the game. Tim Horan's thoughts on the matter were pragmatic: 'If you've got a Ferrari, you don't leave it in the garage!' What he meant was that if you've got the technology (that is, the means to close the roof), then use it. But the debate ebbed and flowed. We wanted it dry, and no doubt the crowd wanted it dry – but the Welsh were more used to playing in the wet than we were and so leaving the roof open made sense to them. As the rain tumbled down, the IRB dithered. Finally the decision was made: the roof would be closed during the week, but would be opened for the game. And that's what happened. The match was played under grey skies, with some rain thrown in for good measure, on a bloody awful playing surface that obviously hadn't yet been properly bedded in and which resembled a sandpit in places. And hanging over our heads was the thought that if we lost this game, we would be going home.

Notwithstanding any reservations about the new ground back then, Cardiff is a magnificent place to play football, a place where the appreciation of the sport is just about unmatched. I count myself as fortunate to have played at both the old Cardiff Arms Park and on the new ground. To hear the crowd singing 'Land of our fathers' is a spine-chilling and unforgettable experience – surely one of the great moments in world sport.

Well, the weather having done its worst, we still managed to beat the Welsh decisively in the quarter-final – 24–9, three tries to nil with George Gregan bagging a double. Back home the newspapers had their doubts. 'Wallabies win but still wobbly' was one headline. Sometimes I used to wonder if they knew *anything*! Sure, it wasn't *the* most convincing win in history, but three tries to nil, 24–9, in the heartland of Welsh rugby isn't *too* bad. We were in the semis, we had conceded only one try and we had ten days to prepare for South Africa, the defending champions. The media might have had its doubts, but the Wallaby campaign was on track. We were down to the serious business. I recalled the look on the faces of our supporters at the airport in Perth in 1995 when we flew in . . . just as they were preparing to fly out to watch us play. I'm sure we all felt some guilt that these people had saved up their money to give us support, and we hadn't made it. But it was also a lesson and a spur to the eight of us who made it through that Cup to this one.

Game 5, Semifinal: South Africa
The team pact of those next few days was simply this: let's give ourselves every chance of making the final – and of winning it. We

travelled east into England, settling at a place called Slough, about an hour's drive from Twickenham. Anyone who has travelled in England will know the name. 'Slough and the west' read the signs as you motor out of London. It's also where the British TV show *The Office* is located. There wasn't a lot of glamour about the places we stayed on that campaign, but I suspect that was the plan of Coach Macqueen and his support team. The task, after all, was to keep our minds on the footy and on getting the business done. And if the places we stayed weren't exactly the fun capitals of the world – well, we made do.

In the lead-up to the semifinal there was a TV interview organised featuring two of the opposing props – Os Durant and Dick Harry. When Os was asked whether he enjoyed a physical game, he responded: 'I don't mind a bit of blood!' When that was put to Dick he came back quickly, looking slightly bemused: 'I hope he's talking about his steak!'

Twickenham was huge. When we arrived there was a 40- or 50-metre walk from the bus to the change rooms. The walk that day was lined with security people, and I remember the South Africans, who were in the vicinity too, saying: 'See you next Wednesday at Millennium', meaning: 'See you in the play-off for three and four.' There was a fair bit of talk going on, but it was water off the backs of ducks. We knew we were going to go well that day.

We realised what awaited us. South Africa would be very tough, very physical. They had bowled over England in the quarter-final with a string of five field goals from Janni de Beer, and we recognised we were going to have to keep him under a tight rein. The match, played in swirling wind and rain, was later described as 'nerve jangling' – and I guess that about nails it. Desperately close, the game progressed from goal-kick to goal-kick, and I was happy I had packed my kicking boots that day.

It was fiercely fought all the way, with the defences of both sides unbending throughout. In nature it was a dour game to play in – with not too much attacking rugby and the penalties punctuating the battle – but gripping for the fans because of the closeness and the drama. Getting close to fulltime the score had climbed to 18–15 our way – all penalties – and it was a matter of clinging to that. There came a point where the bloke on the sideline produced the 'two minutes to go' sign. From that point we played another *four* minutes under Welsh referee Derek Bevan. Then came the moment. Owen Finegan, on his hands and knees crawling over a South African forward in a ruck, conceded a penalty eight minutes into injury time in the second half. Owen was just doing his job, playing to the letter of the law. Well, no, he was cheating – just like everyone else who had conceded penalties in the game! If the final result had turned out differently, Owen might have been given a bit of stick after the game. As it was, no one gave a damn. Anyhow, the indiscretion gave the Springboks a last chance. But in the conditions of the gusting wind and a slippery ball it was a tough kick – from 30 metres or so, and out wide. De Beer steps up and knocks it over for 18-all. I remember standing under the posts and catching the ball and thinking, 'Holy shit! We've got to go *again*!'

I was shattered. I felt I had given my all. But at times like that you have no choice but to dig deeper still . . . and find some more. As we trudged off, the boys were upbeat. Later, on video, we saw the reaction of the South African coach at the moment of the successful kick – a clenched fist raised in triumph, as if they had won.

It would have been handy motivation at the time . . .

You might imagine that a change room would have been a chaotic place at such a time. In fact, at the end of that bruising 80 minutes, it was quite the opposite. It was calm, and the message concise. It was there that Steve Larkham took on board the quiet word from backs coach Tim Lane to have a shot at field goal. And

I remember saying to Nathan Grey as we went back out: 'We've got to get into a position to pot a field goal.'

We ran into the wind in the first half of extra time, slipped behind 21–18 when de Beer booted a field goal, then climbed back to 21-all when I kicked my seventh goal. Near the end of the first ten minutes of extra time I got absolutely smashed after a scrum play we tried, and for a time my head was a little bit out of it and I don't remember exactly what was said in the short pause that followed. But the break was good – Ealsie took control and everyone was actually quite calm. We all knew what we had to do and he just reminded us – go through the process. Don't lose your head, just go through the process.

One of the real positives about the Australian side was that we always played for position – always tried to work ourselves into position to score tries, so that if a penalty was conceded instead we'd be able to take advantage of that, too. So it was as the wind gusted at our backs in the final minutes of 1999's Twickenham marathon. From a lineout we drove the ball upfield: Nathan Grey took it up and we got some quick ball and some more metres. On the right-hand side there was Steve 'Bernie' Larkham, Dick Harry and myself – and the ball came to Bernie. I could see that the South Africans didn't have many at home on that side and I called to him to run it. Meanwhile, Dick was calling, 'chip, chip, chip', urging a little kick over the top. Ah, how the mind of a prop forward works.

Ignoring all of that, Bernie instead hit a drop kick and the ball sailed off in the direction of the stratosphere and end over end all the way over the posts – and would still have done so if they had been 55 metres away. Later it was called one of the worst dropped goals in history – but from where I saw it, it was beautiful – just perfectly struck . . .

24–21.

But it wasn't over. There were still seven minutes to play – time enough for them to steal back another penalty or score a winning try. And it was desperate stuff all the way to the line. I managed to knock over another penalty from wide, 40 metres out – but at 27–21, a try and a goal would still have won it for them. Right down to the wire they were still throwing everything at us, but our defence wouldn't flinch. Then, right near the end, Henry Honniball put up a bomb and it swirled in the wind, but I caught it safely and shouted: 'Mark!'

The next few seconds live on in my mind. I walked up to make a divot where the mark had been called and given, thinking: 'I've got to put this out somewhere up around the 40 metres line.'

And then I heard the referee's soft Welsh burr: 'If you put the ball out, the game is finished.' I changed my angle – and booted it high over the sideline and up into Row M. The game was over. We were going to the World Cup final.

In that match, realistically, we created all the play and we should have scored a couple of tries but they just hung in there as South African teams tend to do, and kicked their goals.

We kicked everything that we needed to, and Burkey slotted a fantastic kick in extra time that put our noses in front. And, obviously, Steve Larkham's goal gets a lot of publicity – and fair enough – but Burkey kicked some real pressure goals that kept us in the match. If he had missed those, it probably would have had a negative impact on the team.

George Gregan

The 100 minutes of that match was an amazing experience, and one that gave us all pause to reflect. I suppose you could say that sport doesn't ask many tougher questions than the one posed to the two sides that afternoon. We had sustained our mental application and our physical presence – and we had won the football match. And every one of us was totally shattered. The coach drive west to Slough was the quietest I can ever remember after a big game. I think we were all in our own little worlds, thinking about what we had just come through.

And thinking about what lay ahead. Would it be France or New Zealand (the other semifinal)? The view was unanimous: it would be the All Blacks we'd be facing in seven days' time.

Instead the French came out and scored 33 unanswered second-half points to beat New Zealand 43–31 in an amazing game at Twickenham, one of the best matches I have ever seen. The fantastic second-half rally by the French prompted a complete re-focus in the Australian camp. We had really been thinking only of New Zealand and another match-up with our old rivals – now it was going to be the French instead. Something remarkable had happened. Our video analyst, Anthony Wakeling, faced the toughest job and might have been the only bloke in the camp cursing the result of the semi. He had piles and piles of videos ready of the All Blacks, of Bledisloe Cup games and key moments, and now he had to sweep them all aside and start delving into the French material, and cutting and blending all the pertinent stuff. Hours and hours of work lay ahead for him.

On that Monday, most of us were still pretty fatigued after the epic match against the South Africans. At the team meeting, there was a run-through by the manager, the doctor and the physio – and then our trainer, Steve Nance, had his turn. Steve had come to the Wallabies from the Broncos (rugby league) in 1998 and made a big impact. I suppose we all thought we were fit before he arrived, but he took it to another level. Before his first session at Caloundra back in 1998 we had been advised not to eat too much at lunch because it was going to be a big afternoon of running. He didn't let us down! He introduced a new plan for getting us fitter – an increase both in the weights program and in running. During a media interview he did one day in France, a French journalist suggested that the Australian team was 'on' something. 'You're right,' said Steve. 'It's called BHW.' The journos were immediately on the alert. This sounded like a big story. 'Yeah,' Steve continued. 'BHW – bloody hard work!' And he walked off with a laugh, having ticked one up against the media.

At our Monday meeting in finals week, World Cup 1999, Steve complimented the team on its victory and then said: 'We're going to do a 21-minute fitness component this week. It's set for Tuesday.' Heads around the room went straight up with such a snap there was a serious risk of whiplash. We all had sore and fatigued legs, and God knows what Steve had in mind. We all looked at Ealsie with glances that said: 'Mate, *no* chance.' The plans were duly reshuffled, to Steve's disappointment and our relief, and our training week was pretty low-key, as it needed to be.

The media obligations were a big part of it, and we continued our policy of doing what needed to be done. It culminated one afternoon in a big gathering in a fitness centre, which turned into a two-hour media scrum. When my turn came, there must have been ten cameras and 30 or 40 media people gathered around. I was having a bit of a laugh more than anything else. I don't think the impact had really sunk in then – for us, it was just another game of footy. The aim was to prepare for it as we would for any other game.

Match day in Cardiff was amazing, although just getting to the game proved to be a real challenge for us Wallabies. We came through the hotel foyer at about 12.30 to be greeted by a bloke from one of the supporters' tours who trailed us around and played 'Waltzing Matilda' – very badly – on his bagpipes when-ever we appeared. As soon as we stepped into the foyer the pipes would strike up, and it was so out of tune it made us cringe. I know he was doing his best to 'inspire' us, but the blokes mostly put their heads down and hurried through the foyer. So chaotic was the parking in Cardiff that day that we couldn't get the team bus out of the car park – until the 'double dirties' had bounced four cars out of the way to give us enough space to get through.

It was a huge day. The streets and the pubs were chockers. It was a great feeling to be heading through that tidal wave of excitement – knowing that if we played well, we would be champions of the rugby world.

Game 6, The final: France
Finals and grand finals in the rugby codes are rarely classics. There is too much at stake. Perhaps that was a fairly widely held view of 1999's final at Millennium Stadium. We set out to subdue the Gallic flair – and did it with a relentless display of defence, backed by taking our chances. At 35–12 it was the biggest winning margin in a World Cup final – only two tries to nil, but no one could argue that it wasn't decisive. My memories of the game are something of a kaleidoscope . . . of us playing smart . . . of Ealsie giving it to the referee over the eye-gouging that was taking place, and even motioning that we would go off the field if it continued . . . of the penalties I kicked . . . and the two great tries we scored . . .

My own contribution of 25 points (seven penalties, two conversions) was a World Cup record, one more than I had scored the previous week – and obviously a source of satisfaction to me. I was gratified to have done my job in a match in which we won the William Webb Ellis Trophy. For a long way (65 minutes), the game was try-less, although our penalty goals had punished indiscretions and enabled us to get away to 21–12. Then, after some slick interchange among the backs, a series of forward drives marched us into the French 22. There, George Gregan exploited a half-gap in their defence and the ball travelled from Horan to replacement flanker Owen Finegan and on to Ben Tune, who scored in the right-hand corner and broke the fullback's arm in the process. Timmy Horan did a great job in that drive towards the line, handling the ball three or four times.

Our second try came from a lineout move in which there was some underhand tactics going on. The video clearly shows Bladesie (Andrew Blades) holding one of the Frenchmen back just enough for Owen Finegan to get into a bit of a gap. Often in football you only need that half-metre or so to get into some clear ground. Owen had the ball in his paws after taking a reverse pass from George inside the 22; he was looking for some support – and he just kept running. The defence held off waiting for the pass – but on the TV coverage the BBC commentator had it nailed. 'Go for the line!' he called in his crisp English accent. And Owen did, aided by the force of the driving Australian forward pack when he was tackled five metres short. The momentum carried him over two or three of the small French backs, and across for the try.

There were eight minutes to go and we knew we had this game pretty well sorted. As the match ran down to its ending, the French spilled the ball over the sideline. I ran over to retrieve it, with a quick lineout in mind – then backed off. The whistle blew and it was over – the winning football in the hands of M. Burke. If you ever happen to see the video of the celebratory moments that followed, you'll be able to pick me out, my arms above my head – and the ball in one hand. The football remains in a safe place in Sydney. My place.

It was pretty convincing in the end, but more of a craftsmanlike display than anything else. We played smart and hard, kicked our goals and got in front, and played some football then to wrap it up.

The Queen gave us our medals, and in the process Dick Harry managed to stop her in her tracks. All of us had voted not long before in the referendum back home, on the question of whether Australia should become a republic. 'Congratulations,' said Her Majesty as she handed Dick his medal. 'And congratulations to you, too,' said Dick. She looked a bit perplexed and he explained: 'You had a victory in Australia today: we're still under the monarchy.'

We gathered then in a big huddle, the Cup in the middle – dragging everyone in, the guys who played, and the guys in the suits who didn't, and we sang the national anthem with gusto, and that was pretty special. It was the culmination of a concentrated seven weeks' work – and the couple of years before that, too – to get to the point we had arrived at that afternoon, to be able to produce such a strong and special performance on the day we needed to do it. By the time we did our lap of honour, with Men at Work blasting out 'Down Under', just about everyone who wasn't Australian had left the building, but those who were left made plenty of noise anyway. In the dressing room we stood in a circle and passed the Cup around, chanting the name of each person in turn, with the accompanying words 'World Champion' – and for some, 'Double World Champion'.

Later the media guys asked me to try to put my feelings into words. 'That's the greatest moment in my rugby life,' I said. 'It is just great to be part of this team . . . Forty-four guys came away, and we all succeeded. It was a tremendous reward for everyone and for our very loyal supporters.'

On reflection, I would say that our achievement was the result of an enormous amount of work produced by an exceptional group of people who shared a perfect spirit. In more than seven weeks away from home, we maintained an excellent and harmonious atmosphere and a good understanding with the coaching staff. Men such as John Eales and other leaders gave us great direction. We lived in near-perfect balance. On the question of management it was important to highlight the influence of the 'specialists' on the principal facets of the game: Steve Nance for physical preparation, Tim Lane for the backs, John Muggleton for defence, and Jeff Miller for his work with the forwards.

I guess it's timely for me to talk about John Eales at this point – as he stands with the World Cup clasped in his hands. Ealsie's leader-ship was different from that of other captains I have played under over the seasons. But of the big bloke, who was such a command-ing figure in the game, you could fairly ask the question: 'What could he *not* do?' He was a great package, really – a smart player, a physical player – albeit not so much an *intimidating* player. As a forward he was a worker, but not a crash-through type of player – not the bloke who was going to charge through the line and race away. He was more the athletic one – an all-rounder capable of making a diving tackle, of putting someone away with a short ball, of kicking a goal just when you needed it. And he was a captain who would talk to you in a way that provided a sense of direction and a sense of belonging to the team. Blokes used to seek him out, looking for the words of inspiration that Eales, the captain, could offer.

I don't think he ever won a 'Players' Player' award in his time with the Australian team. Sometimes I have felt the sorts of things that I suspect he felt, such as the expectation always being very high whenever you ran out on to the field. Even if you performed at your peak – well, it was just sort of expected, and you didn't get much recognition for it; you had just played your 'normal' game. I think it's fair to say that the 'Players' Player' award generally goes to someone who is very 'visible' in a game, a breakaway making a nuisance of himself with his non-stop work at the breakdown, or a No. 10, because they are in exposed positions. John Eales certainly did enough to have a few of those awards in his trophy cabinet. He used to do freak things week in and week out. It was a very good and positive experience to have played under his guidance and leadership.

At the official dinner on the night of the final, I received a paperweight, a model of Millennium Stadium, for finishing as the tournament's second-highest points-scorer, behind Argentina's Gonzalo Quesada, 102 to 101. The grog flowed, and the evening became particularly rugged up at the bar, where the front rowers from the four countries involved in the finals (Australia, France, South Africa and New Zealand) took over the territory as their own. Going to the bar for a drink progressively involved taking your life in your hands. The testosterone level was high, and it was a near certainty that if you ventured into that territory you'd come back with no sleeves on your shirt, or your pockets ripped off.

As the night wore on, several people approached me with some 'news'. The conversations all started roughly along the lines of: 'Did you hear what Gordon Bray said on TV back home tonight?' Well, no, I hadn't. It turned out that Gordon, fuelled by some information from David Fordham, had announced as I lined up a shot at goal: 'And here's Matt Burke lining up his fourth shot at goal. His fiancée Kate made the ultimate sacrifice of staying home to be part of the wedding of a close friend.' Fiancée? Back home, as I later learned, phone calls were made among family members – and even some champagne was broken out. Basically it was a set-up by David Fordham, who was involved with the coverage back at Channel 7, Sydney. David had been at the wedding of a close friend, and talking down the line to Gordon Bray in Wales, the mention of 'wedding' and 'Matt Burke's girlfriend' somehow became 'fiancée', which 'news' was broadcast a couple of years prematurely.

Things didn't quite work out the way they were planned through the remainder of the evening. The 'double dirties' in the team had done some careful research during the week to find a place where we – the team and some family members and friends – could have a reasonably private celebration. Wristbands to get us into the joint were handed out, and all seemed to be in order. Then in the bus on the way back from the dinner I got really crook: headache, an unsettled stomach – the whole deal. I just lay on the bed in my room for an hour and a half and it must have been 1 am or so when I snapped to attention, still feeling under par, and thought, 'God, we've just won the World Cup. I've *got* to go out!'

With no chance of getting a cab on such a night I paid one of the hotel workers 30 quid, and got him to drive me to the venue of our 'private' celebration. When I arrived there, it was a mad-house. The original story was that they were going to cater for just 300 people. There must have been 3000 people there! I showed the blokes on the door my wristband and they just looked at me blankly. Eventually I gave it away, and with Tim Horan, and his wife, Katrina, I took the long walk back to our hotel. Installed at the hotel bar there were about half of our crew – and the party went all the way through to morning. There was just time to duck upstairs, take a sobering shower, pack up and hop on the bus that was taking us to London, from where we would fly home, accompanied by Bill.

For reasons that escape me, I was in charge of the Cup. At Heathrow I stuck it in a duty-free bag and wheeled it around on my trolley. It certainly wasn't on show – but on the plane Dan

Crowley re-enacted a scene from 1991 when he filled the Cup with beer, and carted it around, making everyone on board have a sip.

It was a lively trip, as you might imagine, with no shortage of beer. The lack of sleep the night before guaranteed some peace and quiet for other travellers, though, as tired and emotional footballers gradually succumbed to sleep – me included. At Bangkok, where we had a stop-over, I was just about to tuck into some breakfast when Ben Spindler, our gear steward, plonked a bourbon and Coke in front of me. 'Drink this!' he said. More drinks followed on the last leg home, until about two hours out from Sydney the thought struck me: the senior blokes, at least, would face a big press conference in Sydney, and when I looked around . . . well, I was one of the senior blokes. I ordered coffee, and then more of it, as we winged our way home – our spirits bright, and mission accomplished.

As much as anything, winning the World Cup was a relief. All along we knew there were friends and family at home – a whole *country* – banking on us winning. A squad of 44 blokes, from players to management, all contributed to making victory possible – so when we won, it was just a great thrill. As much as the selected 22, it was down to the guys who didn't get a start, the guys who were the double reserves. As far as I'm concerned, they were just as much involved in the victory as the players who took the field. It was fantastic to realise that we had won the World Cup and that we could claim the status of world champions. And to have done it with a great bunch of blokes who put in so much time and effort over the preceding three years to make it a possibility was something very special.

Chapter 16

THE WORLD CUP FADES . . . AND REALITY BITES

We came home from the UK to a week of frenzy that started from the moment we stepped out of the customs hall at Mascot. With Ealsie in the lead, we pushed our trolleys out into a sea of faces and were soon swallowed up in the surge of people. I was grabbed and steered towards the press conference. But I held my ground. 'Not until I've seen Kate,' I said. And finally there was my girlfriend, Kate, pushing through the crowd – and it was fantastic to see her.

A pretty mad week followed – highlighted by a Sydney ticker-tape parade from Circular Quay up George Street to the Town Hall, where the lord mayor, Frank Sartor, presented the Wallabies with the keys to the city. It was a surreal experience to be in the middle of that huge, happy crowd. We were a pretty humble team, really. We were proud of our feat, but didn't feel the need to flaunt it to the world. It was a bit embarrassing, actually – all this adulation, just because we had won a football match! I think most of the guys would have preferred to sit quietly in a pub somewhere and share a few beers. There were a lot of laughs along the way, though, and notably when a Channel 7 interviewer grabbed a few of the boys seeking their views – and finally got to Daniel Herbert. 'Daniel,' she said. 'Daniel? . . . DANIEL? . . . Oh, well. Obviously Daniel doesn't want to talk at the moment,' she said to camera. What had happened was that she was on Herbie's wrong side. He's a bit hard of hearing in one ear, but it looked like he was brushing the media – and the boys got a good laugh out of that.

It was a long, long day, moving into a lengthy signing session stretching over five or six hours as we wrestled with 400 jerseys, 300 balls and 400 prints at the Australian Rugby Union – the ARU positioned itself quickly to cash in on what we had achieved. George Gregan loves an occasional cigar, as do I. John O'Neill, the ARU chief, provided the cigars on this afternoon and George suspected they might have come from the nearest service station, judging by the burn effect on the back of the throat. They weren't premium Havana, that's for sure. Some fun was had with George's shaven head as the afternoon progressed; gold pens were produced and George finished up with a sort of Roman helmet on his nut. There was a huge dinner for the team and about 2000 people that followed the signing session at Darling Harbour, where the beer and red wine flowed.

It was a frantic night, with throngs of people lining up for autographs. It was draining, at a time when it would have been nice to sit and relax – but for all that it reinforced to us how much the achievement meant to people, and how proud they were of what we had done. The night carried on happily and boozily at the Wallaby Bar at Cockle Bay Wharf, with more beers and laughs. Late, and the worse for wear, eventually I got home. It was good to be there.

And that was just day one of the week of celebrations.

We went on to Melbourne for a lunch, and to Brisbane for another tickertape parade and a reception, and to Canberra for a civic reception. We were paraded at Parliament House and dined at The Lodge, at what I suspect may have been one of the best and rowdiest dinners ever hosted there by Prime Minister John Howard. It was the PM's son's birthday – and everyone had a drink out of the cup, the prime minister included. That dinner was the end of the celebrating, and the signal for normal life to resume. It was a great way to finish a pretty amazing few days. Reality awaited – a brief break, followed by training for the new season. Roll on 2000 . . .

The lights finally faded on the World Cup, and the actuality of a new season and new challenges rolled in through the summer of 2000. The Waratahs – eventually – had a new coach, Ian 'Speed' Kennedy, a lovely bloke and a hard worker, replacing Matt Williams. But the selection of the new coach became quite a complicated process when Greg Smith, who was on the panel charged with making the decision, stepped down from that role and put his hand up for the job! So it came down to a choice between Smith and Kennedy, successful coach of the NSW and Australian Under 21s.

Second rower John Welborn, representing the players, had a vote on the board – and John canvassed widely among the players to determine their preferences. The overwhelming majority were for Kennedy. But pressure was put on Welborn to abstain from voting on behalf of the players. Like Smith, he was an Easts rugby man. But John held his ground and voted the way the players wanted him to – for Speed Kennedy. Instead of being 5–4 for Smith, it was now 5-all and it came down to the casting vote of chairman Ian Ferrier. Justice was done when the nod was given to the new man, Kennedy. What a travesty it would have been if the players' opinions had been ignored.

With Speed Kennedy came a completely new support crew, all the team that had been with him with the Under 21s. I think Speed, such a decent bloke, made a fundamental mistake at the kickoff that conspired against what we were all working for and hoping to achieve. Coach of the elite team of NSW rugby, he approached the job as if he was still coaching kids. And he wasn't. We had 30-year-olds in the side, and a communication problem developed between some of the players and the Kennedy team. The dress code was one subject of debate. The new dress code was meticulously spelt out, and ridiculously strict. Touring football teams staying in hotels of course need to adhere to a certain standard of dress and behaviour. But under Speed there were some silly rules – such as everyone having to wear long trousers at lunch. It all blew up when we were in South Africa. After a long morning training session in hot conditions, the stipulation of 'longs' for lunch seemed absurd. We weren't lunching at the hotel, but at some place nearby, and there was a mini-rebellion. Everyone turned up in shorts and shirts, but still looking respectable. The coach was furious and some strong words were exchanged. Tiann Strauss tried to calm the situation and inject some sense, saying that it was all a bit of fun. But the coach wanted none of it.

This incident represented something of a breakdown in a year in which we had all set high targets. It's logical to think that the tension created contributed to what was in the end a fairly dour year for the Waratahs.

An incident involving me in the match we played against the Northern Bulls in Pretoria, our second game of the Super 12s campaign, still gets a laugh whenever the video is shown, such as at my farewell lunch in 2004. It shows me flinching, some might say cowering, when a huge flash of lighting was quickly followed by an ear-splitting clap of thunder directly overhead just as I was about to take a kick at goal. What a night *that* was! Our kickoff was 7.30 pm, and in the early game played at Ellis Park in Johannesburg, not very far away, a huge high-veld storm had rolled over the ground, virtually flooding it. The storm was headed our way, and there was growing speculation through that early evening that the game would have to be called off. But it went ahead – foolishly, as it turned out – considering that the weather forecast was spot-on. The storm arrived as predicted and as fierce as you could imagine, dumping such a body of water that playing became a health hazard. There was the real risk that if someone had been pinned at the bottom of a ruck they could have drowned, so deep was the surface water. The threat of the lightning I'm sure worried everyone, and the rule book was checked by the refereeing team in the second half on the score of 'abandoning for lightning'. Most of us were golfers and we knew the deal – when there is thunder and lightning over a golf course, you get the hell out.

As a kid, your parents teach you about thunder and lightning – how you count between the flash and the arrival of the thunder-clap, and that tells you how far away the storm is. It was just as I was about to take the kick that lightning hit the grandstand – and as the video graphically shows, it scared the shit out of me. I cringed, then shrunk lower still when the thunder roared. The only thing that possibly saves me when the moment is revisited on film is that the referee, New Zealander Steve Walsh, reacts even more like a frightened rabbit, jumping in the air. I have reminded him of that once or twice. Somehow, I kicked the goal, declaring later: 'Let me tell you, it was almost time to change the strides.' We won the game 33–13 and were happy just to get out of there after such a night.

The referee jumped three foot and changed colour, and Burkey took a couple of steps back and calmly slotted it over. It was an amazing feat.

Jason Little

The TV commentary on the moment, which I heard later, went something like this: 'Matt Burke just about jumped out of his skin there! That lightning was close. Well, this is a true test of his temperament. If he can drop this over, he can drop anything over . . . His left foot slipped, he had that lightning strike and still the ball went over the crossbar!'

It was now eighteen months from the day I had dislocated my shoulder, but I was still struggling with it to an extent – and some coach-inspired flak in the media during the early rounds of the Super 12s about my (and Nathan Grey's) supposed 'flat' form didn't make life any easier. It's a one-way street when it comes to coaches and footballers. The coaches can say anything they like to the media about their players – but the player never gets the right of reply. That's just the coach–player relationship, I suppose. Some coaches reckon it's a 'motivational device'. My attitude has always been, 'If I'm playing poorly or not doing what you want, come and tell me personally and I'll do my utmost to fix it.' The last thing a player wants is to be reading that stuff in the media. But I was copping some of it then: a 'hang-over from the World Cup' was one theory. We weren't going too well as a team, and that didn't help either. And my shoulder remained a problem – it was still sore and stiff and not what it had been. Six years on, it's still as tight as a drum, still needing work now and then to release it and to give me more freedom of movement. When you play a hard contact sport, you have to expect a chronic problem like that.

A gloomy start to the season (two wins in the first six games) was spectacularly reversed on the night we played the Brumbies, competition leaders and rated the best defensive side in the competition. We had been playing terrible football – but in the space of a couple of minutes late in the first half, before the biggest crowd ever to watch a Super 12 game in Australia (33,987), it all changed. Scott Staniforth scored a try on the right-hand side and almost immediately I gave 'Whits' (Chris Whitaker) a call and he put a kick over the top that was just perfect. The ball kept bouncing down the paddock, then sat up sweetly at the end and I snared it one-hand and was over for a try. They came back at us, but we held on that night and beat them 30–25. Channel 7's Gordon Bray posed a fair question as to how a team that hadn't managed two tries in a match so far in the year had somehow come out and beaten the competition favourites. For me it was a night when the ball came sweetly off the boot; I missed only one of nine shots, and *it* hit the post!

The next week we went from the penthouse to the basement. Wellington Hurricanes' Jonah Lomu was sent off in the first half for spear-tackling Nathan Grey, and twice in the second half the Hurricanes were reduced to thirteen men on the field – yet they beat us, 27–20, thereby killing off any lingering semifinal hopes we may have held after the Brumbies game. In the end we limped home ninth, in a field of eleven. I told the press that night I thought New South Wales had 'white line fever' – that we were out to score off every play, and we weren't doing the necessary building. We were a bit like chickens with their heads chopped off.

By that time of the year, Chris Latham and I were locked in a terrific tussle for the Test fullback spot. Over the years I had what you would call a long-running battle with Latho for the No. 15 jersey. It was an ongoing contest – and I've got to say that in 2000 he had a fantastic season, running the ball with great confidence from the back, and winning an award as the best Australian player in the Super 12s. When the *Sydney Morning Herald* polled eleven experts on the question of the Test fullback, seven of them picked Latham, and only three went for me.

The duel was a healthy thing for football and a spur to both of us. There were times when one or the other of us thought the selectors had got it wrong. But for all the rivalry over a fair lump of time, we got on pretty well. After my last Test match in 2004, Latho came over to me in the dressing room and said: 'Mate, thank you very much for the time we've spent together. It's been great battling with you, and great for me to have seen the things you have done.' I thought they were kind words, and strong words from a man who had been my 'rival' for a long time. He could easily have walked away from that, but instead he showed conviction and genuineness and a man's touch in offering such words. They meant a lot to me.

Not long after all the bubbling media speculation surfaced about the pair of us in 2000, the struggle for the Australian fullback job was dead in the water. Amid the heavyweight program that confronted the senior players, a waste-of-time game brought me down and pretty much killed off my domestic season. A Ricoh Cup match in Sydney – described not unreasonably in the media as a 'meaningless interstate game' – left me with some teeth knocked out of my head and a buggered ankle. The teeth gave me the most immediate pain, but the ankle was the problem. I captained New South Wales that night, and we lost 14–19 to Queensland.

To make matters worse, I suffered the injury tackling Chris Latham! The problem was identified as damage to the syndesmosis ligament, which is between the tibia and fibula bones down near the ankle. The worst-case scenario for treating the injury is to get your ankle pinned, because the bones separate. But the pressure was really on me to get right – especially so with the Wallaby domestic season still to come – and I underwent some treatment that, in retrospect, I wish I'd never been subjected to. They jabbed me full of cortisone, when my own preference was to hold off on treating it for a short while, to give it a bit of time to recover naturally. I should have put my foot down. Instead I bowed to expert opinion – and soon was out running on the bloody thing, and no good at all. Every time I had a run, people would say: 'Mate, you're going well,' when I knew the ankle was terrible. I couldn't run on my toes, I couldn't stop and turn, I couldn't take off. The back of my ankle was giving me more grief than you can imagine. It was suggested that I have more cortisone shots. It was at about that time that I had a yarn with our Waratahs doctor, Sharon Flahive. After I explained the situation to her, she said: 'You've got to stand up for yourself. You've got to say, "Look, no more. This is obviously not working."' It wasn't easy to do, but she was right. And all of it came from a game that meant nothing.

The injury to the ankle turned into something of a saga in what became a very strange and troubled season for me. Australia had a busy domestic program – a two-Test series against Argentina, followed by the Tri-Nations. It was a peculiar situation where I was training with the Wallabies (in Caloundra, and then Coffs Harbour) but not in the side and sort of on hold in case the wheel fell off the goal-kicking. To get some game time and prove my match fitness (and I sure wasn't fit!), I played a club game against Randwick and probably shouldn't have. And on the day that Australia played New Zealand in Wellington, I played on the wing for an ACT President's XV against West Japan. The Australian selectors were holding me in reserve – and for my own part I had plenty of reservations, because I knew I wasn't fit. I scored three tries and kicked nine goals (from eleven) in the game for ACT, but

I certainly wasn't fooling myself. Meanwhile, Stirling Mortlock was kicking goals for the Wallabies, so I wasn't urgently needed there.

After the Canberra game I knew for sure I wasn't right . . . and wasn't getting right. Mortlock had handled the goal-kicking well against South Africa, so back in camp in Coffs Harbour I sought out the team doctor. 'Doc, Stirling has kicked well. Obviously he's going to be in the team and I won't be needed. I'm thinking I'd like to be a little more selfish and look after myself.' I told him I would like to get a second opinion on my ankle, and he was sweet with that. In Sydney the next day I visited the specialist ankle surgeon, Kim Slater, and in a procedure that lasted about fifteen seconds he performed a test on my ankle that made me scream. 'I'll see you on Wednesday,' he said, meaning 'I'll operate on you on Wednesday.'

After a moment's reflection I asked him, 'Any chance we could make it Thursday?' I hadn't walked or played golf for more than a month and there was the chance of a hit at Concord on the Wednesday. I thought I might as well take it. I knew I wouldn't be able to do much for a month or so afterwards.

Doc Slater operated on the Thursday, as requested – and a month later I was back running, feeling at long last that I was on the track back. I had missed a large lump of the 2000 domestic season for reasons that, to put it mildly, were frustrating. There was the personal frustration of knowing, during that bad period, that I wasn't anywhere near right, and yet failing to make any progress via the recovery program I had been set. And then there was the matter of the hip pocket nerve. *Not* playing for Australia, and therefore not sharing in the perks and bonuses, is a costly experience for a professional footballer.

I wasn't made any happier when the ARU initially bucked at offering me a further contract. 'We'll have to wait and see how you go, how your form is on the upcoming European tour with that ankle,' they said – which I regarded as a real kick in the teeth. In fact, I was livid. I was only 26 and, without beating my own drum, I had been able to achieve a fair bit in the recent seasons, including playing my part in a World Cup win. None of it seemed to carry any weight, which is what upset me most. I believed I had shown commitment and loyalty. Now they were hedging, disinclined to show *me* any. John Fordham, by then my manager, sorted it out eventually, spelling out why I should be re-contracted. By the time I got back from the Wallabies' short European campaign, the contract was there – an offer, signed eventually in February 2001, that stretched until after the World Cup of 2003.

At the start of spring 2000, I was named as one of just three Waratahs in the 27-man Wallaby squad to tour Europe. 'The sad, sorry state of NSW rugby was exposed again yesterday,' wrote Greg Growden in the *Herald* when the side was picked. The team, with Rod Macqueen as coach, was largely built around the Brumbies – meaning we would play Brumby-style football, and the skinny NSW representation was a reflection of the sort of year we had had. But I was happy to be there.

It was something of an offbeat tour, which kicked off at the impressively named Prince Chichibu Stadium in Tokyo. It was there, against the Japanese XV, that I made my return, as a winger. Chris Latham had the jump on the fullback job, which of course didn't mean that I didn't have my eye fixed on it. But it was nice to be back, and seven goals and a couple of tries made me feel like a footballer again in our 64–13 win. It was sort of bizarre to have gone through that long battle of trying to play football in Australia – and then finally to get a game in downtown Tokyo. It was here, after the game, that I earned the nickname of 'Malcolm Buck'. It came from something that happened at a function held at the

Australian Embassy after the match against Japan. The party was a pleasant event, and near the end an elderly woman approached a group of players. 'I've got everyone's autograph except one,' she said. Fletcher Dyson asked, 'Who's that?' And she said, 'I think his name is Malcom Buck.' Fletcher kicked it around in his head for a few seconds: 'Malcolm Buck . . . MB . . . Oh, Matthew Burke! Malcolm – of *course*!' he yelled out to me. I signed her book 'Malcolm Buck'. And I still get called that today.

The Test match against France in Paris, before 63,000 people, that followed was a far greater jolt. The French are right up there in terms of how the game can be played at its most elite level – and it was something of a shock to the system to be pitched into that after not having played for a while. It was fine, though, and my return to that level of football was reasonable. The kicking boot was in shape and I landed six (penalties) from six shots in our 18–13 win, and I think I scored a 'Man of the Match' award on the strength of it. We fielded a team that represented something of a changing of the guard.

I reckon that we were all half-asleep for that match. It had been a long day, considering that the game didn't kick off until 9 pm! Football is always a bit different in France. There was a moment in the game that was a bit about gamesmanship and about how tough the struggle is at Test level. French centre Richard Dourthe took a shot from a fair way out, 45 metres or so, and the ball gained hardly any height. It went low and hard, and the way I saw it, it cleared the crossbar by half a metre. 'Missed . . . missed,' was the call. Chris Latham caught it cleanly and I called to him: 'Mate, put it down. Dot it.' And he did, and we started running back to the 22. The touchies thought about it – and ruled no goal. And by the time we got back to the 22 the French were really blowing up about it. There was no replay or further correspondence entered into. I suspect that was just before the video ref came into play. So it was no goal, a bit of breathing space – and we got away with the match.

From my time in France, I received a very unusual tribute. A player of the 1950s, Vincent Cantoni, who played with the legendary rugby league fullback and goal-kicker Puig-Aubert ('Pipette') on the famous French tour of Australia in 1951, compared my ability to kick goals with that of Puig-Aubert. It was quite an honour – and much appreciated.

For me this was a comeback tour. But for most of us on the campaign, it was also a beer-swilling and pizza-munching tour. When we were in Edinburgh, for example, we lived just off Princes Street – right across the road from a nice pizza and pasta place. And we gave it a real working-over, eating there just about every lunch- and dinnertime. I hopped on the scales one day during the Scottish leg of the tour and I was 103 kilos, the heaviest I have ever been. As I tell this story, I weigh 90 kilos, which is about right for me. Carting all that weight around felt somewhat bizarre. But it didn't seem to affect my form in the cold conditions over there. (Maybe the extra lard helped!) Against the Scots at Murrayfield I had another good day, with a try, three penalty goals and three conversions. We won 30–9, and I picked up a 'Man of the Match' award, playing on the right wing. For me – at least *that* day – big was beautiful. I was certainly playing with enthusiasm, and genuine delight at being back in Test rugby.

The Poms beat us in fairly shonky circumstances at Twickenham in a match best described as 'controversial'. In the second half, Chris Latham was sin-binned, followed by Matt Cockbain, and we were down to thirteen at one stage – yet England could only scrape home on a try that should never have been allowed. David Giffin had been binned in the first half, adding up to a troubled afternoon. Winger Dan Luger was awarded the hotly disputed England try on the last play of the day when it seemed he hadn't grounded the ball properly after a kick through. Luger looked like he might have got an elbow on the ball and nothing more after a chip kick. As it was shown on the big screen, referee Andre Watson was receiving plenty of Aussie advice, roughly paraphrased as: 'Mate, you can't give *that*. No way that was a try!' But the decision, of course, rested with a higher authority, the bloke up in the grandstand. And the video ref, offered only a couple of angles by what rumour suggested was a one-eyed TV producer, decided he would press the green button. Later there was talk of dark deeds – of the video ref *not* being shown other angles that cast the most serious doubt over the 'try'. Anyhow, Jonny Wilkinson scored 17 points, and England beat us, 22–19, much to the delight of the fans.

My own game was personally pleasing; I scored all 19 points and was rated the Wallabies 'Best on the Day'. But overall, it was very disappointing. We kept playing them on tours, and coming away as losers. The circumstances of this one made it hurt even more. It was a bloody shame. It was a happy tour involving a good bunch of blokes, and up to this point we had really got the job done – and would have completed it 100 per cent with a fairer fall of the cards at Twickenham. For me it was special – to be with great travelling companions and to be back in big-time football after the saga of my injured ankle.

My thoughts on Rod Macqueen, who led us in the World Cup and through that campaign, and beyond, are a bit of a mixed bag, and I guess it is timely to talk about him at this point. To me, his management skills were better than his coaching skills – and I suppose that's why he always surrounded himself with good assistants. He had real success, and positives and good qualities, of course.

Macqueen was coach of Australia at the right time. He had a lot of good 'cattle' around him – and anyone who knows the game understands that a coach has to have the right players in order to succeed. In addressing the subject of coaching in the book he wrote, he talked about management structure and pulling the strings, directing those around him. And I guess that sums up the way it worked under his coaching. There were certainly times when he wouldn't be at training and the practical stuff would be left to the other coaches and the players.

I played under Rod's coaching for four years and in that time he guided the team through some magnificent victories – Bledisloe Cup, Tri-Nations, Cook Cup, World Cup and a series win over the Lions. It's a great trophy cabinet, and more so when you consider that all the trophies were held at the one time.

I think that Macqueen would be the first to admit that he had some fantastic players running around the rugby grounds of the world, especially with Eales captaining the side, and Gregan, the little terrier, as vice captain. In the leadership department, we were well off. Guys like David Wilson, Tim Horan, Jason Little and Toutai Kefu weren't bad players to guide any team around a football field.

He took over at a time when Australian rugby was in some turmoil – with an embarrassing loss to South Africa signalling the end of Greg Smith's reign as coach of the Wallabies. Macqueen seemed hesitant to take over the team – perhaps because he felt he was inheriting some 'old baggage'. But he accepted the job – and took a Wallaby team to Argentina, where it became apparent that changes needed to be made, and drastic ones at that.

He had the foresight to implement a master plan that centred on the training camp scenario, which is still operational today. The vision was to get players out of their comfort zones – and out of hotels and into self-contained apartments. It started at Caloundra

– a long way from home for most. Very likely that original vision was to have players concentrating exclusively on the game of rugby. That was a step forward – leading to what Australian Rugby has at Coffs Harbour now with Camp Wallaby.

Not surprisingly there were some teething problems, but the overall outcome was a positive one. The results came, and 1998 turned into one of the most successful years Australian rugby had ever had. Wins over England, New Zealand, South Africa and Scotland provided strong direction towards the World Cup. There, all the lead-up work to our famous victory in Wales was meticulously planned by Macqueen and Co. – down to the day, the hour, the minute.

Macqueen did some coaching and provided direction – and careful planning was always guaranteed in the preparation for Test matches. But most of the coaching was handled by Tim Lane (backs coach) and Jeff Miller (forwards coach), supported by Alec Evans, who came on to the coaching staff during the World Cup, along with John Muggleton (defensive coach). Like all head coaches, Macqueen went 'over the top' sometimes, when he felt it was necessary.

In the wider view he will be regarded as Australia's most successful coach – and no one can deny him that ranking. In my opinion, his ability to look outside the square was arguably the defining quality of his coaching. Rod Macqueen took on board opinions from other coaches and also listened to his experienced players – and that input no doubt helped with the success he had. All football coaches, I'm sure, dream of ending their careers at the top – of being able to make their departure as winners. Rod Macqueen was able to do that through the historic Wallabies win over the Lions in 2001.

A match for the Barbarians against South Africa at the Millennium Stadium, Cardiff, was nice icing on the cake at the end of 2000. There is a whole rigmarole of good rugby and social things that go with a Barbarians event – and they are inevitably enjoyable. There is even a football match. All of it revolves around a bloke named Micky Steele-Bodger, who played for England years ago and is one of the world's nicest guys. He is a heart-and-soul rugby man, revelling in the whole thing and with a fund of great yarns. It was a privilege for me to be part of a game like that, alongside a smorgasbord of international players – the likes of Brian O'Driscoll, Neil Jenkins, Andrew Voss, Lawrence Dallaglio, and the Kiwis Carlos Spencer, Christian Cullen and Mark Hammett. Fellow Aussies Daniel Herbert, Dick Harry, David Giffin, Chris Latham and Jim Williams were in the side with me.

The South Africans sort of spoiled the party in the second half by playing real rugby that was fairly distant from the free-and-easy Barbarian tradition. We couldn't compete and they ran away to win 41–31 after we had led them 31–17 at halftime. Basically, with a Barbarians event, you just turn up and play. The whole exercise is always considerably more about what goes on off the field than on it. The spirit is free, and you rely on your physical presence and reputation to get you through. I remember at the first training session, New Zealand's John Hart, who was co-coach of the Barbarians with Bob Dwyer, made the point: 'This game is 10 per cent set play and 90 per cent counterattack.' He put us through a routine of kicking the ball downfield with all in pursuit – and then it was switch, pass, cut, loop, until we worked our way back up to him. 'That was pretty good . . . Now I want you to add a few more things in there as well,' he said – booting the ball downfield again. We did that about eight or nine times, and were blowing hard at the end of it. By now there was some muttering among the players. This, after all, wasn't the Barbarians' style – to be grinding away on the training paddock. There was a quick word to the manager . . . and a quick word in turn to the coaches. Next day, training consisted of a walk-through on the tennis court. Life was as it should be.

During the week of the Barbarians game I was paid a tribute that was as appreciated as it was mildly embarrassing. In the match program were these words: 'If John Eales is the finest forward in world rugby, the remarkably relaxed and ridiculously accomplished Sydneysider [me!] is the most complete back. Only injury, the unwanted gatecrasher at every player's party, has interrupted Burke's climb to the top of the pile. He kicks goals like Neil Jenkins, gathers high up and unders like Matt Perry, runs as powerfully as Joe Roff, cuts angles like Tim Horan, tackles like Va'aiga Tuigamala and thinks his way through a game like Hugo Porta and Isaiah Berlin combined. A rather decent player, one way or another. He could go far.'

Phew!

A big highlight of the Barbarian experience for me was the chance to meet Welsh singing legend Tom Jones at a nightclub. It was around five o'clock in the morning, I suspect, when we shook hands. Home from a big night out with the boys, I bumped into Neil Jenkins, something of a rugby god in Wales, in the foyer of our hotel. 'Do you want to come and meet a mate of mine?' Neil asked in his lilting Welsh burr. 'It's Tom Jones. He's down at the pub.' About the only words I really picked up were 'Tom Jones'. We were all mumbling a bit at that stage of the night. But before long, I was sitting and chatting happily to the man himself. 'Do you mind if I get a photo?' I asked. 'No problem,' said Tom. 'Has anyone got a camera?' I just stood there for a few seconds, then said: 'Oh, yeah! I think I've got one in my pocket', knowing full well that I had grabbed it before leaving the hotel. So the photo was taken, and remains in the Burke collection.

Chapter 17
A LEAGUE OF THEIR OWN

The arrival in rugby of league star Wendell Sailor from the Brisbane Broncos, Queensland Origin and Australian sides created huge publicity at the kickoff to the 2001 season. There was debate as to whether or not rugby had come up with a winner in pinching a senior, elite player from league. That was the politics of it. My thoughts were that any player who comes to the game at the top level has to earn his stripes. And so it was with Wendell. The big challenge for players who make the crossover is to learn the ins and outs, the nuances and subtleties, of rugby. On the face of it, the games are very similar – you make tackles, you score tries, you kick goals. But there are intricacies and differences that take some time to learn. And I think Wendell would be the first to admit that he was a little lost at the start. But his attitude was great and he had a strong desire to reach the top level. He pushed on in the face of the knockers, and worked on the different options that confront a rugby league player – and finally he got there. I think there would have been relief all around – from Wendell, and from the bigwigs who had decided to chase him in the first place – the day he was handed his Test jersey.

Luck played its part in the opening that came for Sailor – but that's just football. Ben Tune was injured and out of the first Test of the season against the Maoris, and then his replacement, Scott Staniforth, had injury problems, too – so Sailor got the call. It was a classic case of someone's misfortune representing someone else's good luck. Sailor played in both Tests that year against the French, although he wasn't picked again in the squad until the end-of-season tour when he replaced Ben Tune in the Argentinian Test and went on to start in the remaining Tests against Ireland, England and Italy. There was a classic flip-side of the role that luck can play when, in 2004, Sailor pulled a hamstring in the warm-up at Suncorp before the Test against England. Clyde Rathbone got the late call-up and scored a hat-trick of tries in a match that Australia won easily.

The Sailor signing attracted huge publicity for rugby. Wendell has a vibrant sort of personality and happily talks himself up, and he commanded vast space in the newspapers. Maybe his chirpy nature worked against him a bit, too; there were people who backed away, rating him a bit of a show pony. I think that with Wendell there were so many opinions of him, the best option was to wait until you actually met him. Then you realised that he worked as hard as anyone else, and injected the sort of enthusiasm that could lift a team. He's a big talker and rarely shuts up. Sometimes that can be a good thing. When he came to rugby he was a work in progress – and no doubt he still is. We *all* are, in fact. I know that I'm still learning stuff all these years down the track.

The subsequent signing of Mat Rogers in 2001 and a wider courting of rugby league players, driven by ARU boss John O'Neill, created some unease among established rugby players, and despondency among the younger brigade. I believe it was largely an ego thing from the ARU's point of view. I think John O'Neill was trying to prove something – to say, 'Look, we're a big and growing game – and hey, we can entice some of the top guys over the fence from rugby league.'

The signing of Rogers, in particular, caused some uncertainty and discontent among the contenders for Waratah backline positions. A talented all-rounder, Mat could play pretty well any position except halfback in the backline, so the pressure was widely spread. Blokes asked themselves the inevitable question at this and the other signings: 'Don't they have faith in us?' Within the team there was some resentment. But once Mat Rogers came on board, he was accepted with an open mind. Like anyone, it would be up to him to prove himself.

The league signings have generally been positive – Wendell Sailor, Rogers and later Lote Tuqiri . . . and Nathan Blacklock to a lesser degree, considering that he returned to league. The signings certainly put the pressure *right* on anyone who aspired to play wing or fullback at the highest level in rugby. I was pretty comfortable with it all, established and hoping that what I had done in the past would hold me in reasonable stead. As long as I kept playing good football, I would be chosen.

But I really felt for the younger blokes. There was a lot of despondency at that level. Rugby had always been built on an ethos of nurturing the game from its very roots, bringing youngsters up through the various levels and all the way to the top. Now, for some, the chances of playing for Australia were lessened by these big-money signings from another game.

The rugby league influence was further strengthened in rugby's ranks when Lote Tuqiri and Nathan Blacklock came on board in 2003. In 2004, in South Africa, Lote came out with one of the funniest calls I've heard on a football field. Penalised, and given a yellow card (he'd had a few of those for technical fouls when he first came into the game), he turned to trot back as the South African kicker walked to the mark. 'Okay, boys. Heads up, heads up,' called Lote. 'They're going for the two!' 'Mate, you're playing rugby union now. It's *three* points,' I reminded him. 'Oh, yeah,' said Lote. 'They're going for the three . . . they're going for the three!' It was a lighter moment in a pretty fierce game, which we lost 38–27.

I think Lote Tuqiri has come on in leaps and bounds as a rugby player. The switch isn't made easily, but he is a young bloke and the learning process has grown game by game with him. He has wonderful natural gifts – and his strength is unbelievable. He's quick, with fast feet that get him off the mark swiftly, a level head on his shoulders, and strength that makes him truly formidable. You quickly learned never to partner Lote in gym work, as you have to constantly take weights off machines in order to do your own work.

Nathan Blacklock came across as a bit of a 'see you later' to rugby league, departing that game on not particularly good terms. The Waratahs gave him his chance, and I'm honestly not sure whether he always had his heart and soul in it. There were times he really put in – and others when he seemed less committed. But he is certainly a player of great instinct, with the ability to score tries – the sort of winger who turns up on that last pass every time. I remember he scored a try. He got a great short ball from Shaun Berne, chipped and regathered at speed and made it to the line. It was just outstanding. His only problem was the boys got to him too quickly with their congratulations – he wanted to do the trademark backflip.

Nathan was a bench player with us in 2003, and I think he was disappointed he wasn't getting a full game. He was an erratic, gifted player who could do some amazing things, but I don't believe he ever had a strong enough grip on the game of rugby to be an 80-minute player. During a trial match in which I was playing outside-centre, Nathan came on and was suddenly out on my right-hand side. 'Mate, what position are you playing?' I asked. 'Left wing,' he replied. 'You're on the *other* side,' I said. 'Oh, yeah,' said Nathan. But he was that kind of player – he would roam around everywhere in attack and defence, and his forte was popping up out of nowhere and scoring a try.

The league guys certainly added a new element to rugby – and provided a new challenge for coaches charged with the duty of transforming their skills developed in one game into those required by the other. Coaching football is, among other things, a delicate balancing act. The state of the art is when the bloke in charge gets the balance just right between the physical and the mental in preparing his football team. In my view, this has become even more vital in the age of fulltime professional football. The move to professionalism didn't automatically mean that training had to become a grind or a daily chore resembling boot camp, just because there were extra hours available. But sometimes in my experience it *was* that way – with a classic case being coaches who automatically wanted to train their teams harder whenever they lost a match or two. Often a far better approach is for a team to train *lighter* – but to prepare better mentally. I think the biggest challenge facing all of today's coaches is just that: to set the right balance for the team. It will continue to be that way into football's future.

My thoughts were on such things at the start of 2001 when Bob Dwyer returned to coach New South Wales. Bob was a coach with a wealth of experience on his side, although invariably with some older views after his long years in the game. I think it may have been the first session that season when he put us through a drill that basically simulates a game. You run for a certain amount of time, and then have three times that amount off. So, if you run for five seconds, you break for the next fifteen seconds, and so on. It's quite a hard drill, and as he was explaining it to us down at Narrabeen, I dropped my head a little. This was 2001, after all, and we had been doing that exact drill back in 1993. I looked across at Gary Ella, the Waratahs' assistant coach, and he was smiling. Gary had done the drill back in the 1980s.

Coaching is no easy job. In a training session there is a certain amount of hard work that has to be done. But if that work goes on too long, it sometimes means the quality is going to suffer. One of the secrets of being a top coach is knowing when to cut it when a session is going well.

Bob was back at the helm in 2001 in place of Speed Kennedy, who hadn't produced the hoped-for results. With a new coach and logo, expectations were renewed for the team, which had never finished higher than sixth in the Super 12s. Under Bob, I was to be both fullback (after there had been talk of me playing five-eighth) and captain – and relished the idea of both. After we had beaten NSW Country (52–11) and then the Chiefs (42–23) in the opening round of the Super 12s, I summed up for the media how I felt about being captain. 'I don't find the captaincy a worry because we play a system where there are captains all around the paddock.' And that was pretty much how it was. I guess you could say that I captained with a fairly light touch. My thoughts on the job certainly were that a captain should provide leadership and direction on the football field. But football players should be masters of their own destiny, to a large degree – and my philosophy was that the players should be left to their own devices. I had a team that was quite rich in experienced players – the likes of Chris Whitaker, Nathan Grey and the blokes in a pretty seasoned forward pack. I had the 'c' next to my name, and my hope certainly was to provide leadership with the quality of my own performance and to take on more responsibility at training and in off-the-field activities – but there were 'leaders' across the board in that team, players in whom you could place your trust. And I did trust them.

For all that, it was a sobering thought to realise that as NSW captain I was following in the footsteps of such luminaries as John Thornett, Ken Catchpole, Phil Kearns and Michael Brial.

I was to be captain of the Waratahs for three seasons, and when I reflect on it now I can say honestly that I enjoyed each one. When it was shaping that way in 2001, that the captaincy was heading in my direction, I made a careful assessment of the skippers I had played under – the likes of John Eales, Phil Kearns, Michael Brial and George Gregan – and thought a lot about the 'mix' that would best suit me.

I think that first and foremost as a captain you must be able to stand up to the coach. Sure, it's good to have a healthy working relationship with him – but as skipper you have to be very much for the players. George Gregan is a great example of that style of leader and I much enjoyed playing under his captaincy. Greegs was certainly for the players, and that must be a beneficial thing – meaning that the players will dig deep for you in tight situations. My further thought is that players at that senior level have to be essentially their own captain. Even though as captain you might have the last say, the final defining words before you run out on to the field, you can't mother blokes all the time. Individual preparation is the basis of what happens on the field – and the most important thing is for players to take responsibility for the quality of their own performances. And that was my style. I see it this way: a captain tosses the coin, decides which way his team is going to run, and strives to put in a high-standard personal performance each week. Other than that, the responsibility lies with the individuals in the team; if blokes aren't aiming up, it's then that the captain needs to intervene with a few words.

What does it take to be a great skipper? It's not an easy question to answer, whatever the sport. Obviously, you have to be ruthless about doing the things that need to be done on the field. You must set a high personal standard, hoping that those around you will elevate themselves to where you want them, and the team, to be. You need to have a calm head on your shoulders, a necessary quality for making the right decisions at difficult times. And while being 'for' the players, you have to be that little bit removed, too – able to impose discipline when required. One thing is for sure: the best players don't necessarily make the best captains.

With the honour of leading New South Wales now mine, I was determined I would give it my best shot. In tune with the reality of Super 12 football, I seemed to please the media back at the start of the 2001 season when in an early match against the Bulls, as NSW captain, I elected five times for us to kick for touch and an attacking lineout to keep the momentum going, rather than take a shot at goal. 'Adventurous captaincy', they called it. 'Who said that the buccaneering spirit of the Waratahs is dead?' was another comment. The first two of those occasions produced Waratah tries. Our approach was in line with the different requirements of modern rugby. The fact is that there are two distinctly different ways of playing top-level rugby these days. One approach covers Super 12s and Tri-Nations games – where you need to score bonus points to enhance your chances of staying up there in the competition. The other is Test match rugby, where the four-try rule doesn't exist and there is only one goal: winning.

The game against the Bulls was one of those nights when we could afford to play with a sense of adventure, and enjoy the running game. The Bulls weren't strong that year and we beat them 53–7, continuing a promising start to a NSW season filled with the usual anticipation – that maybe *this* might be the year – and kicking off with a hat-trick of home wins (Chiefs, Stormers, Bulls).

But being on the road in South Africa brought us back to earth. Against the Cats at altitude in Johannesburg, I suffered a knee cartilage injury that still gives me grief whenever I try to twist and turn. It was just one of those things that happens in football – an awkward fall, and a big lump of a bloke landing on top of me. We lost the game (21–28) after building a lead, when the Cats came out breathing fire in the second half and blew us away in the period after halftime. And as the fluid swelled my knee to balloon proportions, I missed the next couple of games. We went down to Durban to play the unbeaten Sharks and lost that game. Phil Waugh took over the captaincy – and I was doing it really tough. There's nothing worse than sitting there on the sideline watching as your team goes down, and knowing there's not a single thing you can do about it.

When we lost to South Africa in a Test in August 2004 (my final game for the Wallabies), someone did the sums and worked out that since 1996, Australia had won only one of nine Tri-Nations outings there, in 2000. In an attempt to tackle the altitude challenge for the game at Ellis Park, Johannesburg, we had tried all the possibilities – from training hard as soon as we got off the plane, to taking it easy and not doing anything until virtually the day before the game. There had been endless discussion on the challenge posed, and how to beat it. Nothing, so far, seems to have provided the right solution. Australia, and the Waratahs, have struggled there. The Kiwis have had better success over there than we have.

During the 2001 season the question of the Australian captaincy was under public debate. Ealsie was struggling with an Achilles tendon injury. Greg Growden wrote in the *Herald* that George Gregan's 'headstrong, aloof nature' was against him, although George was always the favourite. There was much ongoing discussion: Gregan v Burke v David Giffin v Daniel Herbert. When George clashed with referee Andre Watson in a Super 12s game in Dunedin, there was more controversy. 'You'll never talk to me like that again,' Watson thundered.

But history has long since recorded that Greegs got the job, and as far as I'm concerned he was the obvious choice and the way I expected it to go. From my point of view it would have been great to be captain of my country, and I knew I was just one of a number of blokes capable of doing the job capably. But I have always believed that you don't have to have the 'c' next to your name to have a positive influence on a football team – and I would continue to try to do that. I was happy for George; we are very good friends. And I think the Growden reference to a 'headstrong, aloof nature' was just another way of describing George's very competitive outlook on life. As a halfback, George was (and is) perfectly placed to captain the side. He's right there in the thick of the action, yapping to the forwards. I think you can fairly say that the ideal positions from which to captain a rugby team are 8, 9 and 10. To lead a side from fullback can be difficult – but it's certainly manageable, considering you are back there with a wide view of what is going on all over the park. My full support for George was never in doubt, and I did my best to provide that throughout my career in the Wallaby team.

* * *

The Waratah season was one of under-achievement (again!) after a 4–2 start, although a late season win over the Crusaders (25–22), champions of 2000, was satisfying. The season was a frustrating one, but enjoyable, too, in the harmony that existed in the team. We had all the necessary potential and played very well at times, but erratically so.

The bloody Queenslanders knocked another nail into the coffin when they beat us near the end, 25–20, at the Sydney Football Stadium. We were really ready to go in that match, but were wrong-footed from the start when Chris Whitaker was tackled in the corner from the kickoff – and they just picked up the ball and scored. Against New South Wales over the years, Queensland always seemed to be able to pull out-of-the-ordinary stuff like that from the hat. Many times on paper we looked the better side in matches against them, with more 'name' players in our ranks. But football matches aren't won on paper, and they developed a nasty habit of beating us.

Playing Queensland is a real experience of mind games every time considering the recent history – and they seem to thrive on it. And it's fair to speculate that deep in the NSW psyche there exists a pretty solid doubt every time the Waratahs line up against them. The trick might be to return to basic things and just get out there and crunch them. Yeah, that's the advice from an old Waratah – forget all this psychology stuff, and ignore the mind games . . . Just get out there and rip in!

The international season that kicked off against the Maoris, a game that I snuck into via the back door, was the beginning of my demise as a goal-kicker, although I kicked two from two when I was handed the chance. I wasn't named in the original starting fifteen for the game, but got the call, as a winger, when Joe Roff was ruled out with an ankle problem. The Waratahs' struggling season hadn't helped my cause and Latham was at fullback. They handed the kicking to Elton Flatley. The time had arrived when the blokes in charge of teams were putting their faith in other people when it came to goal-kicking. But we beat the Maoris 42–19 and I was happy to get a run. The international season ahead was a big one, with the British and Irish Lions touring, and I intended to be part of the mix.

Chapter 18

PRIDE AGAINST THE LIONS

British Lions' Southern Hemisphere tours are comparatively rare events on the rugby calendar, and I think it took a while to seep into the psyche of Australian fans that the battle that was to unfold over three games in 2001 was something extra special. After all, Australia had never won a series against the Lions (England, Scotland, Ireland and Wales) in 102 years! And this was the first tour since 1989. Older fans probably had memories of an incident involving David Campese and Australian fullback Greg Martin in that series – but it was a bloody long time ago. In the third Test of that series, Campo fielded a failed drop-goal attempt by Rob Andrew and threw a pass, almost in the in-goal instead of touching down and taking the 22 drop-out. Martin dropped the awkward pass and Welsh winger Ieuan Evans dived on it for a try.

It didn't cost the Wallabies the match – they still had time to recover – but they went on to lose 19–18. The Lions thus took the series 2–1 – and Campese copped plenty of flak in the media over the costly mix-up.

This time the Lions were back with a large and very professional support team, and with a solid lead-up program that would enable them to get their combinations together. We had one game to get us ready – against the Maoris, and we knew the challenge was going to be an especially tough one.

The series kicked off at the 'Gabba in Brisbane, and the big surprise as we travelled to the game was the sight of a red-clad army heading to the ground. It felt like we were heading to a Sydney Swans match! It was, of course, rugby's version of the Barmy Army plus many others – a virtual flood of expats and Lions supporters. At the ground the sight was amazing – a sea of red, with pockets of green and gold only here and there – so much so that the story emerged afterwards of how Lions skipper Martin Johnson had taken one look and then headed back to the dressing room to tell his players: 'It's like a home game out there, boys – we've got *that* much support.' On a wet 'Gabba, with the centre square a glistening mud-patch, thanks to the patter of Aussie Rules feet, we took a real towelling that night, 29–13. I watched the first half from the sidelines. Roffie had come back into the team and he and Andrew Walker were on the wings, with Chris Latham at fullback. They ran through us that night, ran around us, and out-muscled us across the park. I came into the game at fullback in the second half, and struggled. Centre Brian O'Driscoll ran around me and scored a try, and No. 8, Scott Quinnell, barged over me from two metres out to score another. The Australian team felt strangely flat. We were there to play a Test match, but we just didn't seem ready for a match where the intensity was *this* high.

We came out of the game dejected, but not down and out. We

had been overwhelmed by the intensity and pace at which the Lions had played the game. But we knew we could play a hell of a lot better – and that was something to cling to. We had to forget about what happened in Brisbane, draw a line in the sand – and start again. As the Poms might put it, we had to get ourselves sorted.

The performance and presence of the Lions had created such a buzz and so much press that security was enlisted at Camp Wallaby, Coffs Harbour. Coach Rod Macqueen was a little paranoid on the subject of spies, and wary of the media – and training sessions were off-limits to just about everyone, except us. The media was kept on a long leash, well away from the players. This was deadly serious. The first Test had caught us on the hop, to an extent, but we weren't going to go down without a big fight next time.

The game, and the realisation of the Lions' record and the sort of hurdle we confronted, reintroduced passion to the second Test, played at the Colonial Stadium, Melbourne. There was a lot of pride in our ranks, too; after all, we *were* the current world champions. The ARU got busy and organised free scarves and beanies to counter the red army supporting the Lions. Gold, of course. I was back at first-choice fullback and goal-kicker – and delighted to have both appointments.

And we beat them 35–14, a record score for a single Test against the Lions. The second half was hugely gratifying after an intense first 40 minutes. We were down 11–6 at the break and I had the sense that the Lions were very confident they would drill us in the second half, as they had in Brisbane. I'm sure their unbeaten series record over 102 years meant the world to them, even as a composite team, and they were going to finish us off if they possibly could.

For my own part I headed into the halftime break as if in a London fog – courtesy of a collision with Martin Johnson when

I got my head into the wrong position as I made a tackle. I was in gaga land as I sat in the dressing room, the talk going on around me. At such times you push through it and continue, because that's what football is about, but I wasn't real flash.

Within about six minutes of the re-start, Joe Roff had scored two tries and turned the whole series on its head. After the first of them I took the shot at goal – and must have missed by fifteen metres or so. Physio Greg Craig sent the message down the wire: 'Burkey's not real good.' The plan almost certainly was to take me out of the game, but in the next play Andrew Walker busted a cheekbone in a tackle and was gone. All of a sudden Latham was into the game at fullback, and I was on the wing. Just when we needed it, Joe Roff scored his second try, again in the left corner, and our confidence was sky-high. But it was a fierce and bloody struggle, with the Lions doing all in their power to physically batter us into submission. Steve Larkham, a real star that night, was a particular target. They battered him from pillar to post – to the extent that he couldn't front up for the decider in Sydney. There were a number of questionable incidents – but not once did the ref, Jonathan Kaplan from South Africa, look like pulling out even the yellow card. Once we jumped them on the scoreboard, we were mentally on top and matching them physically. We went right to the wire, and near the end Owen Finegan made a great break, threw a one-handed pass – and with some big help from the forwards I was able to drive over in the corner. The try and last goal gave me a tally of 25 points. Notwithstanding the headache, it was fantastic to be back.

Despite what had happened in Brisbane, we always believed we had a chance of coming back to win the series that year. We had a good side and a belief in ourselves – and it became evident that there were some rumblings of discontent in the Lions team, mainly through stories that appeared in the media back in England. There were mutterings that the training sessions went on too long and that the players didn't have enough free time. There was ongoing discontent, too, about a Kiwi (Graham Henry) coaching a British Lions team.

The decider, in Sydney before 84,188 fans at Stadium Australia, was a desperately fought and fitting ending to a pretty remarkable series. We got out to 16–10 at one stage, but the Lions dug deep, with history and so much tradition at stake, and dragged it back to 23-all in the 55th minute. It was anyone's game, but we weren't about to buckle. Twice in the late minutes (66th, 75th) New Zealand referee Paddy O'Brien penalised the Lions, and twice – thankfully – I was able to knock over the goals from right field. After the goal that edged it from 23-all to 26–23 I gave a little fist-pump in the air. Kate asked me about it later: 'You don't usually do that.' She was right, of course. Shows of emotion on the field have never really been my thing. For me that would generally come later, back in the dressing room with my mates. Whether I kicked a goal, and especially when I missed one, I never showed much emotion. There's nothing to be gained from swearing and carrying on. And my belief is that you shouldn't let the opposition see that you are down. Keep your head up, and don't let yourself get caught out in anything. That was always my idea of being in control when it came to the football field. But, there it was against the Lions: a fist-pump – just a little message in a very big match to say, 'We're not far from this, boys!'

At six points clear, we still weren't out of danger. And a late penalty gave them a chance to find touch and get some metres and go for the driving lineout – and maybe the try and goal that would steal it away. It was then that Justin Harrison intervened with his moment that would become part of Australian rugby folklore –

stealing the ball away from Martin Johnson on our fifteen metres line with the Lions in a menacing position. The moment – photographed, framed and signed – quickly became a popular piece of memorabilia.

The steal, and our resultant kick for touch, meant that they had one last crack at us. And amid the huge tension as they played what was pretty close to volleyball, patting the ball from one to the other while chasing the try they needed, it ended up with our Andrew Walker not only going over the sideline, but hurdling the sponsors' signs, too – just to emphasise that the ball was out and the match was over.

The whistle blew. We had won, and made history.

For me, it was a night to remember. It was my 50th Test match, and with that milestone came the honour of leading out the team before a crowd of 84,000 people. The victory and the 19 points I scored were icing on the cake.

Big Justin would never forget it either. His ball steal in his debut Test would be a famous moment in his career forever. And there was also the matter of having the last laugh in his battle with English winger Austin Healey, a late withdrawal from the Test. In the Lions v Brumbies match, Healey had accused Harrison of belting him late after his second try. The pair had sledged each other during the game and again clashed verbally at fulltime. Healey subsequently wrote a column for *The Guardian* in England (ghost written by former Wales and Lions player Eddie Butler) in which he called Justin an ape, a plod and a plank, and attacked everything Australian – our weather, our humour, our male population, Australian culture generally, and called Pat Rafter a 'super-hero loser'. Not our Pat!

The world media being the way it is, the story was back in Australia in a flash and got a huge run in the papers here. It was pretty naïve of Healey if he thought it was going to sneak through unnoticed. I remember coming down late for breakfast at the Parramatta Park Royal where we were staying, on the morning the story broke. Justin Harrison was there, along with one or two others, and as I sat down he spun the paper around, revealing a headline that read: 'A plod, a plank, an ape'. I read the story, trying not to smile. Meanwhile, from across the table, steam was coming out of Googie's ears. I think the point has been made many times that when it comes to Australian sporting teams, it's not such a great idea for the opposition to provide further ammunition when they go into battle. Generally there seems to be enough inbuilt spirit and will in Aussie teams right across the sporting spectrum. Now one bloke (Harrison) was even more fired up to prove a point as a result of some ill-chosen words – and he sure did that!

It was a fantastic finish to the series – and a triumphant exit for coach Rod Macqueen, who had announced to the team that he was retiring at the end of it. He did a great job in preparing us for this, his last game and one that turned out to be a real slice of history for Australian rugby. There was appreciation of how he was able to get us focused on the individual tasks that went towards winning football. Under Macqueen there were big targets along the way – the World Cup of 1999 (the biggest!), the Tri-Nations of 2000 and now the challenge to the Lions' years of supremacy, in 2001. As a coach he was able to finish on a high and winning note. Ealsie wasn't far away from hanging up his boots, either, so the winds of change were blowing through Australian rugby.

For the Wallabies of season 2001, the challenges didn't get any easier. The trip to Pretoria to take on the South Africans two weeks after the Lions decider was never going to be easy. They beat us 20–15 there in a tough one-try Test that wasn't pretty.

* * *

Then came the task of readying ourselves for the defence of the Bledisloe Cup at that most testing of venues, Carisbrook in Dunedin – the ground they call the 'House of Pain'. When it comes to matches there, the logistics are usually quite testing, for starters. Glance at the map and it looks easy; New Zealand, after all, is only just down the road. But for a game of football in Dunedin you generally fly the three hours to Christchurch, with its two-hour time difference, and wait around there before moving on. If you are lucky you can actually fly on to Dunedin. If the weather is a big problem there, which it can be, you might have to fly a bit further down, to Invercargill, and then bus it back up. If the ball doesn't bounce right, it can take you ten – or even twelve – hours to get there – by which time everyone is flat-out weary.

For this big game of 2001 the ARU came up with a different idea. They would arrange a Qantas charter flight to take us direct from the training base in Coffs Harbour into Dunedin. The thing was, Australia hadn't won a Test there in eleven attempts since 1905 (and no individual nation had won there in the period 1908–2001, although the British Lions had beaten the All Blacks there in 1930 and 1971). If we were going to get this monkey off our backs, we needed to get it right.

To make it economically viable, supporters were offered a package arrangement, from Sydney – to join us on the flight to New Zealand. We travelled up front, with the fans down the back. It was good to know we were going to have at least some support over there.

I was crook – riddled with 'flu and feeling very poor and nursing a thundering headache when we arrived. For some inexplicable reason the training run for next day, the Friday – known as the 'captain's run' – was scheduled for around nine o'clock in the morning (seven o'clock NSW time). I went up to the coach before we started and said, 'If you happen to see a picture of me yawning in tomorrow's paper, don't take offence. It's just so early.' So, we were under the pump straightaway.

But there were good signs, too. It was to be an afternoon game, and that was a positive. Dunedin in winter can be a wet and gloomy place – and even if it's not raining, there tends to be mist, and a dew on the grass at night, making conditions difficult. Instead the day dawned chilly, but sunny.

I'll never forget my preparation for the Test. In the two change rooms there were a couple of heaters on, which was unusual. Normally, you don't want to have to go from the warmth of the dressing room to the sudden shock of facing the All Blacks, going off their heads, out there in five or six degrees. Mentally the risk is that you might be still back in the dressing room sipping a cup of warm chocolate when the black avalanche hits. But that day, in the relative comfort of the dressing room, as I nursed my 'flu, I actually slept soundly for half an hour before the game. We had got there early and I'd gotten myself strapped – ankles, wrists, etc – and my boots and gear on. I went and sat in the quieter room, and promptly went to sleep. When I awoke from this decidedly off-beat preparation, I went out into the cauldron of the 'House of Pain' and played the best football I'd played for a long time.

I scored a try from what the media called a 'chip and chase'. In fact, it should have been called a 'shin and chase'. I took a ribbing from the boys afterwards: 'Burkey, can you teach me that shin kick?'

The game started badly for us after we turned over the ball and Tana Umaga kicked through for Jonah Lomu to score in the corner. It was 5–0 after just two minutes, and no doubt there were many people wondering whether this was going to follow the same old script. So often in the Tests I played against the All Blacks, it seemed to go that way – they would jump us at the start, and make it that much harder for us. But on this day we steadied, and settled into a pretty good groove, although for a time the points weren't coming. Then we came down the left side and Bernie Larkham put me through a gap as he is so adept at doing, and I got outside Taine Randell and into some space. The fullback Jeff Wilson was coming at me fast and I knew Joe Roff was back a bit, but not far, and I thought I'd try a chip kick.

If it had been a proper chip kick with a little height, I probably would have been cut down before the line. Instead, I shanked it a bit and it was much more of a *shin* kick as it flew past just inches from Wilson's head. On the slightly damp ground I was able to retrieve the ball and I slid across the line with the tacklers.

It went on to be a memorable night for us in a memorable year. At fulltime, we had won the game 23–15 and retained the Cup after a typically desperate battle between the two teams. Just about everything went well for us that afternoon. There was exciting running and last-ditch tackling. A tackle I made on Andrew Mehrtens not far out from the end, knocking him in to touch with an All Black try perhaps beckoning, stays in my mind. Later, Gordon Bray wrote: 'That single tackle effectively represented two and a half years of gradual confidence rehabilitation' (after my shoulder reconstruction).

A key moment came when English referee Steve Lander awarded us a penalty try after Joe Roff had been knocked over by Ron Cribb without the ball when he was certain to score in the corner. With George Gregan offering him all the advice in the world, Lander ran around and awarded the try under the posts. I can almost hear George now: 'Mate! That has *got* to be a penalty try!' Then, when the signal concurred, I can picture him following the ref around to the posts, about half a metre behind. As the whistle trilled, George gave him a bum pat with words to the effect of: 'Well done. That's a very courageous decision, and especially down here at Dunedin!' The try was a big help in the scheme of things, but on the back of the win over the Lions, we played very well and earned the further piece of rugby history that came our way.

Back home in Coffs Harbour in the wake of it, there was drama involving Andrew Walker. The return flight took us through Sydney, where Andrew, who had been homesick, left the team without permission and headed off to be with his family. He was subsequently stood down from the following week's Test against South Africa in Perth. He did what plenty of us would probably like to have done – but our directions were to head straight back to Coffs Harbour to get ready for the next game.

Among the four or five messages on my phone on the Monday was one that started: 'Hi, Matt. This is Phil Wilkins [rugby journalist]. Could you please call such-and-such phone number . . .' I jotted down the number, but unknowingly missed the end of the message. Sometime later our media manager, Djuro Sen, came to see me. 'Mate, are you aware the media are going to run a story on Andrew Walker and you, and the reason why he broke camp?' It emerged that the phone message had suggested that if I didn't return the call ASAP, Wilkins was going to run with a story that Walker and I had been involved in a punch-up on the Saturday night after the Test – and that the 'incident' had been behind his decision to shoot through. Not only was the suggestion wrong, it was ridiculous. To this day I'm mates with Walks – and I don't think there is anything much that we would ever argue over. I thought back to the Saturday night. With plenty of others, I had been at the casino in Dunedin, at the roulette table for a while – and I couldn't remember seeing Walks there at all during the night. The story needed to be knocked on the head, and quickly. One of the big-value items underpinning the Wallaby teams of my time was that we always got on so well together. A scurrilous story like this wouldn't be helpful to anyone. I can only presume that such a story would have come from a 'tip' – perhaps from someone chasing money. It was quickly killed off, and never saw the light of day in the press. Andrew and I were able to laugh about it later when he rejoined the squad, for the return match against the All Blacks. Later, on 11 October, he went AWOL from Coffs Harbour prior to the UK tour and was dropped.

We drew with the South Africans 14-all in what was virtually a 'dead' game, and the following week we came from behind to beat the All Blacks again, 29–26, in a match that meant more than most, before 91,000 people at Stadium Australia. Marking the retirement of John Eales from international football, it was a game of ebb and flow – with Australia in the lead at halftime, and then the New Zealanders coming back to grab the lead (26–19) and make *us* play catch-up. It was a night on which we had two strong and distinct focal points – to hang on to the Bledisloe Cup, and to send Ealsie out a winner.

I played 65 minutes before an ankle injury forced me on to the sideline. Andrew Walker, back from his earlier week of controversy, then came into the game with an excellent cameo performance – including a superb tackle, a great kick, and a characteristic evasive run, the three of them in total helping to shape the ultimate result of the game. It was a classic example of the input that a fresh and talented bench player can have.

Many football matches are especially remembered for special events. This was one of them – and it belonged to Toutai Kefu. The try our No. 8 scored in the very last breath of the match when we trailed 22–26 was so memorable that I think it's probably up there in the list of iconic sporting moments – one of those events about which people ask the question: 'Where were you when . . .?' It was an absolute ripper – and as I sat on the bench I could only wonder how the hell he had got through there. Steve Larkham had faded across field with the ball then dropped it to Kef, coming through on his left-hand side. Kef burst through the first tackle, palmed off the right-side tackle, broke through another tackle, and then had enough impetus to reach out and place the ball over the line as he was finally felled, just short. It was a truly magic moment from a fantastic player.

The boys leapt on him like a giant scrum – and Ealsie, in particular, was trying to get in there and give him a huge hug and say 'thank you'. 'I'll buy him a beer every time I see him for the rest of my life,' the captain declared later. Kef has a later update on that: 'He seems to run away from me every time I get near him!' It was a marvellous night for them both – and for the team.

I had played with Kef as far back as 1996, when he won his first gold jumper on the tour to Italy. I found him a great guy. Of Tongan heritage, born in Australia, he was as adept at Aussie slang as anyone you would meet. In 1996 when he was named for the trip, Phil Harry, the ARU president, made a point of congratulating him. Speaking in a very slow and deliberate manner in the apparent belief that Kef's grasp of English mightn't have been too hot, Phil shook his hand and said, 'Toutai, congratulations on making the tour. I hope you have a great time and enjoy the experience that rugby has to offer.' 'Yeah, mate. Thanks, mate,' said Kef, sharp as a tack. 'I'm just heading down the road to have a beer with the boys. See you later.'

He was a fine player for Australia – and he scored no better try in his life, surely, than on the night he stole the Bledisloe Cup from New Zealand's grasp.

Chapter 19
IN THE SHADOWS OF 9/11

The Wallabies' Northern Hemisphere campaign of 2001 took place in a world that had changed forever. The horror of the events of 9/11 in New York and Washington prompted a time of introspection and reflection for everyone, including a bunch of footballers getting ready to fly across the globe. I know that, from my own point of view, 9/11 gave me a new perspective on things. We might have been big fish in the world of rugby, but in the wider view, what we did was insignificant.

The rugby league Kangaroos called off their planned trip to the UK, but I honestly don't believe that our trip, scheduled to begin six weeks after the terrorist attacks, was ever in doubt. There was some pause for thought, certainly – and I put my hand up on that score. I talked at length to Daniel Herbert about it, and we were subsequently named in the media as the 'players most likely to pull out'. The strike, after all, had been at the heart of the United

States – and we Australians were close allies of the Americans. So, too, were the English – and we were scheduled to play England before 75,000 people at Twickenham. Could such an occasion be another perfect terrorist target?

It was inevitable that those sorts of thoughts ran endlessly through our heads. I was on the verge of getting married to Kate and starting a new life, and suddenly the world was a dangerous and volatile place. Should we be going overseas at this time? There was a lot of that sort of questioning going on – but, with it, the thought that, notwithstanding the uncertainty and unease, life always had its risks and had to go on.

I was reassured by the thoroughness of the ARU, which was in constant dialogue with the Department of Foreign Affairs, getting all the necessary intelligence and information. When a clear-the-air meeting in Sydney resolved a number of issues, and the green light was given, I had no hesitation. Of course I would be part of it.

There was a new addition to the travelling squad, a bloke who it was assumed generally would be a sort of security person for the team. But when he sat us down for a briefing, his first words were: 'I'm not a guard. I'm not going to take a bullet for you.' He explained that he was, in fact, a security analyst, an expert in assessing possibly difficult situations and working out how to get around them. 'Wherever we stay,' he told us, 'always have a bag packed with your essentials, wallet and passport, close to the door. In case of an emergency, it's clothes on, shoes on, grab the bag – and off.' He talked about places that might not be safe, and about where we might and might not go.

His role, among other things, would be to do some reconnaissance work at places we were to visit, and to come back to the team with his advice. So, he was an important cog in the wheel of the 2001 Wallabies, carrying a fair load of responsibility on his shoulders. In the first week or so everyone followed the plan pretty carefully. But as time went on and we began to breathe a little easier, our security man came to be perceived as more of a tourist. When there was a problem with a map he had prepared of Madrid, where the tour began, I think he lost us a bit and the blokes started to go their own way. The city map was coloured in 'go' (green) and 'no go' (red) areas, but somehow there was a mix-up and the 'no go' areas had been coloured green and the 'go' areas red. One morning, a few of the boys took a taxi to one of the green-marked places. As they piled out of the cab in a decidedly seedy part of town, the driver had a 'what the hell do you want to go *here* for?' look on his face. They took a look around, hopped straight back in the cab, and returned to the hotel to share the story with the rest of the team.

With Ealsie gone, George Gregan was our captain – and he was a logical and popular choice. He had been vice captain and had led the Brumbies to some Super 12 success. He played his football in a position of authority on the field (at halfback). Daniel Herbert was named vice captain – and, again, he was a popular choice. Herbie is a great bloke and was an outstanding player. The choice of two backs as the team leaders was a little unusual. More often in the past the roles have been split – back/forward. But in George and Daniel there was lots of experience – and the forward pack had its own in-built leaders anyway. Eddie Jones was now at the helm as coach, having taken over from Rod Macqueen in the wake of the series against the Lions.

The start of the tour, after a warm-up game against the English National Divisions XV, wasn't flash – with the team housed two to a bathroom-sized room in a hotel in Madrid. Some subsequent muttering and shuffling led to most of us at least having single rooms. Brett Robinson had sussed out the place before the tour, and reckoned it would be okay; it offered reasonable accommodation with playing fields just down the road suitable for training. The match against Spain, one of the developing rugby nations, was a 92–10 cakewalk featuring thirteen tries, ten of which I converted for an Aussie Test record. It wasn't a bad way for the team to celebrate the Wallabies' 400th Test overall. The question is often asked whether those sorts of games are worthwhile. I believe they are – and especially so if they can draw a fair crowd and the team on a learning curve can take away something helpful. They are difficult games to play in, though – always scrappy and lacking real intensity. But this day was a milestone for Spanish rugby and the crowd turned up in reasonable numbers, with some Aussies dotted here and there, so there were a few positives. For our part, we got to experience a new culture – and had a useful hit-out before we played England at Twickenham in the next international.

The Poms beat us 21–15 before 75,000 people the following week, with Jonny Wilkinson getting all the points (five penalty goals, two dropped goals) in a performance that was a sign of things to come. England are a real stumbling block for the Aussies, so the Wallabies' victory in late 2004 at Twickenham would represent a refreshing breakthrough. Yes, England won that 2001 game on Wilkinson's boot – but it's a fact of life in Test match rugby that you'll take victory however you can get it. Later on that tour, when we beat the Welsh 21–13, I landed seven penalty goals. For all the hope and intention of scoring tries, you take victories any way they happen to come, and we celebrated happily that night.

After the England game, their coach, Clive Woodward, launched a stinging attack on Australian rugby union, having a dig at Eddie Jones and letting off steam about the Wallabies now having lost two in a row to England at Twickenham (2000 and 2001), despite being world champions.

Woodward's attack was just another chapter in the running

battle between him and Australian coaches over the years. Woodward and Macqueen have exchanged words; Woodward and Jones have exchanged words. It's just been the way of things with Sir Clive. There has certainly been offence taken by the Northern Hemisphere at some of Australia's attacking plays in recent years. My own view is that Australia have been pioneers in this respect. Some Australian innovations, such as the decoy runner (stolen from rugby league), have caused a considerable fuss.

Woodward was always outspoken when it came to rules and IRB meetings. I am aware of one meeting at which seven out of ten video clips featuring allegedly illegal play were of the Australian team in action. Bloody colonials!

Coaches are enigmatic characters, in my experience, and the sniping that went on between Woodward and his Aussie counterparts was just part of the deal. They all have their own beliefs and agendas. They all seek the 'edge' over their rivals. And they all play mind games to a greater or lesser extent, and I suspect take perverse pleasure in doing so, because they like the idea of having 'control'. If they can put pressure on a rival by something they've said . . . well, I'm sure that blokes like Woodward are more than happy with that.

We travelled on to France after the England game, with the winter really starting to bite now, and stayed at a town that would have been a beauty if it had been summer. But Bandol by then was as dead as a doornail – a typical French seaside town that had pulled down the shutters for the winter. Europe can be a trap in that way. You can visit some town on the water that is bustling with people, and full of cafés and good cheer, in summer. Go back in winter, and it's another world.

So it was at Bandol, where the cold seeped into our bones and training was an endurance test: a 40-minute drive from our hotel, to then be confronted with an icy wind and, very likely, sleeting rain. But rugby is a winter game, and the blokes who play it over there have to learn to steel themselves and make the most of it – whatever the conditions.

We played the French at Marseilles on a field that had wire netting rising about fifteen metres from the fences – to stop any missiles that the volatile crowd might want to throw. We lost 14–13 in one of the world's worst games, with the French lifting to the occasion just a fraction better than we did. I came off injured with a corked thigh after 52 minutes, adding to the disappointment of the occasion. For the French, the win over the world champions meant a lot – and the papers were full of it the next day. I wondered how it might have been if *we* had pipped *them* in front of that partisan crowd. A scary thought.

Living with the reality of two straight losses, and with winter closing in, we had one last chance of finishing as winners in the major internationals before we headed home to the Aussie summer. The men in red awaited us at the Millennium Stadium, Cardiff, and it was never going to be a picnic. It rained on match day, and of course they left the stadium roof open, making life just a little more uncomfortable.

The game turned into a penalty shoot-out. Wearing brand-new boots that had proved to be no good-luck charm in the games against England and France, I managed to land seven penalties, and we beat the Welsh 21–13. The score looks reasonably convincing, but there was little continuity in our play that day and at the end they were actually getting on top of us and scored the only try of the afternoon. Before the game I had decided that the boots were going straight into the bin if we lost again. Instead, they stayed in my bag, ready for another day.

A few of the older guys, me included, were rested for the final game of the tour, against the Barbarians. With some of the guys who hadn't been given much opportunity on tour now getting their chance in an Aussie side that featured a very mixed bag of positions, there was good spirit and some enterprising play – and a 49–35 Wallaby win at Millennium Stadium. That made it two straight to end the campaign and breathe just a little life into what hadn't been a great tour for Australian rugby.

In such a year, it was bloody good to get home.

This was a special time for Kate and me. I was introduced to her by a friend when Kate was working at a bar in North Sydney, and some time later we got together. Kate's background is in nursing and she worked at the Royal Prince Alfred Hospital. She was on the oncology ward for three years, in staff health, and finally in the haemophilia centre before we moved to the UK. Kate really enjoyed working in these areas as it gave her great satisfaction to help people and she fitted right in. Everyone who knows her realises what a caring person she is, so it was hard for her to leave nursing behind, especially knowing how difficult things might be in England.

My proposal of marriage, in late 2001, would undoubtedly have disappointed the women's magazines and the Mills & Boon crowd. There were no soft lights, or violins playing, or bunches of red roses or bended knees. We were sitting at home and I just said: 'Would you like to get married?' When I think back on it now, it was pretty pathetic, really – a poor performance by M. Burke. But even without all the traditional romantic stuff, I was as nervous as a kitten. Thankfully, Kate said 'yes'. The news leaked to the papers and the *Sun-Herald* suggested: 'Matt Burke, a favourite among female fans [Hmmm], popped the question to longtime girlfriend Kate' and that it had happened on a 'romantic stroll'. Well, they got that part wrong! We did go for a walk but the key question was asked at home. None of it rated too highly in the romance stakes but I'd like to think I've made up for it since.

Kate and I were married at the end of 2001, following a small gathering of friends and family at home. It could be called an engagement do but it was really one of those nights that just grew, with the usual crew there until the early hours of the morning. The garden wedding, held at the home of Kate's mum and her husband Nigel, was hardly traditional – a stand-up cocktail party (featuring karaoke later in the evening). We had a couple of marquees in the garden – one with a dance floor and the other where people could sit down and have a chin-wag. It was all we wanted – just to have the people who mattered most there. Kate and I had decided we didn't want to do anything formal. We didn't want to get married in a church, we didn't want to have a cake, we didn't want to do the bridal waltz and all that stuff. We basically wanted to have a big party. That was probably a source of some dismay to my parents – I think they would have loved us to have a big church wedding. There was nothing fancy; Kate walked out of the house at 4.30 and by about 4.38 we were Mr and Mrs Matthew Burke. The music kicked off – and away we went. It was a very, very happy occasion and I think everyone who came along remembers it fondly.

Instead of the bridal waltz, Kate and I finished up doing the karaoke thing, singing three songs and doing an admirable job, I might say. Well, at least the crowd was singing along, which probably made it sound better. Apart from the wedding ceremony, the karaoke was the hit of the night. Dick Harry, an extroverted sort of bloke, led the crusade, and there were rock stars everywhere by the end of it. There was a lot of laughter and a lot of fun. Scott Wisemantel, a mate from footy at Eastwood, threw his undies to Kate à la a Tom Jones concert. It was a funny night. And life has been great since.

Chapter 20

NIGHTMARE IN CHRISTCHURCH

Having copped a fair bit of flak over the years on the subject of my hair, I did something in 2002 that I had wanted to do for a long time. I had my head shaved. My hair had been the subject of considerable fun over the years, notably from the likes of Phil Kearns, who made special mention of it at my farewell luncheon in 2004, as you will read a little later. There had been heaps of flak about how it was always neat – even when I emerged from the bottom of the fiercest ruck. No matter how I wore it – long, parted, fringed – my hair was the subject of some chuckles. It was quite famous, in fact.

It was over a few relaxing beers one day at the home of some friends that I made my decision. Ben Spindler and his cousin, both of whom sport the shaven look, were there and at a certain point in the day I decided that I'd get myself a haircut, too. Ben and his cousin, Chelsea, didn't muck around. 'Well, let's do it now,' they said – and then reached for the clippers.

I came to realise that the short-cropped style has a sort of reverse-Samson effect. It's a psychological thing, but wearing your hair like that makes you feel a little fitter, and a little faster. Well, it did *me*, anyway. When I turned up for Waratah training soon afterwards and ripped my cap off to reveal my shaven head for the first time, the reaction could be pretty well summed up as: 'Oh, my God!'

Kate was happy with the cropped look, however, and I was too – and I had it done again for the Leukemia Foundation's 'Shave for a Cure' fundraiser, which aimed to help elevate public awareness of the need for leukemia research. The only problem was that they put the camera on me when my turn came and the bloke doing the shaving really butchered it – which isn't easy to do when you're just doing the shaven-head thing. I could feel his hands shaking, and he forgot to put the number one blade on and started with a sweep that left me looking like I had a mown cricket pitch on the back of my head.

In 2001 Mat Rogers, son of a rugby league legend (Steve 'Sludge' Rogers) and himself a very talented Test player, had come to rugby – and by the Super 12 series of 2002 I again found myself switching position, which has been the ongoing pattern of my career. Waratahs coach Bob Dwyer sat me down one day and started out on a somewhat roundabout conversational journey: 'It seems to me that we need someone in the three-quarter line in this team who can catch, pass and tackle,' he said. I knew what was coming. In the blast of publicity surrounding his signing, Rogers had made it very clear that he didn't want to play anywhere but 15. 'Mate,' said the coach. 'How do you feel about going back to play outside-centre again?'

What I *really* felt was pretty filthy. I would have preferred to stay at fullback. After all, I hadn't played at 13 since 1995. But I understood that a decision had probably already been made. Whatever the reasons behind it – whether it was part of an agreed deal when Rogers signed – it was what had been decided.

I didn't buck. When the media asked me about it, I took the diplomatic line and spoke positively about how it was going to be a challenge, and all the usual rugby-speak. Part of that was just me being a bloke who rolls with the punches to an extent and is disinclined to make a fuss. But also, by that time, I knew not to give too much away to the media, some of whom wouldn't hesitate to beat it up. Nevertheless, there were times in my past when I would have been happier if I had come out and said the things that I *really* wanted to say.

Whatever my deepest feelings, there were positives in the switch to the centres – as there are in most changes in life. I knew I had enough talent, knowledge and understanding of the game to do the job well. It has always been that way with me. I have played rugby with confidence over the years of my career, and continue to do so. I have never found it *hard* to play the game, whatever position I happen to be in. I hope I don't sound like a bit of a tosser here, but it has always been an easy and enjoyable game to me. I was now going to be in the game more, have the ball in my hands more, and from the captaincy point of view I was going to be in a position where I was strongly involved and from where I was well placed to lead the side. I made a decision that it was going to be good: the change would reinvigorate me, create a new focus, and teach me some new things in the ongoing learning process of playing rugby. And Eddie Jones assured me that the switch wouldn't affect my being considered at fullback for the Wallabies.

So, I was, once again, an outside-centre.

* * *

When it all kicked off in 2002, with a 107-nil win over NSW Country in Wollongong, I had alongside me a big, bustling bloke called Sam Harris, who weighed in at 105 kilos and could really play. Sam had all the required skills, and was the sort of player that any team would love to have in the ranks. But, for whatever reason, the coaching staff held the view that he wasn't going to make it. Eventually, Sam was lost to rugby league and in my view it was a sad loss; he had the talent to make it in rugby at a high level.

We headed into the Super 12 season with a 42–25 win over the Chiefs in Rotorua, New Zealand. In my rev-up speech before the game, I said to the guys: 'Look around – there's no one here!' There wouldn't have been more than 500 people at the match. So much for home ground advantage!

Playing 13 for the first time in a number of years was like a brand-new experience. I made a tackle near the end of the game, close to the touchline, and one of our trainers said to me: 'C'mon, mate. Keep it going, keep it going!' And I just looked at him and said, 'I can't move. I'm that tired, I can't bloody move.' At fullback you do a lot of running, but there are breaks. At 13, as I rediscovered, you are in constant motion, either with the ball or without it. The experience of that day got me up to speed pretty quickly.

On the South African trek that followed, I found myself on a dressing room floor at one stage covered in towels and shivering uncontrollably. We were playing the Stormers, and before the game I was as crook as Rookwood, flattened by some awful bloody gastric thing. I played 40 minutes and dragged myself off to talk to the doctor. Was there anything I could take that might help? The answer was 'no' – it wasn't worth the risk in these days of drug-testing. So I went back out for twenty minutes and then just couldn't go on. My only recollection of the latter part of the match – a thriller in which we got home 26–25 – was of lying there on the floor at Newlands in Cape Town, listening to the ebb and flow of the crowd, and feeling bloody dreadful. There was a huge roar at one stage. Later, I learned that it was for a 75th-minute Stormers try that had swept them to the lead. Soon afterwards there was a groan, followed by a painful silence. Nathan Grey had landed a field goal, and we had won the game.

My other vivid memory of that time in South Africa was of a training field in Cape Town on a stinking hot afternoon before we played the Bulls in Pretoria. Bob Dwyer put us through a training session that lasted over two hours. We went through every play in the book. At the end of it, Bob declared: 'Right, reserves in now.' And on came the bench players. If you didn't happen to get one of them in your position (and I didn't!), you had to go through the whole bloody thing – all the plays – *again*. We were absolutely shattered at the end of it, at which point the coach gave us one of his best sprays. So vitriolic was it that the manager came over at one stage to try to calm things down, and he was told where to go as well. I have been on the end of an occasional good spray from Bob over the years – but this one was high-octane, and I think it turned a few people's opinion of him.

We beat the Bulls 51–19, making it three straight on the road, and came home to such newspaper speculation as: 'Could this finally be the year for the Waratahs?' My immediate response to that was to turn the page and just get on with (rugby) business. After all, we had had promising starts before, and they had come to nothing. Nothing was going to happen for us as a result of news-paper theories. It came down to doing the work, preparing as well as we could for the next game . . . and the next. I admit, though, to getting a bit of a buzz when experienced rugby journo Norm Tasker wrote of my switch to the three-quarter line: 'Matthew Burke's union of strength and deception in the centres makes some of us wonder why he ever played fullback.' I guess it mirrored my own thoughts – that the move I had been nudged into making was going okay. A lot of it was down to the blokes around me – a talented Waratahs backline, behind a solid forward pack who were really doing their job. That was a darned good backline – the likes of Chris Whitaker a fantastic halfback with great vision, one of the best I have played with; Duncan McRae: a considerable loss to New South Wales when he was told in 2000 that he wasn't wanted for 2001, but who had now come back from the UK to rejoin the team; Nathan Grey: a centre with a great will to win, and exceptional drive and courage; Mark Stcherbina: another highly talented player who ended up unwanted by the Waratahs and headed overseas; Scott Staniforth: fantastic power, speed, a high work rate – and a lovely bloke to boot, also lost to NSW after the 2004 season; and Mat Rogers: a player of undoubted talent, thoroughly enjoying being behind a backline such as that.

We were batting five from five following big wins over the Cats and the Sharks by the time we faced the Auckland Blues, and finally stumbled there in a photo finish loss, 22–20, which was disappointing. Against the Highlanders (a 31–13 win) I became the most capped Waratah in history, with 92 games, edging past a good mate, Sam Payne, who, in turn, had slipped past Tim Gavin's record. To be up there with such great long-service blokes was a thrill for me. Sam called me from France to offer congratulations and have a bit of a chat. He also called me a bastard, if I remember rightly – but I know he meant it in the nicest possible way. My reaction on achieving a milestone like that is to become quite reflective. I had some fantastic memories, sure, but also some painful ones. I thought about all the training sessions I had been to, and how many times I had strapped my ankles.

When we beat the Super 12 defending champions, the Brumbies, 19–11 in a game that ranked right up there on the scale of ferocity, tenacity and physicality, it meant the Waratahs had secured a Super 12 semifinal spot for the first time. There is always great venom in the mix when the Waratahs line up against the Brumbies, and this game before a record home crowd of 41,645 at Aussie Stadium was no exception. Now that I'm living overseas, I'll still wait nostalgically for the quotes when the game comes around – from Bill Young and the boys, saying how much they hate New South Wales. But we out-toughed them that day, then beat the Hurricanes 19–13, and the chance of a semifinal spot – a *home* semifinal spot – was real.

Against the Wellington Hurricanes, a fiery game that produced that tense 19–13 victory, my 11 points represented a personal milestone. I was now the first NSW player to reach 1000 points. I was a happy camper. Someone asked me if any of those penalty goals and tries and conversions making up the 1000 especially stuck in my mind, and a fantastic passage of play in a match against Wellington in 1996 came to mind. Christian Cullen set off from fullback on an electrifying run during which he ran around five blokes but stepped left once too often and got caught. We won the ball from the ruck, and with Campo at five-eighth I called on him to put a kick over the top. He obliged with a perfect kick into space – and I chased it hard, from a position about 70 metres out from our tryline. Forty metres down the paddock I got a fair kick on the bouncing ball, although it was wandering close to the touchline. Heading the chase I then got the bonus of an absolutely super bounce near the tryline, caught the ball in mid-air and dived over, finishing with a big slide. Cullen got one back on us that day, though – a brilliant length-of-the-field try that showed the bloke's speed and ability. On a field that is 100 metres long, he ran probably 120 metres – across, around, forward, sideways . . . and then under the posts. He really could score a try.

A penalty kick? My first thought is of a game against the Bulls at altitude, at Loftus Versfeld, Pretoria. At training the day before, a few of us had been taking shots from 65 and 70 metres out, with the ball really flying in the thin air. When it comes to game day, you obviously don't shoot from that far out. But when in the match we were given a penalty 55 metres out and about sixteen metres in from touch, I convinced Tim Gavin that we should go for goal. It never looked like missing, and certainly ranks as one of my best career goals from a penalty shot.

A conversion? Probably the wonky goal I kicked on cramping legs against Otago in 1997 to win the match. As described earlier, the circumstances of that kick made it unique – the cramping, the reverse curl, the weird suggestion that it had hit another ball booted simultaneously by a ball boy before scraping over. The kick was pretty close to a shank, but it made its scratchy progress over the crossbar and so was stored in my memory bank as something special.

When Queensland beat us 31–24 late that season on 5 May, 2002, Coach Dywer told the press he thought we 'froze on the Ballymore Stage'. I don't agree. Queensland just out-muscled us (again) – but there was very little in it. I got penalised for an intercept that would have represented a ten-point turnaround, although if you happened to ask Latho the question he would probably tell you he would have caught me. I reckon it was a fair intercept, and would have been a fair try. I simply took a gamble in a desperately fought match – and their fly-half, 'Flats' (Elton Flatley), hit me fair on the chest with a perfect pass. I was off and away. But for the referee it was one of those moments when they look up and ask themselves the question: 'How could he have got up there *that* quickly?' I had gone for it, *that's* how. Anyhow, he called me back – and our seven points up the other end became three for them. We had lost the match – but the semifinals still beckoned.

* * *

Queensland had been going along solidly enough that season –
but their psyche is such that for them to come out and beat New
South Wales (and especially second-placed New South Wales!)
wherever they happen to be placed on the ladder makes everything
okay with the world. It's a bizarre mindset – but, you know, maybe
it's what the Waratahs need to do: make the Queensland match
a do or die commitment. Win *that* one and you can turn around
any season!

For us, it all ended in tears.

As NSW captain in 2002 it's not easy for me to talk about the
nightmare of the following week. At Jade Stadium, Christchurch
on 11 May 2002 the Crusaders, Super 12 leaders, bashed and toyed
with us in about equal measure and won an 80-minute football
match 96–19. You might wonder how such a thing could happen.
But it did – and from this distance of a couple of years, I can only
laugh about it.

So, what *really* happened that night?

Well, for starters, the Crusaders were on fire. We were flying for
a couple of minutes and then . . . do I *really* have to talk about it?

I know that there was a moment in the first few minutes when
the Crusaders were definitely thinking, 'Phew, hang on, we're in for
a fair game tonight!' We had started the game with a real lightning
strike, a planned move involving our numbers 13 and 10 which
sent 10 (Manny Edmonds) haring through the world's biggest gap
and off on an 80-metre run to the try line. We didn't score, but it
was a good moment in a not-so-good day.

But from that point, everything *they* touched turned to gold.
Four of our blokes would be herding one of theirs into touch and
at the last second he flicks the ball back inside and the player who
has just been tackled is back on his feet and off for a try – that sort
of thing. Again and again!

We went into the game under-strength through injury, including the heavy loss of Nathan Grey for the season – and we lost Mat Rogers early with injury. Wrestling with the problems, Bob Dwyer had decided to pick a team quite different from our first-choice team of that year. I don't think that's any excuse (and there can be none for that sort of scoreline) – all contracted Super 12 footballers should be ready for the intensity and aggression of the kind of contest we found ourselves in that night. Adding to that, because the Otago Highlanders had beaten Queensland over there, knocking them out of the semis, we knew before the game that we were to host a home semifinal, whatever the outcome of our match. Yet, to play well and be highly competitive against the Crusaders was, of course, our goal.

But we just got bashed – and some guys went really quiet. As captain, there wasn't a lot I could do as the procession unfolded. They had 63 points on the board by halftime. Sixty-three! It's unheard of. And to really rub it in, even though they were scoring all over the park, and some of them out wide, Andrew Mehrtens was knocking the conversion over every time. It was real black dot stuff, and behind the posts I was willing him to miss one. Mate, give us a bit of a break . . . don't make it a seven-pointer *every* time. But he just kept kicking them and ended with thirteen from fourteen. The one he missed hit the post.

The match was an aberration, something that can happen occasionally in football. I remember talking down the track to Wendell Sailor about it and him recalling a league State of Origin match in which New South Wales were red-hot, and toying with the Maroons. Wendell recalled how the Maroons would gather behind the posts and the talk would be, 'Don't let them get to 30' . . . then, 'Don't let them get to 40' . . . and then, 'Don't let them get to 50!' Just occasionally a team is unstoppable, and it was that way that night. And, as captain, there's not a lot you can say. As much as you try to tell blokes that pride is on the line, the fact is the avalanche continues to roll and there's no one out there to help. It's up to you.

I'm sure that to anyone watching, it must have seemed that they had 23 players out there, while we had about six. The fact that we managed a few *Keystone Kops* moments too, with blokes falling over at inappropriate times, didn't help the cause either.

The (almost) hilarious thing was that we went close to picking up a bonus point for four tries. We managed three, and near the end of the game actually had the ball for a few minutes. That would have been a hoot – to get beaten by 77, and still earn a bonus point.

At the end of it, the cameramen were there in force to capture our dejection – and especially mine, as captain. But no way was I going to give them what they wanted: a shot of a loser sulking, head down, dragging himself off the park. I made sure I walked tall – and the photo that appeared after the match was a beauty, with me sporting that 'my pride can't be dented' kind of look. We had been smashed, sure – but I wasn't going to give the media the chance to rub it in further.

I believe his greatest moment as a captain was the way he handled the situation after that devastating loss against the New Zealand side. I remember ringing him – I didn't actually speak to him, but I left a message – just to congratulate him on the way he handled all that. The media, the situation – he did it all with dignity and a certain calmness and perspective that really summed him up. He just keeps everything in place and he treats the success and the fame and everything else with a certain simplicity and humility that is great and that stands him in good stead when things are tough. That day things were tough and I thought he handled it magnificently.

Brother Anthony Boyd

In the dressing room afterwards, I was so deeply disappointed at what had taken place that I decided not to attend the post-game press conference. Chris Whitaker stepped up and handled it for me, and I'm forever indebted to him for that. I honestly wouldn't have had a clue as to what to say.

Later that night, some of us sat in one of the hotel rooms and watched a movie – Whits, Scott Staniforth, Mark Stcherbina and a few others – and gibbered away about nothing in particular. But every so often someone would say, '96–19!' – and we would all cringe and wonder what the hell was going to be waiting for us when we got home.

To make it a bloody lot worse, the Queensland players were at Christchurch Airport when we arrived there for the flight home. Their own season had ended with a 40–26 loss at Carisbrook against the Highlanders, leaving them with absolutely nothing to crow about, and they had been on the town much of the night. But at the airport they gave us an absolute mouthful, saying things like: 'Here comes the NSW cricket team!'

Considering what I had achieved in rugby in the past, I wasn't going to let one night, one match, bring me down. It was a blemish on the careers of all of us who played that night and something we weren't proud of. But as the Queenslanders carried on, I chose to ignore them. As far as I was concerned it was crap – and some of it coming from blokes who had never played a Test or who were new to the game. The boys handling the cargo at Christchurch Airport couldn't resist having a go, either. As I sat on the plane, looking out the window and watching the bags being loaded, I saw a container on which was written in large letters: 'Waratahs, you are the weakest link. Goodbye!' I wasn't going to let it get to me. But some of the other guys took it all personally, and it wasn't a happy trip home.

* * *

At Mascot Airport I was about as disappointed with a team management decision as I have ever been in my career. As we were rounding up the bags and getting ready to head out and face the music, our media manager came up to me. 'Matt, you're right for outside?' he asked. I told him I was. I had expected that the media would be there in large numbers. 'I'll just be as honest and straightforward as I can be,' I told him. 'Yeah, that's good, mate,' he said. 'Look, Bob's [Bob Dwyer] not going to answer any questions at the moment. We've just taken him out a side door – he's going to do a press conference tomorrow.' I said, 'Are you kidding?' and then thought to myself, 'What a cop-out.' It was the first time in rugby it had felt like 'us' and 'them'.

Outside the customs hall, the media guys were swarming around Mat Rogers. Spotting me, they were over in a flash and the questions started. 'You must have been embarrassed by what happened over there . . . You must have been embarrassed for the fans,' someone asked. What I had learned about dealing with the media was not to repeat the question. It seemed to me they were trying to get me to use the word 'embarrassed', but I wasn't going to say it. The microphones were crowding into my face. 'Mate, do you mind?' I said to one bloke. 'Give me a bit of space and I'll answer all your questions.' I consciously set out to slow the whole thing down, and in the end I think I did okay.

I had been thrown into the Colosseum, but I remained calm. I didn't get heated, angry or otherwise emotional. 'Obviously we are disappointed,' I told them. 'But we have to set that aside and concentrate on the Super 12 Finals.'

And I managed not to say 'embarrassed' – not then, anyway.

But I can say it now: I was *totally* embarrassed by what happened against the Crusaders, as any footballer with any pride would have been. But I wasn't going to provide a cheap headline – a picture of

Waratah skipper Matt Burke with the word 'EMBARRASSED!' splashed above.

Next morning, a Monday, a photo of me wheeling my trolley out of customs to face the music was on the front page of the *Sydney Morning Herald*. It's the only time I've ever made page 1 of the *Herald*. Elsewhere we were lampooned as the Horror-Tahs. These weren't great days.

The week ahead, preparing to play the Brumbies, was never going to be easy. To be beaten so badly would shake the foundations and confidence of *any* side. We were heading into what should have been a really exciting time, but when I look back on it now I'm sure we had blokes in the ranks who were scared then. The mindset was going to have to be especially powerful to turn everything around in a single week.

We didn't manage it. We competed okay against the Brumbies, and a tear-away first-half intercept try by Scott Staniforth gave the team a lift. But it was only a matter of time. They broke us, and they broke our spirit – and they beat us 51–10, and scored plenty of tries in doing so. The papers didn't miss us next day: 'Wara load of rubbish yet again', was one headline.

This Super 12 season of great promise and hope was over. Worse than that, it had ended in near-disaster. Heading for the semifinals we had leaked almost 150 points in two games. The 2002 Waratah season will be remembered forever for its terrible finish, rather than for its successes, of which there were more than a few, and especially the milestone of a Waratah team making the semis after years of disappointment. We went into that season with great spirit, yet in just a couple of weeks it all went sadly wrong.

When I reflect on it now, I have no doubt that we headed into some games with the wrong mindset. The players of 2002 have to accept some of the responsibility for what happened. But I believe the coaching staff also have to put up their hands.

Chapter 21

THE GOAL AND THE
GOLDEN GIRL

Christchurch notwithstanding, some amazing and wonderful things happened in my life in 2002. I booted a goal against the All Blacks that pitchforked me into the newspaper headlines. And I became a father for the first time.

I'll kick off with the event that mattered most . . .

The day I became a father, 23 September 2002, was one of the most beautiful of my life. My daughter, Harriette, was born that morning at the Royal North Shore Private Hospital, and as a new dad I got to spend a little time alone with her before Kate came back into the room. It had been a fantastic experience, though a tough time for Kate going through her first pregnancy and with many ups and downs. A terrific doctor, Vijay Roach, made the experience very comfortable for us, and helped ease us through.

Now I was a dad – sitting there with my child – my offspring – in my arms. Harriette and I had about 40 minutes alone together, and I just sat there petrified. She started to cry at one stage and I looked around: 'God, isn't there someone here who can help me?' I don't think I moved in that 40 minutes; I just sat there with my arms cramping. I was too scared to move even an inch.

You soon get over that and become quite adept at holding and carrying them, changing and dressing them. But this first morning it was as if I was set in stone as she lay there asleep in my arms.

I have to say that I have loved every minute of being a father – and just as much now when we have two, Harriette and her little sister, Edie Grace, born on 16 March 2004. For me, being a dad is super.

As I'm sitting here in Newcastle, England, thinking about the kids, I can hear Harriette singing. Kate's mum taught her the nursery rhyme 'Three blind mice' and she sort of mumbles it: 'Wee bwind mice . . . wee bwind mice . . .' It's great. Becoming a dad is one of the very best things that has ever happened to me. My life has changed – but certainly for the better. To have Harriette wake us in the morning, calling out 'Daddy' or 'Mummy' is one of the best sounds in the world.

Harriette was born four weeks before I headed off on the wide-ranging Wallaby tour of 2002, so I had a little time to get to know her. Then Kate was left holding the baby – literally! And I came back to a daughter who had doubled in age. She was still a chubby little one, but had grown and changed even in those short weeks.

The goal came about seven weeks before Harriette's birth – at Stadium Australia on 3 August, to be exact. In order to re-live what I suppose was the most famous goal of my career, it is necessary to wind the clock back a few minutes. It was Australia v New Zealand, the Bledisloe Cup at stake and the stands filled to the brim. With seven minutes to go in a game that was of the typically desperate do-or-die nature of Bledisloe Cup football, Mat Rogers scored a solo try close to the ruck to make it 13–14 . . .

All goal-kickers in high-level football have lived through it – that moment late in a game when suddenly it's pretty much all down to you. I suspect the heart might give a jolt at such moments and the blood pressure climb a little. But it's just part of the job. And when I walked up to take the kick, I went through the routine, did my best to blot everything out, and lined up the ball. I gave it a great hit – and the ball thundered into the left upright full-on – and bounced back.

Though not usually one to show emotion on the field, as I have explained, as I ran back, my jaw clenched, I hurled the kicking tee as hard as I could towards the sideline. At that moment, as I realised later, the camera was panning on to Mat and showing him giving me the filthiest look, as if to say: 'I've done all the hard work and scored the try, and now you've missed the bloody conversion!' I said to him afterwards, 'What was *that* for?' 'Mate,' he said. 'I thought you would have got that one for us.'

But we knew we had plenty of time. As I was running back I glanced at the clock. Seven minutes to go – there was still time to play some football. And we attacked hard and ended up getting a penalty. Mat picked up the ball and gave it a bit of a kiss, pushed it into my chest and encouraged me to kick it for him and for the team – and to think of all the endorsements I would get when I landed it! I had a bit of a chuckle and perhaps that helped to make light of the whole situation, but watching it on video now it looks like I just didn't care. Those images of me walking up to take the shot show me laughing and joking. Maybe some people saw it as arrogance – but it wasn't that. I was just chuckling at what Mat had said.

I just had a bit of a joke with him, actually, to try and lighten up the moment because there was a lot of tension in the air. The crowd was really buzzing and the hooter was pretty much just about to sound and I said to him, 'Kick this goal, mate. It's money in the bank. The endorsements will start rolling in and your memorabilia pieces will skyrocket!'

Mat Rogers

It was right on fulltime that referee Andre Watson penalised the All Blacks on their own quarter, ruling that replacement Leon MacDonald had his hands in a ruck and providing this last-gasp opening, a chance to win the game. The penalty we received had come from an advantage decision, and when George Gregan missed a snapshot at field goal it came back to the original call – and the penalty our way.

The day before, when I had been practising goal-kicking in blustery conditions at the stadium, Phil Waugh had been trying to distract me by imitating the fulltime siren each time I approached the ball. Phil was giving me stick, pretending he was the hooter – and later that all came back to me.

The penalty was awarded *exactly* at the spot where I had missed five from five the previous day and was a slightly tougher kick than the conversion I had missed. Chris Whitaker knew it, and on the bench where he was posted with the other reserves, mentioned my efforts in the wind the previous day.

On Fridays, at the last training sessions, Matt usually stays around and has a few kicks from different positions around the field. He missed five in a row from that exact same spot the day before – and he actually picked up his kicking tee and walked off and didn't bother kicking any more. So when the kick came in the game I looked at Brendan Cannon, who was sitting next to me, and I said: 'Oh, no. He missed five from there yesterday!'

Chris Whitaker

The positive thing was that the conversion I had missed seven minutes earlier had been from close by. I now had my chance to do a correction on the line of that kick. When people ask me about the moment, which they do now and then, I tell them that the situation was akin to an Ambrose at golf, where the putt of the bloke before can give you a chance to read the line. I thought to myself, 'Just don't do anything different. You've been here a hundred times. Kick the ball well, strike it well.' So I aimed it just a fraction out to the right, a little further out to the right from the previous kick . . .

I thought of John Eales, and of his match-winning goal in 2000 for Australia to beat the All Blacks 24–23 in Wellington, and of Stirling Mortlock's kick from touch to beat the 'Boks 19–18 in Durban three weeks later. I was now in the same position – with the chance of winning a big football match for my country.

The thought of the kicks I had missed at training on the Friday never came into my head. But as I lined it up, I glanced at the big screen, directly behind the posts, and there was a full-screen image of Eddie Jones, biting his nails and looking worried. And I thought, 'God, just bundle some *more* pressure on me!' The swirling southerly wind that had been around all night continued to gust.

I think the thing that I remember most is that, when we were awarded the penalty, Burkey had a wry smile on his face as he walked towards the spot and that just showed, certainly not over-confidence or arrogance, but his confidence in his own ability and, I think, the actual enjoyment of the challenge. I think guys like him who are born goal-kickers enjoy those moments. They're the moments they practise hours and hours for.

Eddie Jones

All the practice you do – all the repetition, the countless thousands of practice shots in gales, in dead calm, in driving rain – is about getting ready for moments like this. I approached the kick knowing that I had landed many similar goals before and that kicking was like riding a bike – you just do the same thing. And I hit it sweetly and it rose in the night air and went straight through the middle. It was one of the best feelings I have ever had in rugby.

I just knew he would kick it. It's funny, and it's easy to say after the event, but as soon as the penalty went up I sort of knew he would kick it – first because he had missed the one after Matty Rogers' try . . . When you play golf with him you know that he is going to hit it right down the middle – that's the way it works. He never makes the same mistake twice. And that was the way it worked out. He set himself up and just whacked it over. I'll bet it just didn't move from the black dot. So it was no surprise to me. But it told you a fair bit about him.

George Gregan

We had retained the Bledisloe Cup, for a record fifth successive season. The fulltime whistle followed before the ball had returned to earth – and then there was pandemonium.

I suppose relief was my main emotion. I have been in that situation a few times in my career – and have kicked the goals that needed to be kicked, and missed some as well. I recall a miss in South Africa in 2001, and one in Perth in 1998. On those occasions you feel terrible. But on this night, all was well, and the celebrations that followed mirrored the emotions of the match.

Next day the newspapers made much of the fact that I had missed three of five shots in the game. Andrew Mehrtens had missed, too – three shots, I think – so it wasn't a great night for the kickers.

But the god of goal-kickers had smiled when it mattered, and I was thankful for that.

That season of 2002 was played out in the shadow of the World Cup. I'm sure that every single bloke who played in the international series that followed the disappointing NSW fadeout from the Super 12s had firmly fixed in his mind the thought of being part of a home World Cup the following year. We beat the Maoris in a tough game in Perth, 27–23, to kick off the Wallabies' program. The match produced a strong message about 'opportunity' in football. Ben Tune, a first-choice winger, was out injured as was his likely replacement, Scott Staniforth. So, Wendell Sailor got the call-up, scored a try, and was able to build early claims to be a permanent member of the team. Sailor was a regular up until the 2004 season when he pulled a hamstring, which knocked him out of the match against England – and so opened the door for Clyde Rathbone. In football, the wheel turns . . .

We then played the French in a couple of typically physical games, featuring some questionable off-the-ball stuff, and beat them twice – 29–17 in a scrappy match in Melbourne, and 31–25 at Stadium Australia – which was encouraging, considering they were the current Six Nations champions, had won ten matches on the trot and were playing some pretty good football. In the Sydney game, the second, I scored a try that featured about four knock-ons, all of which the referee, Paul Honiss, managed to overlook, leaving me to run 50 metres or so when plenty of players had stopped in their tracks, waiting for the blast of the whistle. The second game had gone right down to the wire – to the moment when we stopped their No. 8, Imanol Harinordoquy, right on the corner, when everyone was just about out on their feet, trying to defend the lead we had built. It was a good start: 2-nil over the unpredictable French.

Before we played New Zealand in the first of the Tri-Nations games that year, their coach, John Mitchell, made the understatement of the season. 'We are playing in August, in Christchurch, at night,' he said. 'It's not going to be balmy.' He wasn't wrong; in fact, it was bloody freezing, and pouring with rain throughout – the worst conditions I had played in for a long time – and we got beaten 12–6 in a tough and frustrating match. Why the hell they persist with night games over there, I don't know. Maybe it's tactical . . . maybe it's TV . . . maybe a bit of both. Someone described my contribution as 'my best game' – and it was a night I certainly got heavily involved. I was trying to keep warm!

I remember the match for the referee, Jonathan Kaplan, failing to make a key decision: to award us a penalty try. At the 72-minute mark, Steve Larkham charged down a kick and I chased it through and retrieved the ball five metres from the line. I was tackled, but got a pass to Daniel Herbert, who, in turn, was tackled *before* the ball reached him. Kaplan produced the yellow card, but didn't take the next step – ruling that a try for Herbert was only 'possible', not 'probable'. It was one of those tough calls for a ref.

Winger Ben Tune was the man in the hot seat when we played South Africa in the first of the Tri-Nations games in 2002 – and I have rarely seen a team bond and celebrate together as we did when he powered through three tackles on the end of a backline move to score a great try early in the Test. Ben was under fire. Some time before, following knee surgery, he had tested positive to a prohibited steroid prescribed by a doctor who hadn't gone through the accepted process of declaring the medication. The positive test hadn't been made public, and Ben was stood down from Queensland matches until cleared by the ARU – which he subsequently was. The handling of the matter, and the decision, hadn't gone down well with some.

Against the South Africans in Brisbane, he copped plenty. The build-up became something of a war of words, and in the game itself Ben was sledged and called a drug cheat – leading to an ill-tempered match that sparked a brawl and the sin-binning of two of our blokes, Justin Harrison and Jeremy Paul. Ben was in the middle of that. Retaliating against something that had happened earlier, he bopped Springbok skipper Corne Krige on the nose – and then it was on. Ben, one of the best wingers I ever played with, gave us a brilliant start with the try he scored early – and it was the springboard to a strong performance and, ultimately, a 38–27 victory. Krige squared up in the return match in South Africa and he and Ben then called it quits.

The first Test was a match of intimidation where the rules of the game were stretched – exactly what you expect every time you line up against a South African side. They play a hard, ruthless brand of rugby, with some off-the-ball stuff usually thrown into the mix, and so it was that day in Brisbane.

Continuing my 'back to the future' role with the Waratahs, I played in the centres that day, at 13, and found myself with a mountain of work to do in defence. In conversation with Glen Ella afterwards, it emerged that I had had the opportunity for only three attacking runs in the 80 minutes. Playing 13 can be like that – a position from which you can find yourself doing a lot of dummy running. Sometimes the chances with the ball actually in your hands are very limited – and that day there were occasions when I was screaming out for the ball – and it never came. Matches like that are very frustrating, and I imagine every outside back in the game has experienced one now and then. And it's after a game such as that you can get branded, as in: 'Burke's not running enough with the ball.' Through Glen Ella and coach Eddie Jones we did some tweaking in the aftermath, the result being that the numbers, in terms of me touching the ball, rose dramatically the next week when we played New Zealand and took the Bledisloe Cup.

The Tri-Nations went to New Zealand that year, in an absolute photo finish when we lost to the South Africans 33–31 in Johannesburg. That match featured a huge Aussie comeback from a seemingly impossible position – from 26–9 down after an hour to lead 31–26 in the late stages. In the end they won it on a goal that shouldn't have been allowed under the rules as written. It prompted something unusual in my career – an exchange with the referee, Paddy O'Brien, after the final siren. A new rule had come into rugby that allowed kickers a one-minute limit to shoot for goal. Werner Greeff took forever to line up that last kick, and under the new rule the goal should have been disallowed. I told the ref so at fulltime.

Earlier in the game I had been strictly subjected to the rule. On a windy night the ball had fallen off the tee as I shaped to kick. The ref had already told me I had only fifteen seconds to go, once the tee arrived. Now the ball was on its side and he was intoning, 'You've got fifteen seconds.' Down the paddock one of the South African players was ticking it off in a loud voice: 'Fifteeen, fourteen, thirteen, twelve . . .'

At times like that, all the routine stuff goes straight out the window – the breathing, the setting up, the first approach to the ball. All I had time to do was plonk the ball on the tee, take three steps back with no pause, and move in to give it the best thump I could. It sailed straight over the black dot – casting serious doubt on just how relevant is all the pre-kick routine stuff!

But when fullback Greeff lined up his kick at the end, after he had barged over for a try for 31-all, he took forever. Finally he was ready, paced back and booted it straight between the posts. Immediately the game was over, I was into the referee. 'Mate, what's going on here?' I asked him. 'That was terrible. He must have taken a minute and a half. You should have blown it up and called it off.' Readers might take note here that we were in Johannesburg, one of the scariest places you're ever likely to visit on a rugby assignment. And that's why I chuckled at O'Brien's response. 'Mate, I've got balls,' he said. 'But they're not *that* big!' I couldn't help laughing. He was still miked up at the time and the comment came over TV. I understood. It would have been the bravest of decisions to rule the kick out of time and call the game off.

The international program ahead was a heavy and varied one, hopefully hardening and settling the team for the challenge of the World Cup. We flew halfway around the world to tackle one of the game's toughest assignments – a match against the Argentinians at the famous River Plate Stadium. If there is a place in world rugby, over all others, that screams intimidation and home ground advantage, this is it – ahead of even Johannesburg's Ellis Park. There are streamers and whistles and balloons and flares – a constant cacophony, and the chance that you might get spat on. As we left the dressing room, the local officials guided us into a tunnel that took us out safely through the fans and on to the ground.

We knew it wasn't going to be any easier out there in the middle, and it wasn't. The media back home reported how we were 'gouged, spat on, punched and kicked' and headlined 'gutter tactics' – and that sort of gives you the drift. It was a tough game, far from the best spectacle in the world, but we won, 17–6, albeit unconvincingly before a crowd of 40,000. Straight away the media was on our backs. The press guys expected more from us than we had shown there.

In Argentina, everything seemed difficult, although the handing over of a little team gear here or there could help to ease the path – such as when we crossed the border into Brazil. That seemed set to be a long and laborious process, with all individual documents and passports to be stamped – but after we handed a few Wallaby shirts and bits and pieces over to the border guys, we were quickly on our way.

The South American experience had its very special moments, though – such as a visit to the amazing Iguaçu Falls, which can be a difficult place to fly in to, owing to the volatility of the weather. A previous touring team had been turned around and despatched back to Buenos Aries after flying for an hour into a monsoon; we knew that story and were happy to make it this time. We had a terrific night out in Brazil, going to several different places to experience authentic Brazilian food (steak, specifically!) and various aspects of the country's culture and dancing. The sight of one Brazilian dancer missing an attempted tumble and crashing to the floor during the show was one highlight. At the next place we visited, the compere was a bit confused as to where we were from and they started playing the *Austrian* national anthem. But it was all lively and colourful and good fun – one of those experiences that can help make a football tour memorable.

From Argentina it was on to Ireland – and truly atrocious conditions at Lansdowne Road. There, in the wet and the cold, the Irish beat us 18–9, Australia's first Test loss at the ground in 34 years. Irish five-eighth Ronan O'Gara kicked six penalties from six shots, I landed three from three – and that was that. With Mat Rogers out injured, I played fullback, my first run at 15 for quite a while. It wasn't a night to be trying out something different, and I played terribly. I wasn't alone. We were trying to play dry weather football in conditions that wouldn't allow it, and only when some common sense came into our play late, did we threaten. The local press wrote it up as a great Irish performance. Back home our media called the Wallaby performance 'wretched'. We were back to being the Wobbly Wallabies and had been given a World Cup wakeup call. And that's football. Winning is everything.

Added to the rather negative focus now on the team, there was great controversy back home surrounding skipper George Gregan's decision, after the Ireland game, to fly home for the birth of his second child – something that had been agreed to by the ARU and coach Eddie Jones before the tour. George would be back for the next match, against England. I can confirm that as far as the team was concerned, everyone was behind George's decision to make the trek. We understood. Greegs had the support of the team, both as a player and as our captain. If the media saw it differently – well, that was their choice. As far as we were concerned, George was a bloke who led from the front, a players' captain who would stand up for his team-mates against officialdom if it was necessary. If he thought a player was getting stiffed, he would go to bat for him. And I think the senior blokes, especially, understood the weight he carried as captain – doing his best to juggle the awkward role somewhere in the middle between players and coaches and administrators.

I was vice captain on the 2002 campaign, replacing Daniel Herbert in that position at the start of the season, but I always had the feeling there was an element of tokenism about the appointment and the position. Yes, I was certainly proud to be vice captain of my country's team. But did I have any real impact, or a wider involvement that should ideally reflect what a vice captain would do? Probably not. As a senior player I certainly did what I could, generally and at training, to make sure it all worked. But when it came to leadership of that team it was basically George as captain, Eddie Jones as coach – full stop. I had the feeling in rugby that the vice captain's role was given and taken away pretty easily – rather than being any long-term designation or commitment.

When England beat us 32–31 in one of those games where it was a case of 'you score, we score', we were batting one from three on the tour, and the times were fairly gloomy. It wasn't a happy tour. It had been a long season, the weather was consistently crook, and we were training really, really hard. There was a fair bit of angst around the place. There was discontent with the amount of training we were doing, and it got to the stage where there were guys who just didn't want to be there. The England game was something of a mixture. Steve Larkham played fullback, Elton Flatley was at 10, and I was back in the centres – moves that were designed as a bit of a ploy. Elton ran in a couple of really good tries; and late in the day, after the scores had fluctuated back and forth, we had a chance to win the game. Near the end I had a shot at goal from 45 metres out, pretty much in front – but the kick faded right. On a tour on which we were struggling to an extent, that was disappointing – for me and the team.

We finished the game in Italy, in Genoa, where it poured with rain non-stop for seven days. There wasn't a hint of sunshine the whole time we were there. In my view, Genoa falls short of any number of other places in Italy when it comes to things to see and do. I think really the only highlight came when Aussie supermodel Megan Gale, the face of Vodafone in Italy, turned up at a press conference. Her appearance made the week for all the boys, and put a bit of a spring in their step.

Against an Italian team we were expected to outclass, we were no more than tradesmanlike, and won 34–3. It was nothing flash, and our attitude probably wasn't great, but we did the job against an opponent now in the Six Nations lineup, although still regarded as minnows to an extent.

I came home to newspaper opinion that my days as a fullback were probably over, and that my permanent future lay in the centres. I couldn't argue with that. I had reached the point in my career where I no longer wanted to be the all-rounder, shifting from position to position. If I were to play in the 2003 World Cup, it would be as a centre.

Chapter 22
FEVER

From the moment we stepped off the plane from Italy at Mascot and back into the summer sunshine, there was really only one game in town. Even if World Cup fever wasn't quite yet raging in Sydney, it was at least brewing nicely just beneath the surface, threatening to cast a very large shadow indeed over all other sports in 2003. Yet, for us, the players, it was a *long* way down the track. Between the large bunch of 'hopefuls' and a spot in Australia's World Cup squad, there stood many weeks, and a heap of football.

The Waratahs rode through the early 2003 Super 12 season never too far off the pace – and a semifinal chance right up to the last breath, in fact. In the end it came down to us not scoring *one* more try in the final-round match against the Chiefs, whom we beat

25–14. We needed four tries for a bonus point, and we got three, and so finished fifth. Prop Matt Dunning copped a whole heap of flak for kicking a field goal just at a time when we needed a try. But as far as I was concerned as skipper, there was no blame. It was just one of those things that can happen on a football field, and when you miss out on something by a fraction at the end of a long campaign, there is no way the blame can be assigned to one bloke. The kick was a bit of a head-scratcher, for sure, but it did show Matt's diversity of skills! At such a time your mind tends to rove back over the whole season, thinking of the things that got away. You rue losses against teams whom maybe you should have beaten, and you recall chances missed. A semifinal berth would have been great – but Mad Monday, the now traditional 'let down' day at the end of a season, was big, anyway. The theme was 'dress up', and I went as Elvis Presley. That's all you need to know.

There was some new blood in the Waratahs lineup that season. Lote Tuqiri, Nathan Blacklock and Ryan McGoldrick had come over from league, and young blokes like Adam Freier, Matt Hodgson and Al Campbell had taken the next step up. Bob Dwyer was again at the helm. McGoldrick subsequently was quite a loss to rugby when the game turned its back on him and he went back to league to play with the Sharks. He was a very talented player who showed great enthusiasm for his rugby, and on his form in the trial matches that year thoroughly earned his chance in the opener against Auckland, a match played on a wet track in Sydney. But in that game, which we lost 31–18, Rupeni Caucaunibuca ran around him at one point and scored a try. McGoldrick was dropped after the match and virtually never got another shot at it. Next thing, he was a rugby league first-grader. The bloke who had run around him, Caucaunibuca, had done the same to some of the best players in the world! I didn't have much doubt that Ryan McGoldrick would have made it in rugby union.

Nursing a sore knee from early on in that Waratah campaign, I had reached the point in my career at which all long-term foot-ballers arrive. I was now in my 31st year, and my mind roamed occasionally over the possibilities that might lie ahead. The media had a crack at it, too. Would I continue on in rugby in Australia? Or would I go overseas? Or maybe give it away and get a *real* job out of football? The World Cup lay just ahead, and I hoped, of course, to be part of a winning Australian campaign. But after that? Another year with the Waratahs, perhaps? I'm a bit of an idealist, I suppose. I'm certainly happy to share my own dream here. Deep down, I wanted nothing more than to stay on in Australia and finish my rugby life where it had begun all those years ago. I believed that my form was good enough, and the experience I brought to any outfit useful enough to make that a reasonable prospect. Maybe I've always been a bit naïve. But if I can fall back on a cliché here, I perhaps placed a bit too much faith in the goodness of mankind. I had been loyal to rugby – knocked back rugby league offers now and then – and given the game the best I had. And I had been part of the rugby 'family' for a long time. And yeah, I really wanted to stay on and play with the Waratahs.

These matters were on my mind as we headed into the Super 12 season that would be the springboard for ultimate World Cup selection. On 8 March 2003, I became the first Waratah player to reach the 100 games milestone. It happened a long way from home, at ABSA Stadium in Durban – and it would have been nice if I'd been back in Sydney in front of our crowd. We beat the Sharks convincingly, 49–36, which was a good way to celebrate.

The World Cup cricket tournament was being played at the same time, and I suspect a few of the supporters had read that I would be far away from home when I reached my century. Anyhow, a bunch of blokes turned up in the stand at King's Park, toting a sign that read, 'Burkey, 100 not out.' I was chuffed, and the more so when they hung around after the game and presented it to me when I came out of the change room. I still have it. Thanks, guys – whoever you are.

Later that night in my hotel room I let my thoughts stray back over all those Waratah years – right back to the first game, against Fiji in 1992, in the big boots. I had torn my hip flexor on a cold training night before that match, creating serious discomfort, but there was no way I was going to miss the game. I had experienced rugby making the change from an amateur game to a professional one. I had seen coaches come and go – Macqueen, Sayle and Smith, Hawkins, Williams, Kennedy and Dwyer – and I had outlasted most of them. A generation of players had been and gone. I remembered the beginning, of being the quiet young bloke who used to sit in a corner at after-match functions while the 1995 World Cup men like Kearns and Gavin did all the talking to the sponsors – all the way to now, when *I* was the bloke doing the talking, while the young fellas stood in the corner. I'd encourage them to go and have a yarn with someone. And they'd ask me: 'What should I talk about?' And I'd suggest that they talk footy, because that's what had brought us all together there. Rugby is good like that; it helps develop social skills, because there is a lot of mixing to be done. I have seen so many blokes come out of their shells, gradually developing confidence and skills in handling people that will benefit them in their lives beyond football. I always encouraged the younger players to use their experience in football to build a platform for the rest of their lives.

After the match the papers recorded that I had scored 1047

points (33 tries, 156 conversions, 189 penalty goals, one dropped goal) in the 100 games.

Someone asked me to pinpoint how rugby had changed, in the progression from amateur to professional. Among other thoughts I offered the following: 'We used to be beer swilling idiots in my early years in the game and you'd just get as drunk as possible after the game. Now it just doesn't happen.' I would probably rephrase that answer if asked again today. But there was truth in it, of course. With professionalism had come a maturity factor and the acceptance that with the amount of work you are expected to do, you just can't go and destroy yourself the way we once did. Guys still get on the booze, of course – but it's nowhere near as frequent as it once was. There is always a training session await-ing. Fines are imposed if you're late, and so to turn up late *and hungover* would have severe repercussions.

But I think the ethos of the rugby game remains, and that the fundamental things are still more or less in place. I hope it stays that way. Call me old-fashioned if you like, but I believe there is strength in the old traditions and the old ways – and reasons for still doing some things the way they have always been done. In 2004 I had a conversation with Lote Tuqiri, who was agonising over whether to stay with New South Wales or go to the Brumbies. I was upset about the way things had turned out for me by then (more of which later) and I told Lote exactly the way I saw it: 'Mate, if you want to play good football in a team that plays a good style of football, you'd go to the Brumbies. But if you want to play your football in a better city and a city with a better lifestyle, you'd stay in Sydney. It comes down to that.' Tuqiri started to say, 'I know that Ewen McKenzie [the NSW coach] wants to get rid of the old . . .' Before he could finish, I butted in:

'What, the old *blokes*?' 'No, no,' he said. 'The old *culture*.' And I just said quietly, 'You know, mate – sometimes it's that old culture that keeps things together.'

That 2003 Super 12 tournament became something of a personal physical battle for me. I did a medial ligament in my right knee in an early game against the Bulls, had a break – and then came back too early, re-injuring myself in the match against Queensland and putting myself again on the back foot in what was such a big year. It was a juggling act: the World Cup was much on my mind, obviously, but balancing that was my inclination to keep going and contribute whatever I could to the Waratah cause. As captain of the Waratahs, I was certainly not going to walk away. I knew that even if I was a fraction below par physically, I could still help the cause through leadership and experience, and I wanted to do that.

The beginning of the downhill path that later saw me dumped by the Waratahs for 2005 could perhaps be traced back to an event midway through the 2003 domestic season. The newspapers ran with a story that Eddie Jones wanted me to take a break from football – to rest my injuries and freshen up for what lay ahead. I had been under media fire to an extent for my 'below par form' as I struggled along on a painful right knee. I was quick to reassure Waratahs coach Bob Dwyer that I wouldn't be stepping away to take a break – that I intended to battle through and play my way back into form. But I talked to John Fordham about it – and subsequently met Eddie one morning at a café at Castlecrag to discuss where it all stood. There, while I took a phone call from Fordo, Eddie was flicking through the morning papers that carried stories speculating I was about to take a break for three weeks. I asked Eddie where such a story might have come from. 'Well, it wasn't me. I don't know *where* it came from,' he replied. I never did get the answer on that – whether the coach had been straight with me. The story had been leaked to the press by *someone*.

I really started to wonder, then, where I stood in the game. Was I offside with John O'Neill because I was a member of RUPA (the Rugby Union Players' Association) and there had been a few tiffs between the association and the ARU? Tony Dempsey, the CEO of RUPA, had virtually been at war with O'Neill over a number of issues concerning the players. I didn't know the full answer to that question, but I knew for sure that there had been a change in the relationship between O'Neill, the boss of Australian Rugby, and me.

Eventually I *did* take a three-week break from football – but later, when the Super 12 season had finished and the home internationals were beginning – and then sat fidgeting elsewhere as Test matches were played against Ireland (Subiaco), Wales (Stadium Australia) and England (Telstra Dome, Melbourne), thinking only that I would love to be out there playing. Essentially, the program and the plan as laid out was for me to have a rest, but I was put on a formal schedule of doing weights three times a week, plus running. It almost seemed as if there was a blueprint to drill me into the ground. During our talk over coffees at Castlecrag, Eddie Jones had also suggested that I might think about going back and having a trundle at club football to keep my hand in.

A really positive event during this up-and-down World Cup year came around that time in the production of a DVD about my life in football. I had had an association with Denis Handlin of Sony Music Australia for quite a while – and Sony Music did a fantastic job of putting the DVD together. Inevitably, Aussies being the way we are, I copped some good-natured flak from team-mates (including the new nickname 'Decade' – as in *A Decade of*

Excellence, the title of the DVD – to add to various others), but I took all of it with a grain of salt. And as a father myself by then, and with the thought that maybe I'd even be a grandfather one day, I could only think that it was fantastic to have something like that to be able to share with future Burke generations. The DVD was good fun to make, too – with positive contributions from a lot of people. The 'roast' came later – at a farewell lunch in 2004 when a collection of speakers dished me up pretty well.

But even the DVD wasn't trouble-free. There was a tussle with the ARU over the image to be used on the cover – and by then I suspect I wasn't the most popular bloke on the block at ARU headquarters in North Sydney. As far as I was concerned, the days when I would be taken for a ride and would say no more than 'yes sir, no sir, three bags full, sir' were over. I made a conscious decision that it was getting late in my career and thus it was about time I started looking after No. 1. Very likely I was seen then as a bloke who was starting to stir the pot. But I figured I had paid my dues – been the 'nice guy', available for years for anything they wanted me to do, and been used up a bit because of it. Now I was going to pursue a harder line, be a little more selective. I have little doubt that at least a couple of people at the ARU had their noses put out of joint because of it.

Everything in rugby at that time was looked at through the prism of the World Cup. And the point was made often enough that for the backs it was going to be very tough, and very competitive even to make the squad. As early as July 2002, the *Daily Telegraph* had run a page of mug shots on the back page – with the headline, 'Seven of these players will be dropped for the World Cup'. The blokes pictured were all backs. There was talk of an 'embarrassment of riches', and it was true that the ranks looked healthy. No way were they going to leave out the league trio (Sailor, Rogers, Tuqiri), Gregan and Larkham were there, and so too Stirling Mortlock, on his way back from a shoulder injury, but a fantastic player. Looking at all of those faces, I knew that it wasn't going to be easy. I had goal-kicking as an extra string to my bow, plus big-match experience – and I hoped that those things, allied with good form and good health, would get me across the line. But missing the Tests against Wales, England and Ireland wasn't a help.

I did what Eddie Jones had suggested and went back and played a couple of games for Eastwood. Eight goals from eight shots against Northern Suburbs and nine from ten against Manly showed that my goal-kicking was on song, and I did my best to play quality football, too, to reinforce the point that I could still play, still make an impact on the rugby field. It was a time of getting myself sorted, mentally and physically – while biting my lip in bitter disappointment that I was out of the loop while Test matches were being played. The thing that really hurt was that I had been ruled out on an excuse that suited *them* – when I was fit. I agree that my form had been a bit below par, and sure I had medial ligament soreness, but this red herring about my fitness was an 'out' for the blokes picking the Test teams. A perception that I wasn't fit, and therefore wouldn't be considered, made life easier for all of them. It was World Cup year and I wanted to do everything I could to be part of it!

For someone who had been in the game at a high level for a long time, there were times when I started to feel like an outsider. When the Welsh came to town I had no intention of going to the Test, but in the end I got hooked up in a promotion for one of the sponsors that required me to be at the ground. I parked the car fifteen minutes before I was due to do my interview spot, endured the interview, which was conducted by a woman who, with all due respect, seemed to have very little idea of what it was all about, then hopped in the car and drove home. I had no interest in watching the game, beyond hoping that my mates in the Wallaby team would do well. And I'm sure that my body language and the clipped answers I gave made that pretty clear as I hurried my way through the interview that night.

But things can change, of course. England beat Australia 25–14 in Melbourne, and Chris Latham was dropped from the side, along with four others (Turinui, Grey, Sharpe and Paul). It was a tough call – I always think that to drop a fullback after a team has lost makes him a scapegoat. Suddenly, I was back – for an assured tough game against the South Africans at Newlands, Cape Town. We lost 26–22 in a tight game, and I marked myself hard. I did a few things right, but a few things wrong, too. My game ranked as about an 'okay' in a disappointing general team performance.

The pressure was coming at me left, right and centre now. Before the start of the Tri-Nations Tournament, blokes like Russell Fairfax and David Campese were calling it my 'last chance'. I didn't care what they were saying, but the principle of it continued to irk me: that old players, who had been good players but, like all of us, with deficiencies in their games, would come out and bag current players. It remains the pet hate of the Wallabies. And if I ever do it, you can come and give me a good clip over the ear. My belief is that you don't criticise where you came from. Comment, by all means, and strongly and constructively. There are ways of saying things without bagging. Tim Horan proved a master of that during the World Cup. They wanted him to be more controversial, but it's just not him. His comments throughout were expert, honest and insightful – which is the way it *should* be, surely? But there are some who are constantly negative, and Dan Crowley is one who springs to mind. I know they're paid to do it, and good luck to them. Just don't ask me to do it. In that time, when the pressure weighed heavily, I was heartened by the support of those who knew me. One day I received a text message from Brett 'Pappy' Papworth, ex-international and Eastwood club-mate. It read: 'the easiest job is that of a critic/don't forget how good you are/one of the best'.

In the first couple of minutes against the All Blacks at Telstra Stadium I was there to finish off a good move down the left-hand side and score a try. Back at ya! But it was all downhill from there. We got smashed 50–21 and I was taken out of the game just after halftime, replaced by Chris Latham – and far from happy with that. 'End of the world' was one headline the next morning.

The week leading up to that game had been a massive one for the forwards. They got smashed from pillar to post at training and must have set a million scrums and lineouts. One of the guys who wasn't playing made the comment that if after all of that they could hang and do well in the match, it would be a superhuman effort. But there was no petrol left in the tank in the second half, and they ran right through us.

From a game in which we were thumped so comprehensively, Australia made one change. The fullback. Game two was against the South Africans in Brisbane, and I could see the writing on the wall in huge letters. The selectors would have been lynched if they hadn't picked Queensland's favourite son for such a match.

I got two minutes on the paddock against the South Africans that night – in a match that produced a great win for the team (29–9) and was a big confidence booster. It was a night when the Wallabies played very smart football. George as captain chose penalty goal, penalty goal, penalty goal, just to break the spirit of the South African team, and it was a very professional win. Two minutes on the paddock counts for a cap – but it's a token thing, and you'd really rather not go on. You don't work up a sweat and you feel like you've contributed absolutely nothing at all – which is generally true. As soon as I hit the field, I thought: 'I'm going to get a touch of the ball, at least!' There was a move on down the blind side and Wendell Sailor stepped in, stepped out, stepped in again, and was finally tackled. I went in to join the ruck and then I thought, 'No, I'll get out of this and fly across the other side. I'll get a touch there.' And the ball headed that way and suddenly there was a bit of a gap, and Steve Larkham had the ball in his hands. To make a short story even shorter, Bernie cut me out, passed to Phil Waugh who was tackled, the ref blew fulltime and that was it. See you later. At that point I walked up and touched the ball, just to know that I had.

It's times like that I really felt for Chris Whitaker, who had spent about half his life sitting on the bench as George Gregan's understudy, hoping to get a game. Whit's mindset, commitment and uncomplaining devotion to duty have been fantastic.

At the match function after the South African game I was with a group of people connected to one of the sponsors, and a bloke asked me: 'How did you go tonight, Matt?' I said, 'Well, you *might* have seen me. I spent 78 minutes running up and down the sideline warming up.' Everyone laughed, including me. But deep down it was frustrating not to have been able to make a contribution.

The next week, against the New Zealanders in Auckland, I played half a match on the wing, replacing the injured Wendell Sailor. We lost the game 20–17, but I was reasonably satisfied with my performance – and with the thought that I was still thereabouts in the mix for the World Cup as the countdown continued.

There followed a nervous pause, between the end of the domestic season and the arrival of the World Cup carnival. We were all fully in World Cup mode by then – but the powers that be sent numbers of players back to club football, blokes who hadn't had much of a run in the rep season. I think it was a bad call. I played a couple of games for Eastwood and didn't want to – much as I loved the place. The World Cup squad had only one focus now, and there was always the chance of suffering an injury in the club arena that could end a player's lifetime dream.

The other angle on that situation was that the World Cup squad was training bloody hard. Camps had been organised where the emphasis was on getting the team a whole lot fitter, and that meant a heap of running . . . and running . . . and running. The trainer had endless stats on individual fitness levels and how much work we needed to do. All of us got to the stage where we were running fit, but at what cost to the body?

Not long before the Cup was to begin, I was despatched to play for Eastwood, against Lote Tuqiri's side, West Harbour. By now, *no one* wanted to play club football. But you can't go in half-hearted, because that's when you *do* get injured. Before the game we had a solid week down at Manly, where we were training. At the end of it I felt like my hamstring was falling off the bone. But however much crap we backs tend to give the forwards – and rightly so – I have to say that the Wallaby forwards had done an *enormous* amount of work that week. So when the Eastwood representatives – Matt Dunning, Justin Harrison, Jeremy Paul and Bill Young – opted out of playing against West Harbour, they were right to do so. But they really rubbed salt into the wound. When I ran out there, the four of them were sitting together and cheering me on: 'Do it for the 'Woods!' they shouted, unable to hide their smiles.

I had to laugh, even though I felt like my leg was falling off.

We lost the game, which was disappointing. But at least I got through relatively unscathed, and the World Cup dream lived on.

Chapter 23
CROCODILE COUNTRY

In anticipation of the pre-summer hot weather arriving with the World Cup, we flew to Darwin to do our final segment of training. In fact, the Cup, when it kicked off, was accompanied by a cool to mild spring – perfect football weather. In the tropical Northern Territory we laboured away in daily temperatures that reached 38 degrees Celsius – and it was bloody tough going. The days were just too hot for full-scale training sessions, so those were scheduled for dusk – one simulated game, fifteen a side, absolutely full-on with the only difference being that the coaches chose the starting point – a scrum here, a lineout there, a penalty here. We did our gym work and lifting in the morning, then tried to dodge the heat until the sting had gone out of it just a fraction in the late afternoons. One day we visited a crocodile farm and I took some photos with one of the twenty disposable cameras Jeremy Paul had bought for the team. When I spoke to Kate that evening and told her about it, she asked if I'd included some of the guys in the photos – as a personal memory of the occasion. Of course, I hadn't – just crocs, which all tend to look pretty much the same after a while.

Notwithstanding the heat, I trained hard and well. I felt refreshed and certainly motivated to succeed and to advance my claims to play in the Cup. I think by then just about everyone had conceded the outside-centre spot to Stirling Mortlock, but I wasn't going to go down without a fight.

Up there, far from home, part of what we did was the hard physical stuff. The rest added up to a unique bonding exercise among members of the team that would defend the Cup. The centrepiece of that was a pretty memorable experience: 24 hours in Arnhem Land. At the end of the Darwin training program – with some of the blokes almost out on their feet, so tough had been the preparation – we flew there in a small fleet of six-seater planes, landing on a dirt runway in what seemed to be the middle of nowhere. Land Rovers conveyed us to what we were told was a five-star campsite, comprising tents and bungalow-type buildings. Sleeping rough, out on the deck, wasn't something this boy from Sydney was used to – but after experiencing it I decided I wouldn't swap it for a comfortable bed and a doona. For a bloke who had never seen too much of our own backyard, outback Australia, it was something very different.

We split into two groups on the day of our arrival. One group went barramundi fishing, while the other headed out on a two-hour bushwalk, which seemed to pass in no time at all. We visited caves dotted with wall paintings thousands of years old, and learned about survival techniques and some of the bush foods that can keep you going if you happen to get lost out there. It was another world.

At dusk, we linked up with the blokes who had gone fishing

and headed back in boats towards the camp. Soon someone spotted a big croc on the river bank 500 metres or so downstream from where the boats had been moored. We made our way over there and manoeuvred close to get a good look and some photos. Remembering what Kate had said, I passed my camera over to John Muggleton and asked him to get a shot of the croc, with me in the foreground. We nudged up *very* close, about six or seven metres away, and he was a big 'un. We were at about two o'clock from the direction the croc was facing, which was smart, because, as we later discovered, crocs tend to head in a dead-straight line when they take off. The other boat carrying the rest of the players had pulled up nearby and some of the boys were making baby croc noises, trying to stir up the big fella.

All of a sudden, he *did* take off, scaring the bejesus out of everyone. Muggo skilfully snapped his pic just at the instant he was scampering across the water. The problem was, the croc headed straight for, and rammed into, the front of the other boat. Lote Tuqiri, who was standing up front in what was basically just a flat-bottom tinny with a cover on top, went about two metres up in the air and almost over the side. At that moment, the guys on the other boat were shitting themselves! Their tinny almost took on water. After it happened there was 10 seconds or so of absolute dead silence, and I'm sure that everyone on board was toying with the $3 million question (that's how much the 'cattle' in the boat were worth): 'What would have happened if he *had* tipped us over?' Then there was an outburst of relieved laughter, and Lote was crowing about how quick he was to have got out of the way. In fact, everything had happened at such speed that no one had any possible hope of reacting.

Back at the camp, at dinner that night, there was dancing by some of the local Aboriginal people in spectacular ceremonial paint (ochre) and dress. It was fascinating to learn about the meaning and significance of each dance. George Gregan got out there and was painted up, and they invited the rest of us to do it, too – and everyone got involved in what turned out to be a fantastic night.

Watching and being a part of these ancient rituals way out there in the bush, so far from anywhere, helped to draw us even closer together as a group. Afterwards we sat together and each of us had the chance to speak, or to decline if we chose and pass the opportunity on to the next person. Most of the guys had their say, including some of the quieter ones who seemed to open up as we sat there under the stars. The tins supplied by our sponsors, Bundy Rum, were a help, no doubt. I talked about it being my third World Cup, and of the experience of the first, at which I was a young bloke, just part of the group, and of the second, which we won, and how good that felt. And I told a few stories because the blokes sort of give it to me about that – they reckon I re-run stories all the time. And I talked about this 2003 Cup, and what winning it would mean and how by doing that, all of us could proudly hand on that legacy to the next bunch. The night ended at about 3 am with some skylarking – boys being boys.

I joined the fishing group the next day – although fishing had never been my thing. Might as well give it a go, I reckoned. I was in a boat with George Smith, Joe Roff, who was below par as a result of the big night the night before and who just lay quietly in the bottom of the boat, and George Gregan. We went really well for city-dwelling boys. We caught *heaps* – trees, reeds, logs; in fact, we caught everything *but* barra. Never even got a nibble, in fact. But it was a great time all the same – just out there on the lake under a cloudless sky, yarning and joking, with football talk drifting in and out of the conversation.

The Northern Territory experience was both physically testing and a lot of fun. Up there we made a resolution that we would take a no-holds-barred approach to winning the Cup, and that every one of us would do everything in our power, both physically and mentally, to try to win back-to-back Cups. We wouldn't die wondering.

We talked about how one big difference between this campaign and that of 1999 would be the amount of media attention. In 1999 we were in the spotlight as one of the 'gun' teams, but it would pale into insignificance compared with 2003. The media focus on the team was always going to be huge, and so too the demands on our time if it were allowed to get out of hand. We would have to find a balance between the private space we needed and the public space that came as part of the deal. It was great to be able to reflect on all this up there in the Territory, far from the epicentre – and I believe that subsequently the team handled the media attention well. We were buoyed by the certain knowledge that this time we would have the full backing of boisterous home crowds wherever we went.

Chapter 24

THE GREATEST SHOW
ON EARTH

I was over the moon to win selection in our first game of the 2003 World Cup campaign, against the Argentinians. Eddie Jones confirmed my selection a day or two before the start of The Greatest (Sporting) Show on Earth. 'Mate, you're in the team.' Beauty! But it wasn't subsequently presented in the public arena quite the way it should have been, although I was immensely proud when I was handed my World Cup jersey, with its sprig of wattle embroidered on the side, to differentiate it from the standard Wallaby jumper. In the wattle were ancient echoes of Australian sport; the green and gold that became the traditional Aussie sporting colours in the 1920s were struck on the foundation of 'gumnut green' and 'wattle gold'.

There was fierce competition between Stirling Mortlock and me for the outside-centre spot; we both knew that playing in the opening game would give one of us an edge on the other. On the Thursday before the game, Stirling came down with a gastric virus, and the clear impression was given that I was in the team (and he wasn't) for that reason. In other words, I was 'second choice'. It wasn't true, even though some of the stories and headlines conveyed it that way: 'Burke takes over from sick Stirling' and 'Veteran Burke to seize his chance'. In fact, I later learned, I had been picked on the Tuesday – before there was any mention of Stirling's illness. The *Sydney Morning Herald*'s Greg Growden had got it right when he wrote: 'Sources indicated last night that when the World Cup squad first assembled, Mortlock was tagged the first choice No. 13 . . . But in recent weeks the ACT utility back drifted out of favour and by last weekend Burke had been confirmed as the main candidate for the midfield position. Even before news came of Mortlock's (and Latham's) ailments Burke had been pencilled in on the team list.' I had won the position fair and square. Although it nagged at me that I was presented as a 'fill-in', I said nothing; I pretty much bit my lip and decided I would just try to make the most of my opportunity.

We knew that the game against the Argentinians would be tough. There was idle speculation about the likelihood of Australia winning by 50, but it was never going to be like that. A couple of seasons before, we had been lucky to beat them in Buenos Aires. They had a powerful pack and some very capable backs, and we knew it would be no picnic when George Gregan, captain of Australia in an opening World Cup match, proudly led us out.

The match was nothing spectacular. We played with fair intensity and did what everyone expected, and beat them – 24–8. And we were happy with the win. I really worked to try to get into the game as much as possible, and came off the paddock fairly satisfied.

Against Romania in Brisbane I got 60 minutes of game time, spending much of it waiting for the tap on the shoulder. Mortlock, recovered from his 'flu, was ready and raring to go on the sideline throughout. Again the media had heaped pressure on me ('Safety-first Wallabies overlook Mortlock'). I knew the replacement moment would come sometime, and it did. The situation was far from ideal. I would class Stirlo and me as pretty good mates, so I had no problems on that score. We had played a lot of football together, and with success. But as far as I was concerned, it was him or me for that outside-centre spot – it couldn't be some sort of cosily shared arrangement. The way I saw it, either *I* was in the team or *he* was. I wasn't getting a lot of help from the journos – especially from News Limited's senior rugby man, Peter Jenkins, a bloke who never seemed to me to be much on my side in the latter stages of my career and who was now heavily pro-Mortlock.

As far as I'm concerned, football has always been about getting the job done – no matter how old or how young you might happen to be. If you're doing your stuff for the team, age shouldn't come into the equation at all. But the pro-Mortlock push was heavy then, and I have to say it went a fair way towards spoiling a few Burke breakfasts. Even though you try to dodge the negative stuff that's written, it eats away at you. I even had my old man ringing me one morning, so concerned was he about something he had read. 'Mate, just don't read it,' I told him. But it gnaws away, all the same. I felt it was pretty unfair. If I had been playing terribly . . . well, okay. But I wasn't; I was doing my job solidly for the team. You know that the opinions offered in mass-circulation newspapers or on high-rating TV or radio programs reach many people, and that, no doubt, some of it will be taken on board. A bloke like Campo would give it to you in the paper – and then give you a cheery wave and a 'G'day, mate!' when he saw you at the match. Hang on a sec! The challenge, I suppose, is just to focus on what you're doing and try not to worry about it. But it's not easy.

* * *

The Romanian game brought a big win, 90–8, and a couple of tries next to my name in the 60 minutes. My form was satisfying. Former Test captain Nick Farr-Jones wrote in the *Daily Telegraph*: 'Matt Burke attacked the line, running at deceptive angles which confounded the Romanians. It is hard to see how Stirling Mortlock will wrestle the No. 13 jersey from Burke going forward.' Tim Horan made a similar point in the *Herald*. The match was no great spectacle against one of the smaller-fry rugby nations, and again it was a matter of Australia doing what it was expected we would do and winning the game by a clear space. My goal was specific and short-term: to play well enough to get a start in the next, and first big game: against Ireland.

But before that there was tiny Namibia, absolute minnows of the Cup competition, and taken to the hearts of the fans because of it. This was the chance for the blokes on the Australian bench who weren't going to get much air time in the tournament. Morgan Turinui was one of them – and he got 40 minutes against the Namibians, which turned out to be his only 40 minutes of the entire carnival. Nathan Grey was another, and he got half a game here, too. I got half an hour in the second half. Chris Whitaker captained the side against Namibia. There were those who thought that perhaps I could have been given the opportunity, in line with past tradition when long-service players such as Horan, Little and McCall were afforded the honour. That was for others to debate – I certainly didn't begrudge Whits his chance.

I made earlier mention of my conversation with Mat Rogers on the subject of goal-kicking in this match. Elton Flatley had kicked against Argentina and Romania, and I hadn't kicked in Test matches for a while. Yet, it was part of my game and there was the need for me to keep my hand in. 'Mate, if I get on the paddock, do you mind if I take a couple of shots at goal?' I had asked Rogers early in the week. Mat had no problem with that. But near the beginning of the second half when we scored and I jogged up to take the kick, John Muggleton sent a message down the line: 'Rogers to kick . . . Rogers to kick.' So that was that – adding to the perception that I was on the fringes now. The kicking side of the equation that had been part of my armament was marked 'no longer required'.

The match was won by, almost literally, a cricket score – 142–nil, and Mat Rogers picked up 42 points from two tries and sixteen conversions.

I held on to my spot for the match against Ireland in Melbourne – well, an hour of it, anyway. This was a big game. A win would mean that we had topped our pool and would head on to what was a very winnable match against Scotland. If we lost, it would mean a match against the French, considerably more dangerous and unpredictable opponents. We *had* to win – and in a tough game during which Ireland really lifted, we did win. Just. The scoreboard read 17–16 at fulltime, but only after they had popped dangerously at a field goal in the last few minutes. It was a tense game throughout, spiteful at times. Again I played okay, especially in defence where my workrate was high.

I was replaced by Mortlock at the 64 minutes mark after taking a knock on the knee. I had the sense almost immediately that, barring something unpredictable happening, that could be it for me in the World Cup. As I sat on the bench watching the second half of the game, I said to myself: 'You've got to be ready now for the moment when the coach comes up and explains why you aren't going to be playing in the tournament from now on.'

It happened, as I had thought it would, a few days later, when we were back at our training camp at Coffs Harbour. It was a double-session training day, and before the start of the afternoon session

Eddie came up to me: 'Burkey, can I talk to you for a second, please?' We pulled away to one side and I knew exactly what was coming. 'Mate, I've got some disappointing news for you,' he said. 'You're not going to be in the team this week, and I have to tell you that you won't be in the fifteen . . . *or* the 22. You'll be sitting on the sidelines.' I was ready for the news. 'Okay, mate,' I said, and asked him why. 'We've just got to give the other bloke a go,' he replied. Meaning Mortlock. And that was it – there was no further explanation, although it seemed I was left out because I was not 'effective enough in attack'.

In my view, it was a situation that had to arise. At some point, one of us was going to be genuinely in the team, and one of us wasn't. I had to take it on the chin, of course. Stirling is an exceptionally good player, and the decision was going to be made sometime, one way or the other. I just felt that, given my form, I should have gone on. I was especially disappointed not to be in the 22.

Against Ireland, Matt was all over Brian O'Driscoll, the real danger man in their team. He blotted him out with great defence. It was a terrific performance and I came away from the game with the firm view that he had been one of the best play-ers on the field. I was so incensed by the selectors' decision that I let Eddie Jones know formally what my thoughts were. I was in Melbourne and then later I watched the match tape in full and couldn't for the life of me believe that he didn't warrant retention – if not in the fifteen, then at least in the 22.

John Fordham

It was the end of my World Cup campaign right there. In the days that followed I got to see the other side of life in the Wallaby camp. On the Thursday we headed to Brisbane, where I became a 'double dirty'. It's a different world, I discovered. You train with the team at most of the allocated sessions early in the week, but you are pretty much not required after that and just do your own thing. That week in Brisbane, essentially we weren't needed from Wednesday night until the following Monday. We played some golf on the Thursday and were able to have a couple of beers after dinner. Morgan Turinui and I went to the casino a couple of times and had a bet. I don't mind a spin on the roulette wheel. At training, all of the double dirties were running their hearts out; everyone, I suppose, clinging to the hope of getting the call-up. But after training, it was a completely different world from that of 'the team'. I have never felt so alienated as when I first stepped into that environment in Brisbane. It was quite bizarre, being so different from the other side that had been my experience to that point.

It's on match days that it really hits home. You go to the team meeting, you sit there on the sideline and watch and think, 'What would *I* have done in that situation?' You're part of it, but not *really* part of it. You are still excited for the team and your mates when they win – and the 33–16 quarter-final victory over Scotland was solid enough without being too convincing – but it's not the same.

At training the double dirties run as the opposing side against the Australian team, taking different names as the tournament progressed. Before the Argentinian match they were the Tucuman XV – Tucuman being a team in Argentina. Before Romania, some were saying 'Budapest', but I reckoned Bucharest was the right call. Before Namibia . . . no one knew. Before Ireland they were the Belfast XV. Now, before Scotland, we were the Edinburgh XV – and I was one of them.

In the lead-up to the big semifinal against New Zealand in Sydney, I felt a mixture of relief and frustration. The team was going great now, and that was fantastic – but it was frustrating to be part of it and yet *not* part of it.

Earlier in the year, in June, there had been something of a blow-up when the media learned that George Gregan had stayed with his wife on the night before the match against England at the Telstra Dome in Melbourne, instead of at the team hotel. Unofficially, it was accepted that senior players sometimes stayed at home if they were in their own town, but some former players were critical of George. In *their* day, they said, there would be a dinner the night before the match at which they would discuss the game and the tactics for the next day. But times had changed, of course. We were now fulltime footballers, together all the time – and the last thing you want to be doing is talking footy 24/7. But because of the kerfuffle over George, there was now a rule that everyone had to stay in the team hotel at all times. Despite the rule, during the week the team trained in Parramatta I fulfilled all my commitments to the team, but spent a fair bit of time with the family, too. I was able to drive home after training to be with the Burke team for a while.

Because the New Zealanders had been in such commanding form through the tournament, barely anyone gave us a chance of getting past them to make the final. But I think the All Blacks got a game ahead of themselves on that night. I suspect they were thinking 'final' – while the Australians under Eddie Jones's direction were focused absolutely on *this* 80 minutes of football. It was a great and concentrated Aussie performance, bringing a famous victory, 22–10, and a place in the final.

In the course of such a triumph, the horrific neck injury suffered by our front rower Ben Darwin was as chilling a moment as I have ever experienced in football. It was truly shocking to see him lying on the ground, not moving. Ben, a big, strong bloke, was caught up awkwardly in a scrum in one of those million-to-one chances that can happen when the power is on up front. All of us watching could only hope that things would be okay, that he would climb back off the deck. He didn't, and there was an eerie silence and then sympathetic applause in the stadium as they carried him off.

Yet, strangely, what happened to Ben Darwin, and the inspiring aftermath, was what made me really feel part of the team again. We were united in our concern for him. When he got out of hospital, he came to Parramatta to say a few words to the team before the final. I still get a shiver up my spine when I think about that. I think that, for all of us, it provided a sense of belonging, that we were all in this World Cup thing together. Ben coming back to talk to us as he wrestled with his emotions, knowing already that his football-playing days were over, was unbelievably special. It probably made more than a few of us re-evaluate things. I know it did me. I had been whingeing and feeling sorry for myself – and here was a bloke whose career had finished in the blink of an eye, but who was already moving on. Ben's meeting with the team was an inspiration for the final.

One of the biggest-ever nights in Australian rugby is part of sporting history now. I sat there on the sideline in my suit, raincoat at the ready, along with the other double dirties and watched the marathon unfold. Elation at the early Lote Tuqiri try was dulled by England's smart left-side try, scored by Jason Robinson. Metre by metre it settled into a war of attrition, the scores edging up, goal by goal. Then came the late chance for Australia to square it up and take the game into extra time and, perhaps, an epic victory.

While Flats is lining up the goal attempt, the TV camera is trained on me. What do they want – for me to look *disappointed* if he kicks it? He knocks over an ice-cool goal and it's 14-all. The feeling is fantastic. We're the underdogs – but we're still in it, still have a chance of stealing the Cup, just when the Poms had it ready for their British Airways flight home.

Into extra time, Flats lands another huge-pressure goal to keep the dream alive. And then the ending, with the extra-time period running out . . . and Jonny Wilkinson snaps a field goal shot off his 'wrong' (right) foot and it goes through the posts at the southern end. It's over: 20–17. The World Cup is won . . . and lost, and Bill is off to the UK for the first time.

The feeling afterwards was one of bitter disappointment – to have gone so close, then seen it stolen away by a great kicker. There was talk later that it wasn't a great *match* per se, but it was certainly a hugely dramatic one that will live on in the minds of everyone who saw it. In the wash-up, it was just like any other football match – disappointment in the losing dressing room, post-mortems on how, maybe, it could have been different, a visit to the change room by some of the English blokes to say, 'G'day, and thanks for the game' – and later some beers, and a wind-down, before the next morning pack-up and return to real life.

I was later able to look back on my own involvement in the campaign with some satisfaction. I hadn't let my disappointment show. I had stayed focused throughout and contributed all that I could. Probably only Kate knew how I really felt during this part of my career. I would like to think that my team-mates in that long World Cup campaign of 2003 believed that M. Burke made a positive contribution. But as the curtain fell, I wondered if I would ever again pull on the Wallaby jersey.

Chapter 25
A FEW THINGS ABOUT MATTHEW BURKE

Despite the Jonny Wilkinson field goal snap that killed the dream of a hometown Australian victory, the 2003 World Cup had been a resounding success, drawing huge crowds and giving rugby weeks of unprecedented dominance of the sporting landscape. For the game and all of the Aussie players involved it meant a rise in profile. I guess people 'got to know' many of us over those weeks and there was increased interest in who we were and in the game we played. It seems perfect timing in the aftermath of the battle for the Cup to reflect now on some of the things people asked me at that time and have questioned me about now and then through my rugby years. When I sat down to think about it I realised that I had been asked all sorts of weird and wonderful things about my life in and around football. The queries represent a real mixed bag: how I feel about records, the media, golf; how I deal with pre-match nerves; how I try to live a 'normal' life, without football dominating too much. I hope the following thoughts might throw a little light on my journey in rugby.

Nicknames

I've had a few nicknames over the years. Mainly they've been variations on my surname: 'Burkey' and 'Burkes'. But there have been some others. I have mentioned my dislike for my given second name, 'Coleman'. It still bobs up now and then – as before a Super 10s match one day a few years back, when a couple of blokes sitting behind me in the grandstand called out, 'Hey, Coleman!' I just ignored them.

It was after we had demolished the Canadians 74–9 in 1996 that John Eales came up with the name 'Moses'. I'd had a big night, kicking nine or ten goals. Ealsie, who can be a practical joker and likes to throw out a bit of a niggle, told the media that I'd been given the new nickname 'Moses', because I 'parted the goal-posts like Moses parted the Red Sea'. And, of course, one of the newspaper headlines the next day said something to that effect. (I have a suspicion Ealsie might have been trying to rid *himself* of a nickname here.)

George Gregan landed me with the name 'Valvoline', which had a couple of subsequent variations in 'Slippery' and 'Oil'. It has been interpreted in a few different ways. In my earlier playing days, my hair used to stay in place, no matter what was happening out on the paddock. There was a theory that I used a lot of product in my hair to keep it that way, oils and stuff. Valvoline – get it? But the original version and designation was George's, and it involved a sponsors' golf day we were playing one day up at Coolum, a beautiful part of the world. The format for the day was an Ambrose. Those who know golf will appreciate that there is a fairly complicated procedure to be adhered to on the greens, involving the marking of putts. I won't go into all the details except to say that I was last to putt and my team was looking at a six, unless I managed to sink my long putt – which I did. George, back down the fairway waiting to make his approach, was yelling out, 'Six, mate. Just write down "six".' My mob went on to win the day by one-eighth of a shot.

George, a keen competitor, wasn't impressed – and duly tagged me 'Valvoline', plus just about any other slippery product that was on the market. My golf handicap has been a bit of a worry to George, too. My registered handicap was ten, as we played rugby on Saturdays and trained during the week and I never got the chance to play competitions – competitions being the only way you can reduce your handicap. So I was playing off ten for a number of years, when maybe it should have been a little lower. George reckoned so, anyway. I ended up playing a few good rounds and got my handicap down to seven, but George still thinks I'm fiddling the books. Whenever someone asks me what I'm playing off these days and Greegs happens to be around, there'll be a little cough and some sniggering. He reckons I'm a bit slippery when it comes to golf.

Now and then I still get 'Malcolm Buck' too, stemming from the cocktail party incident in Tokyo that I related back in Chapter 16.

Finally, towards the end of my career in Australia, a couple of the smart young pups in the Waratah side added another name to the list: 'Decade'. It came about after the making of the DVD about my time in football, called *A Decade of Excellence*, courtesy of John Fordham. The boys had a good laugh about that. 'Mash' is another occasional tag – referring to the stories I have been known to tell about my rugby experiences. Some of the boys reckon they're as ancient and long-running as the famous old TV series.

* * *

Golf

A great part of the Wallaby experience for me was the opportunity it provided to play on some of the world's great golf courses. I love my golf, and am a member at both the Concord and Macquarie links, where I am off seven these days. On the Wallabies' European trip of 1996 we were in Edinburgh, which gave some of the team an opportunity to play a round on the famous old course at St Andrews. There were 24 blokes bidding for the twelve spots available; even blokes who weren't golfers put their names down – because it was St Andrews. I was on duty the day the decision was to be made, along with Tim Horan. (We have 'duty boys' each day on tour.) It fell to me to organise the 'sweep' that would decide the lucky twelve, and I wrote everyone's name on a bit of paper and screwed them all up and put them in a bowl.

However, this being my honest life story, I can reveal that I slinked it a little bit. I had written the names of Tim Horan and Jason Little (my roommate) and my own name at the top of a lined exercise book page – and when the names were torn out and placed in the bowl, just a hint of blue line was showing on the back of each slip.

We sat in a semicircle at a team meeting and picked out the lucky twelve. Jason got picked out fair dinkum at about number six and there were smiles all around, considering he was in on the sting. When it got to number ten, Tim, who was holding the bowl, said: 'I'll have a go now.' He dipped his hand in and, amazingly, pulled out my name. He then walked across the room to where I was sitting. 'Let the duty boy have a go,' he said, and held the bowl out to me. I rustled the remaining pieces of papers, spotted one with a flash of blue on it, and pulled it out. Tim Horan!

Well, the place was in uproar. The boys were filthy. For some reason they smelled a rat, and there were accusations of rorting and conspiracies. I surreptitiously swallowed the piece of paper to get rid of the evidence – but there was general agreement among the boys that a heinous crime had been committed.

Needless to say, Burke and Horan didn't go to St Andrews. As it turned out it poured with rain and was freezing cold on the appointed day, so we weren't too miffed about that. But because of our small misdemeanour, we were cited to appear before the team court for our 'punishment'. Usually the penalty when someone stepped out of line was to skol a glass of beer. But the court introduced an outside element: we had to eat a local delicacy, a cold pork pie, without washing it down. That was bad enough. Then we had to eat three raw eggs and drink three beers. I finished the exercise just before sprinting to the washroom to bring up the lot. That was just after the manager had told us the agenda for the next day. 'It's breakfast at eight and on the bus at 9.30.' *Breakfast*? I only had to *think* of food, and I was off and running.

Notwithstanding that small slip-up over St Andrews, I have had some great days on the golf course. I have played in a couple of Coolum Classics, and in a Jack Newton event at Noosa. And one day at Concord I got to play with Craig Parry. A mate of mine, Darrell McGraw, had rung me: was I interested in a game? I told him 'yes', but that the morning was the only chance I had; I was tied up in the afternoon. 'It's a game with Craig Parry,' he said. 'Oh,' I said. 'What time are we teeing off?' So I fronted for the one o'clock start to find quite a crowd of members around the first tee. Craig wasn't long back after playing beautifully and just missing out in the British Open. I have honestly never been so nervous in my life. The club professional and David Campese were the other two in our foursome. The club pro asked me, 'Mate, do you want to tee off first?' 'Geez, no. I'd better go last,' I told him. 'Let me put it to you this way,' he said. 'Campo [who can play] will be down the middle, and as club pro I reckon I can get one down the middle . . . then there's Parry, and you.' I thought about it.

'Righto, I'll go first,' I said. So I lined it up and did all the tricks – walking back from the ball and that kind of stuff. I hit a three wood and I reckon my head came up about a foot before the ball had departed, but I managed to get perfect contact and the ball flew down the middle, to polite applause from the gathering. Milking it, I tipped my hat to the crowd as I walked coolly back to my bag.

It was a lovely day. Craig is a terrific bloke and we talked about family and rugby and all sorts of things. It was so relaxed that I even gave him some stick on one of the par three holes when he landed short, while I was about two metres from the hole. He then hit a little eight-iron pitch and run which went straight into the hole for a birdie, while I missed my putt. I was pretty quiet after that.

A few guys like to tag him with the 'Valvoline' call, because he is just a bit of a slippery character. He puts across this fantastic persona, but skim the surface and underneath there is a guy who's raring to go, jumping at opportunities. He is often the cornerstone of any practical jokes that happen in the side, and he just sits in the corner and quietly chuckles away or tells one or two guys in the side what is going on; he has very much got his finger on the pulse. What to me was disappointing came after he did his shoulder in that clean-sweep game at Stadium Australia. I thought then his golf would be gone. But even on a half swing or a three-quarter swing he could still out-drive me with a one wood, and I think he was hitting a three iron or a four iron at the time – and still taking money off us left, right and centre. I think it might have even improved his swing a little bit! And golf is probably where his nickname originates from.

Nathan Grey

He is the only guy I know who shoots anywhere between 73 and 77 every time I play with him. So, you're talking one to four over par every time – and he still manages to play off ten. I mean, he has been playing off ten for three or four years now, and I have been playing with him longer than that and he always shoots those scores with me, so I can't work it out. That's why I never beat him. He's very competitive – and that's a good example of how he is competitive. He has just doctored the system in terms of his golf handicap. We all know he should be off four or five, but he still punches out to ten, so, as they say, he'd walk over his grandmother to get a result – but in his quiet, guy-next-door sort of way.

George Gregan (2003)

Records

Back in 1996 when I broke the record for the most number of points scored in Tests in a calendar year (189 in eleven games), the bigger question of records and what they meant to me would often come up in discussion. To be honest, they were a nice bonus for a bloke who happened to be a goal-kicker, and a source of some quiet pride and satisfaction – but not much more. To me, the game itself was always the thing – not the gathering of personal laurels.

But there was *one* record I would love to have had and which I dreamed of late in my career – and I admit to feeling a bit miffed that I didn't get a decent crack at it. Michael Lynagh's Test points-scoring record of 911 was in my sights through the last couple of years of my career in Australia. When it all ended for me in 2004, I had 878, so I was frustratingly close – just a handful of tries and goals. Circumstances conspired against me late in my career; I was still part of the Australian team, but I wasn't given a lot of 'air time' or opportunity. The World Cup match against Namibia in 2003, which offered a bonanza of points, was one example. When the word came down from the top that Mat Rogers would be kicking in the second half, I felt like saying to John Muggleton, our defence coach, 'Thanks very much, mate – good on ya.' It wasn't a case of being greedy; I just wanted an opportunity to do what I had done in football for a number of years: kick and do some stuff on the field, and to actually have an input.

The records that I *did* pick up along the way are listed at the back of this book and I am happy to have established them, but I would have loved to have had a more solid crack at the Lynagh milestone. To fall short when the chance might have been there still nags at me a little.

Pre-match nerves

For most of my career I contended with pre-match nerves. I used to get really, really crook before big games, and quite often, while the coach or captain was delivering the final words before battle, I'd be on the loo. With me, it was usually a problem at both ends – and I don't know whether it was a nerves thing or a food thing . . . or a bit of both. It would continue when I got out on to the field. I remember vomiting (discreetly) on the halfway line before a Bledisloe Cup game. And again before the World Cup semi-final in South Africa. I hid it pretty well. I was looking down, sort of crouched over and away from the cameras at the time. Before a match against Scotland in 1996 I missed the national anthem, having to hurriedly retreat to the dressing room as the two teams lined up on the ground. Safely in the cubicle, I joined in for a few lines of the anthem with team doctor John Best, who was in the dressing room. Then, it was back to the battle. Once we got going, I'd be okay.

My pre-match rituals (apart from throwing up!) were limited to sitting in the same spot in the dressing room and being extra certain that my socks were pulled up to *exactly* the same height below my knees.

The fact that most big matches in Australia are staged at night makes it very tough for the blokes who play the game. On those days, you drag through the world's longest preparation, and often, in my experience, you feel terrible for much of the day. Generally you start badly – by getting up late. Then it's a bit of a walk and a stretch, and the likelihood is you'll be as tight as a drum. The rest of it is just waiting around . . . a bit of breakfast . . . a bite of lunch . . . some afternoon tea . . . maybe a snooze. Mainly your mind just nags away at you about what lies ahead, about the preparation, and about what you have to do. It's a long and nervous wait. For the blokes on the reserve bench it's a little different – they can actually relax a little more and enjoy the day, more at ease in the knowledge that they aren't going to be among the fifteen who actually run out. Obviously they've got to do all the preparation, and know all the moves. But if they let themselves worry as much as the chosen fifteen, they'd be an absolute mess by the time they got the call into the game.

Travel

For me the travelling has been a terrific part of a life in rugby, and it continues to be a big part of the way the game operates today. Rugby is a truly international game now, and the blokes who play it are able to see the world. As a Wallaby, there are opportunities such as meeting the Queen, which I have been fortunate enough to have done a couple of times. In South Africa, I was in the same room as Nelson Mandela, though I didn't actually get to meet him. The presence of the man is unbelievable. It was fantastic to see the sights of Rome and Paris, and to be able to go to Table Mountain in Cape Town, all courtesy of rugby. I've had a fortunate life; if it hadn't been for rugby, almost certainly I wouldn't have had the chance to do and see those things.

Showing emotion

I have never been one to show much emotion on the field, although probably I have been a fraction more outgoing late in my career. Generally, over the years, I have kept a balance between confidence and humility in the way I have conducted myself out there on the paddock. I have never believed in mocking the opposition or rubbing it in when something goes wrong for them. Anyone who does that has every reason to expect similar treatment when *they* make a mistake, which we all do! My attitude to mistakes has always been just to grit my teeth and get on with it. I think it's the wrong thing to labour the point at those times by doing the big blow-up, or throwing your arms about, or grasping your head in your hands in anguish. That just magnifies what has happened. It's much better simply to grit your teeth and get on with it, I reckon. My advice to young blokes would be to keep your emotions in check while you're out there. Afterwards, back in the dressing room, you can yahoo and yell all you like.

The media

I have generally walked a fairly careful line with the media. If you let your guard down, you risk an unwanted headline or something being blown up way out of proportion – as I found out once or twice over the years. In 2003, in what seemed to be a pretty light-hearted interview for a Super 12 match night program, I offered a throwaway line on the question of possible improvements in the game. I said that maybe two referees would be worth a try. I certainly didn't hammer the point, just aired it (laughing actually), and even suggested that such a move could lead to a blast of whistle-blowing, left, right and centre. Greg Growden picked up the story in the *Sydney Morning Herald*, and next thing it was off and running. Burke was calling for two refs, and it was suddenly a big talking point in the game. No one ever rang me to ask for any further clarification. And I knew it was right out of hand when I happened to have Foxtel on the TV, and the subject was up for major discussion – with a bloke ripping into me. My throwaway comment had caused something of a media frenzy.

Awards

It was quite a thrill to be named in 2003 as 'Player No. 20' on rugby's Top 100 Roll of Honour – a major promotion conducted by News Limited through the *Daily Telegraph* in the lead-up to the World Cup. It was one of a number of nods of recognition I was fortunate to receive during my football career. This one was certainly special. By then, just under 800 blokes had won a Wallaby jumper over the past 100 years or so. It was really something to have been part of that, and to have had a great time playing the game and travelling the world; but it was fantastic to be recognised as being up there in the top group in terms of my contribution. The Top 100 list started this way: John Eales, David Campese, Tim Horan, Ken Catchpole, Mark Ella, Trevor Allan . . . There were some fantastic personalities and players. I was in special company in a rarefied atmosphere – and was chuffed to be there.

Life–sport balance

My perspective on rugby is that it is a sport, and just one part of my life. I am very competitive and I always want to win when I go out to play football. But I have always reckoned, too, that there is no use holding a grudge or walking around with a chip on your shoulder if you lose. Life is about so much else in addition to the game. My wife Kate, my daughters, my other family and friends, are the most important things in my life. Part of my enjoyment of the game has always been to have the off-field set-up firmly in place. It's when you have *that* that your on-field performance goes well. There has always been a real line of differentiation for me between the game of footy and the importance of getting away from it. It's all about balance. And sometimes when something big happens in the world, and the Asian tsunami of late 2004 is an overwhelming example, it really drives home the point that all of us blokes playing football are just playing a game. It's not a matter of life or death – even if the headlines try to make it seem that way sometimes.

Chapter 26

THE BEGINNING OF THE END

New South Wales had a new coach in 2004 – and for a short time I had a new playing position. A former team-mate of mine, Ewen McKenzie, took over the coaching reins and simultaneously I found myself being pushed in the direction of playing five-eighth. Actually, the hint had been dropped more than once during the World Cup campaign. At about the time I was fading out of the picture on that international stage, Andrew Friend, who was appointed assistant coach to Ewen, let slip rather pointedly on a couple of occasions that it appeared the Waratahs didn't have a No. 10 for season 2004. I probably viewed myself as a locked-in No. 13 by that time, but I knew that Andrew was to be part of the coaching structure with the NSW team and I started to consider the real possibility that things were going to change for me – again.

The summer rolled in. After a short break post-World Cup and in very quick time, it seemed, the Waratahs were back in pre-season training camp where there was every indication that, in fact, apart from me, we had *three* No. 10s: Shaun Berne and squad newcomers Tim Donnelly and Lachlan MacKay. Meanwhile, another newcomer – Ben Jacobs from Southern Districts – was being touted at outside-centre. But all the pointers were towards Burke being converted into a No. 10.

From the very first get-together, the returning Wallabies in the NSW side were put under pressure. The welcome back message was roughly this: 'You guys are going to have to work extra hard, because these young blokes *really* want it.' Just because we were Wallabies, we weren't going to get any sort of a free run, we were told. It was the same each year – degrading and unnecessary. *Of course* there would be challenges for positions. That was a given. It was football, after all. But we didn't need it rammed down our throats. It was a pretty ordinary kickoff, bordering on disrespectful to the senior blokes in the team.

At that same time, Kate and I had had some talks at home about where I/we were heading. I turned 31 that March, and I had some hesitation about whether I wanted to continue as captain of the team. I thought that maybe it was time to pass the captaincy on to someone younger, someone who would be around for longer than I would. To do that might give me some more freedom in my own game, as I would not have to worry about leading the side. That thought, among others, was in my head when I was called into the first meeting with Ewen McKenzie and Andrew Friend. Before long on that day, however, it was made very clear that the decision had already been made and the captaincy was going elsewhere. If there had been a bit of quiet consultation, I would have made my own choice and stepped down, but it had been taken out of my hands. With a jolt, I realised that for the first time in my career I wasn't going to be an automatic first pick for the Waratahs. I was in competition with others for the No. 10

spot – and in view of that, the team management had decided the captaincy should go elsewhere.

There were only two possibilities for the captaincy – Phil Waugh and Chris Whitaker – and I was good friends with them both and respected them as people and as footballers. When it was Chris who got the nod, I couldn't have been happier for him, despite my own disquiet about how I'd lost the captaincy. The powers that be thought that Whit's field position (at halfback), close to the ruck at all times, was better suited to the leadership role than my somewhat roving commission. Plus, there was the issue of the captain having to be a certain selection in the team . . .

As the understudy to George Gregan, Whits hadn't had much of a chance to step into the limelight. But in my view he was (and is) up there with the world's best players. George and Whits are different in style as footballers, but they share the quality of great tenacity. It had been an enormous pleasure to play football along-side Chris in the NSW team. I had always found him to be the most considerate and decent of people, and I was genuinely happy for him. We talked on the phone before it was made public, and characteristically he expressed concern for me. 'Mate,' I reassured him. 'You deserve it. You're a great player and you'll do a great job.' Which, as it turned out, he did. I continued to tell him how much he deserved the chance, and that he would have my full support. As a footballer, Chris was always a wholehearted worker – and team-mates find it easy to get behind those sorts of players.

I thought I did okay in my time as Waratahs captain and that I had the respect of the players, although I guess only they can vouch for that.

Once again in my career I rolled with the punches when it came to the issue of my playing position. I could have dug my heels in, and maybe others would have. I could have hammered home the point to the blokes in charge that I was a current Wallaby squad member as a centre – and that, with no disrespect to the blokes they had gone out and recruited, such as Donnelly and MacKay, if they weren't what was wanted at 10 – well, that really wasn't my concern. There's an old saying in football that you don't weaken one position to fill another – and there was a bit of that in it. Those are things I probably *should* have said. Instead, I did the old Burkey 'team' thing and played the 'nice guy' and said I'd give 10 a go. 'I'll help *you* out of your bind and in the process maybe stuff up *my* career,' were the unspoken words.

I put my head down at training, and before long it started to feel pretty good. At five-eighth I was on the receiving end of fast, flat passes from Whits that hit you in just the right spot. It was a treat to play outside a halfback like him, having the ball put exactly where you wanted it.

We played the Chiefs in a trial game in Newcastle in New South Wales, and in my first touch of the ball at five-eighth I spotted a gap inside my 22 and slipped past the opposing five-eighth. As the breakaway reached me in cover, I popped up a pass for a support – only to see it snared by their No. 8, after which play proceeded at a great rate to our try line for a five pointer! Things got better from there, I'm pleased to say, and we won the game easily, 85–19. But just when I was feeling comfortable, I banged up my right shoulder again, going for the line. The tackle that stopped me just short landed me awkwardly on my shoulder and neck – and was to be something that gave me grief and a lot of pain for a long period.

My goal to consolidate myself strongly at No. 10 was in immediate jeopardy – before a ball had been kicked in the Super 12s tournament. Suddenly it was happening all over again – I was doing my rehab, and trying to get myself right, and elsewhere the

NSW team was rolling into gear. All injured players have had a taste of that experience at some time – the feeling of being out of sight and out of mind. I had gone from captain, and senior man in the outfit, to a bloke with a crook shoulder on the outside, trying to be as supportive of the team as possible – but with the frustration creeping in.

I missed a couple of games (wins over the Crusaders and the Sharks), then eased back into football in a match for Sydney against Queensland A, and made it back into the Waratahs, at five-eighth, for the last twenty minutes of the Round 3 game against the Cats, which we won, 46–10. It was five minutes or so before I got a touch of the ball, but when I did I promptly dropped the bloody thing. Shades of my first Test. I got a bit lost that day in a match we already had well won. I ran on with fresh legs and tried to get heavily involved, but I wasn't really playing as a No. 10. The doubts were back: maybe I should be playing centre or fullback?

But at least I was back in football, and the South African leg gave me another brief chance. Kate was heavily pregnant with our second child when I left, and I had made arrangements with the coach and management to fly home for the birth. With Mat Rogers out injured I got the chance to play fullback in my one game over there against the Stormers at Cape Town, which we lost 27–23. It wasn't my best game, in a team effort that was generally below par, but just as it seemed we were getting into gear, I got hooked. It was about fifteen minutes into the second half, and I was far from happy with that. And that was South Africa – my career sort of continuing its stuttering process.

But a wonderful event awaited me. I flew home for the birth of Edie on 16 March 2004, a very happy experience. She was, of course, the perfect kid (I know all dads say that) and I'm a very lucky bloke to have two darling princesses. After the birth at North Shore Private Hospital I again had the very special experience of holding my daughter for a few minutes alone, as I had with Harriette. That was fantastic. Since day one, Harrie has been infatuated with Edie – or, as she is known, 'EE' because Harriette couldn't pronounce Edie properly, and that makes it even better.

It had been a very tough time for Kate, who apart from being pregnant, was looking after Harriette and supervising major refurbishing of a house we had bought – mainly because the two-bedroom unit we lived in would no longer be big enough for the Burkes. With a footballing husband who was often AWOL, Kate ran the show completely through that pretty amazing time – and my admiration for her was (and is!) unbounded.

A proud father-of-two, and, as it turned out, no longer a five-eighth, I was soon off to New Zealand for further Super 12 commitments, leaving Kate in charge, as she had been. It seemed that a new opportunity was opening up in the Waratahs. Mat Rogers had pretty much succumbed to a bad leg injury, which eventually required surgery and kept him out for months, and the fullback spot beckoned. But for the match against the Chiefs in Hamilton, the selectors preferred a young bloke, Cameron Shepherd, to me at fullback. It was a great thrill for Cameron, and good luck to him, but it was hard for me to watch, sitting edgily on the bench, hoping for a call. It came finally, belatedly, at 74 minutes with the game long gone. We lost 32–17, which meant three defeats in a row for a team that had started the year so promisingly. You could feel the tension starting to grow in the ranks . . .

Up until about that point in the campaign, I had remained very positive despite some difficulties such as the shoulder injury, and had tried to bring enthusiasm and experience to the Waratah mix.

But the events before and during that match in New Zealand didn't fill me with hope that things were going to get any better. In fact, one morning I made a quiet decision that the football I played from now on would be pretty much for *me*, although certainly too for the few blokes in the team with whom I had shared so much – such as Whits, Phil Waugh and Nathan Grey.

The catalyst was Andrew Friend questioning my enthusiasm for the job at hand. To paraphrase, he asked me: 'Are you actually doing enough? Can you lift your levels any higher?' It was about then that I decided it was a lost cause. I had struggled a bit because of the injury, but anyone who knew me would have known that I was giving 100 per cent commitment and effort. I'd like to think it has always been that way in my career. But I realised now that I was dealing with minds that were already made up. From now on, it was sort of me against the world. I would go my own merry way – although I wouldn't share those feelings with anyone. Except Kate.

The circumstances of the match against the Chiefs in Hamilton were depressing, too. I was on the bench, and fine with that. In the first couple of minutes, Ben Jacobs was injured and Nathan Grey was sent into the game. I sat there wondering whether I was covering fullback-wing, or maybe fullback-centre, or perhaps all three. Well, I warmed up for about an hour, at which point the trainer gave me the call: 'Mate, they want you down there.' I trotted down, thinking that at least I was going to get fifteen minutes or so, hopefully enough to put some sort of stamp on it. On the sideline I took a seat, while another ten or twelve minutes ticked by. Finally the match clock got to 74 minutes, at which point our manager, Dave Gibson, declared: 'Burkey, you're on.' And I looked at him with a 'What, *NOW*?' expression on my dial. 'Yes, you're on the wing,' said Gibson. 'Winger!' I said. 'I'm not going on the *wing*? Are you *kidding*?' At that point there was a hurried telephone consultation and then a new instruction: 'No, go to fullback.' So I played the last six minutes at fullback as the match wound down to its already decided result.

A week later, the wheel had turned, as it has a habit of doing in football. With injuries cutting deep into the Waratahs, I was picked at outside-centre to replace Ben Jacobs for the match against Auckland. My first thought was how ironic it was that I had suddenly become a vital resource now that players were dropping like flies. My second thought was more positive: here was a chance to go and play some good football, and to re-establish myself at the higher level. With the Waratah season plateauing, we did what we had done more than once before and headed out on a bonding session, which took the shape of a winery tour. It turned into a court session at which the question of whether the senior players were providing enough support to the captain was debated. Finally, it developed into a pretty big drinking session. Back at training the next day I was reinvigorated by the prospect of being back in the side and being able to provide the sort of senior support that I had hoped to be able to offer through the season to Chris Whitaker.

Against Auckland, I played probably my best game so far that season. But I was in a sour mood before I took the field, thanks to a last-minute 'pep talk' delivered by Andrew Friend. 'Mate, it's a big game for you today,' he said, kicking off our brief chat. The usual rev-up that follows last-minute advice is along the lines of: 'Chase the ball hard, and really work with your wingers in defence.' But Friend continued: 'I just don't know whether you've still got it or not – whether you've got the skills and desire to play football at this level.' By then I was looking straight past him, straight down the dressing room to the wall beyond. And I was thinking, 'Don't say *this* to me . . . You can't say *this* to me.' I was *filthy*. Friend was playing mind games again – but what he said to me just didn't need to be said to a senior professional footballer. It was belittling.

I gave the game my all – and I sure needed the run. When it was over, I was knackered. I have never felt so tired after a football match as I did that night. I sat on the sideline for ten minutes, then lay on a dressing room bench for another fifteen or twenty. I was shattered and sore and nursing a bump on the thigh – but happy to be 'back' and satisfied with my game, although we had lost the match 22–17. I had scored a try, kicked three goals and played okay. I'd had more than a few 'corkies' over the years and knew the drill – ice compression, elevation, and easy on the booze. With a haematoma, a blood bruise, alcohol thins the blood, and tends to make it bleed more freely, which slows the recovery process.

The boys were heading out for a beer or two. Whits and I said we'd catch up with them later, and strolled down to the Auckland waterfront to have a coffee and a yarn about the game and what had gone right and wrong. We jabbered away for a while, then rang the other blokes, who had headed to a different place from where we had originally arranged to meet. We'd heard of a place called the Minus Five Degrees Bar, literally a room made out of ice with ice stools, an ice bar, and so on, where they served only vodka, owing to the fact that it doesn't freeze. It was nearby, so Whits and I decided we'd pop in just for the novelty factor of trying something completely different. You can only stay there for half an hour anyway. We had two drinks, the second shouted by a friendly Canadian bloke behind the bar, and left.

That was it: two vodkas. We walked back to the hotel and I took my tired body and sore leg to bed after some compression and elevation treatment. I was on top of the injury. Next day there was tension at the breakfast table, as there invariably is after a loss. The coaches were under building pressure, with the season heading into a trough. Three straight wins had been followed by four successive losses, and suddenly the ladder wasn't looking healthy. At the airport when we gathered for the trip home, Andrew Friend said to me: 'You played well yesterday.' I thanked him. 'You know,' he continued. 'I didn't think you could play that well . . . didn't think you had it in you.' There they were again: the mind games.

Back home in Sydney, I had one day off from full training. But it was our bye week in the Super 12s, and I knew I would be fine. It was on that first day back that a 'little birdie' – a friend connected in high places in rugby – told me that the coaches were worried about my post-game program in Auckland, and especially about my going out for a drink after the game.

To me, that just topped it off. My professionalism as a footballer was being questioned. I had a sore leg, and I had a couple of drinks. It wasn't as if I had gone out and had 22! I chanced to miss probably the hardest running session of the year but I had played enough football to know the extent of the injury, and to know that I was going to be absolutely fine for the next game in two weeks. Two relaxing social drinks weren't going to make a difference to that. By now the 2004 Waratahs season was starting to become very frustrating, on several levels.

I trained the full session the next day, the Tuesday, and did it well – and then left them to it. By now, early sparring had begun on a possible contract with New South Wales in 2005, and I suspect that stirring somewhere at the back of my mind was the thought: 'How much longer will I be a Waratah?'

Chapter 27
THE ORDER OF THE BOOT

I'll make it clear right now: I wanted to play for the 2005 Waratahs. I was keen to finish my career in Sydney, where it had all begun. That is where my heart and my loyalty lay. On my personal wish list, staying a Waratah was a long way ahead of any other possible option. When, during the 2004 season, I was made aware that I was to be denied that wish, I took it on the chin because there was no other choice – and I made sure I chose my words carefully when the media asked me how I felt about it. Now, time has passed and the caravan has moved on. With my career progressing into its latter phase a world away, I'll share the story of how I was dumped by the team I had represented for thirteen years, and of how deeply disappointed I felt.

Negotiations concerning the future plans of M. Burke, rugby player, 31, began halfway through the Super 12 season of 2004.

Part of my deal with the Waratahs was an option covering 2005, which was in the NSW union's favour.

My manager, John Fordham, kick-started the negotiations in the autumn of 2004, making first contact with the NSWRU. It was a bit muddy at that stage, as the union didn't have a chief executive officer for a time and the question sort of hung in the air. Who would make the decision: the chairman? The board? The coach? The correspondence flittered back and forth between the Union and Fordo, with the new CEO, Fraser Neill, then coming on board to be part of the mix.

Back from New Zealand, I was suddenly a first-choice player again (at outside-centre). In a brief purple patch of form we beat the Hurricanes 49–31 and the Brumbies 37–29. The latter match was a milestone in my career. My 22 points in that game took me to 950 overall in Super 12 football, topping Andrew Mehrtens' 936, and to a new record. My comments about Mehrtens were described in the media as 'statesmanlike'. They were also sincere. 'To pass a player like Andrew Mehrtens is something special . . . to be on a par with him, to be mentioned in the same sentence as him, I'm stoked,' I said. And I was.

As a married man with two young children and a new home, my preference by a fair space, as I have indicated, was to stay with New South Wales, where my heart was.

The Waratahs lost the final two games of 2004, pipped 29–28 by the Highlanders and then stumbling – again – against the Queenslanders (7–23) in a match that I felt would very likely be my last for New South Wales. We were described as the 'ever-choking Waratahs' following the Highlanders game at Aussie

Stadium, blowing a 28–7 lead against a team who were down to fourteen men for the last 37 minutes after second-rower Filipo Levi had been sent off. On the fulltime bell I missed a shot from in front that would have won the match, the ball cannoning into an upright. Peter Jenkins called the second half collapse 'the greatest implosion in Waratah history'.

I was pictured in the Sunday press, head swathed in bandages to contain a deep cut – and ruing the moment of the missed kick. I told the media of my disappointment – both at missing the kick and at the team letting the game slip from 28–7. The Queensland match brought no more joy. 'Tahs humiliated – Hillbillies put bitter rivals in their place' was one headline.

Another NSW season had ended disappointingly – and short of the semifinals. But I had played the last five full games at outside-centre, contributed 57 points in those games and found some consistent form. I knew my career had some more 'legs' yet.

The premature end of the Super 12 season had arrived as a jolt. Looking ahead, professional football had dried up for me, apart from the prospect of some club footy with Eastwood. Basically, I wasn't included in anything; I wasn't in the elite Wallaby squad, and in mid-May I wasn't named in the train-on squad. Eddie Jones explained that, in their view, I hadn't been consistent enough with my form in 2004. But Eddie did ask me if I planned to play again in 2005. And when I told him 'yes', he said he thought that was the right call – that I still had something worthwhile to offer. As it turned out, his view conflicted with the one that was taking shape within the NSWRU. But it was all sort of fading away. With just a single match to go, against the Pacific Islands team in June, the Waratahs were winding down.

* * *

On the afternoon of Friday, 14 May 2004, after a NSW training session that I had left fairly quickly on its completion, I took two calls at home. The first was a message from NSW coach Ewen McKenzie. 'Mate, I wanted to have a talk with you this afternoon, but I missed you. Give us a call.' Soon afterwards, John Fordham was on the phone. He had been officially informed that day that the NSW Rugby Union had decided not to pick up the option and extend my contract. I wasn't wanted and had been terminated.

I rang Ewen and arranged to meet him at 7.15 the next morning, at Aussie Stadium. I was aware of what was coming, and I had thought it over during the night. I knew what I was going to do: I wasn't going to get upset . . . I wasn't going to plead my case. However gut-wrenching the decision, it had been made – and I had to live with that.

To his credit, Ewen spelled it out clearly to me. The message, essentially, was that I hadn't been consistent enough through 2004, and on that basis the decision had been made not to continue my employment with NSW. He talked about how I had been 'up here' as a player but had slipped back a bit, while some of those around me had pulled themselves up close to the level I had set. I just sat there and took it on board. There was no point in arguing.

I could have asked the question, of course: 'If I'm still "up there", above these other blokes, as you say, why wouldn't you sign me for next year? If that's the case, what's the problem?' But I wasn't going to debate the issue; I understood that my playing level that year probably hadn't been as high as in some previous seasons. I was realistic enough to know that.

The coach went on to talk about his own experience – how he had been through a similar thing near the end of his career and had left the Waratahs to see out his playing days with the Brumbies. 'Mate, my worst fear would be to have you sitting endlessly on the bench next year,' he said. 'I don't want to do that to you.'

I understood where he was coming from, and yet . . . The thought nagged: if I was good enough to play – well, why not let me play?

I shook hands with Ewen and thanked him for his honesty. I appreciated the fact that he had been up front.

The following are some excerpts from the letters that brought the issue of my future as a footballer to a head.

Letter from John Fordham to Fraser Neill, CEO, NSW Rugby Union, 13 May 2004:

As I indicated at our meeting yesterday, Matthew Burke's preferred option is to remain contracted to the NSW Waratahs and Australia for season 2005.

Having assessed his own playing capacity, his interest level and his desire to continue playing, Matthew is of the firm belief that he still has much to offer NSW and Australian rugby. It needs to be remembered that in the past month he clearly outplayed the current Australian and New Zealand No 13s, winning selection in the best Super 12 teams of those particular rounds.

Already newspaper reports are focusing on Matthew's future. The Australian today suggested his Test career "looks over", while a similar piece is likely to appear in the Daily Telegraph tomorrow. It is clearly in the best interests of the game that a decision regarding the option clause is made as a matter of priority.

Letter from Fraser Neill to John Fordham, 14 May 2004:

On the basis that you are looking for an answer immediately, I must inform you that at this point in time, the NSWRU would not be seeking to take up the option to extend Matt's contract.

In terms of Matt's final decision, I believe it is important to stress that we are very mindful of his exceptional contribution to both the Waratahs and New South Wales Rugby.

Suddenly, the working out of my future had gone from being straightforward (New South Wales) to a blank page. It was a strange situation. Under the terms of my contract, the clause relating to 2005 guaranteed that my wage wouldn't be less than what I had been paid in 2004. New South Wales would pay a percentage, and the ARU would come over the top and pay the rest. Eddie Jones's view had been that if New South Wales were worried about the money angle, then yes, the ARU would weigh in to make sure it was okay. But now that New South Wales had said 'no', it was all academic.

I thought back to the conversation I had had with the coach concerning Lote Tuqiri, and realised that I was regarded as 'old culture'. As such, I had been swept aside, despite my own wishes to play on.

The public support I received in the days ahead was amazing. My dad was devastated and kept saying, 'You've got so much support . . . You've got so much support.' And it seemed to be the case, judging from the messages I received.

Later in the season, as discussion about the decision continued, there were strong, supportive and very public words from two of the game's most respected players, Simon Poidevin and Phil Kearns. Poidevin told the *Sun-Herald*'s Danny Weidler, 'I may be biased, because I had the chance to play with Matt and I know how good he is, but I can't see how NSW can afford to let him go. It is definitely a mistake. I don't think NSW can afford to be without him for next season . . . He is the type of player people want to come and see and he is a player that kids aspire to be like. He is a huge loss.'

Phil Kearns added his support: 'It is a blunder not signing up Burke. I don't usually comment on these things because there are other people who are closer to the situation than I am, but you just have to look at how he has played for the Wallabies to see how well he is going. When you look at the balance of the team and the level of experience in the backline for the Waratahs, it stands out that Matt Burke would have been ideal in that side. I really can't understand the thinking behind the decision not to keep him.'

Wherever I go, people seem to say the same thing – that the Waratahs will rue that day they let him go. There seems a great understanding of what Matthew brought to New South Wales over the years and of his qualities. Among many people I talk to, there is an air of disbelief that he was shown the door. It should be remembered, too, that Matt is the same age as George Gregan, who recently signed for three more years with the Wallabies.

John Fordham

Support came from outside the game, too. I heard from a couple of the boys that HSBC CEO Stuart Davies had got up at the annual Waratah Golf Day (HSBC being sponsors of the Waratahs) and said that my presence was missed at the event, and that I had been an integral part of the Waratah culture and makeup. All of it was appreciated.

Most of all at that time I appreciated the great support of all those friends and family who really knew me as a person and of those who understood the game and its workings because of their own involvement. I would also have to thank the public for their unwavering support. People whom I had never met would stop me in the street and convey how disappointed they were by what had happened; sometimes you don't realise until it's time to go how much of an impact you have made.

The obvious support I received from mine and Kate's families was always going to be there, but was still so very reassuring. My father was so upset by what had happened, he cancelled his long-standing season ticket booking with the Waratahs for 2005.

The support extended by those in and around the game, like the Fordham family, Alan King, Sharon Flahive, Tony Dempsey, Greg Craig, Jeff Miller and all of my mates, was so needed at the time. The likes of Alan Jones, John Laws and Mike Carlton showed support through the public domain, and there were also those who supported me on a professional level outside the game, like Denis Handlin and Graham Hardy.

However, the support that I received from players and ex-players was probably the most significant of all. These are the people who have been there and done that, and know how fickle it can all be, the ones I really respect. I would like to make mention of them – without sounding like a name-dropper, they are my mates: Chris Whitaker, Phil Waugh, Morgan Turinui, Nathan Grey, Joe Roff, Phil Kearns, Jason Little, Tim Horan, Jeremy Paul, George Gregan, John Eales, Richard Harry, Adam Freier and Shaun Berne. The day I left to go on tour with the Barbarians, my mobile phone was inundated with messages.

From my point of view, it was a case of: what should I do now?

This last season in Australia proceeded along what was for me, at least, a seriously strange path. Another twist arrived out of the blue: Eddie Jones told me that, notwithstanding his concerns about my 'consistency' in 2004, I was certainly still in the running if the Wallabies happened to strike injury problems. The message essentially was that if there was an injury to the

Wallaby 13 (Stirling Mortlock) I'd be in the squad straight away. In the official Wallaby view I was still the No. 2 outside-centre in the land. Fine . . . I would keep toiling, even if I was a bit confused.

Early one morning at that time, I took a call from 2UE break-fast announcer Mike Carlton, a bloke who had been a supporter of mine over the years. He asked me about how things stood with New South Wales, and I told him of the uncertainty there – and mentioned that I had spoken to the national coach and it seemed that I might still be somewhere in the plans at Wallaby level and that for the time being I would keep training, keep fit, play some club football and hope for the best.

Next thing, Eddie was on my message bank giving me some-thing of a pizzling for having opened up to Carlton. 'What we speak about is private,' was the message. 'I don't expect you to go and tell the world. If you have a problem with that, give me a call.'

I wasn't going to leave it at that, and I rang Eddie back. 'Mate, I'm sorry if anything I said was out of order, but you've got to understand my position,' I said. 'I've just been sacked from my job (with New South Wales) and then when I've spoken to the national coach I've been given a ray of hope that I might still get to play for my country. I just hope you can understand why I might be enthusiastic about that.' There was some frustration at both ends, but I think he understood where I was coming from. It wasn't as if I had been giving away deep, dark secrets. I think by then most people in rugby knew the position.

Eddie and I talked again before the Test match program swung into gear in 2004. I had received an invitation to play with the Barbarians in a three-match tournament in England in late May, and the coach wished me well. 'Go away and have a good trip and find some form,' he said – and in the same breath asked me what my hopes and intentions were beyond that. I said that I still wanted to play Test match football, that I still had the desire, and that if the chance came I would grab it with both hands. I found a question like that immensely frustrating. After giving a decade or so to the game, and achieving at a high level, and loving the experience – *of course* I wanted to keep playing at the highest possible level and for as long as I felt I could still do it. And to find some form in the ad-lib, muck-around, high-enjoyment atmosphere of Barbarians football? It's not really the place.

I had never been to Europe in the summer and I found a new world of sunshine and green fields and long twilights. In Bristol I had the honour of captaining the Barbarians against Wales in the second match of the Staffware Challenge tour. I played two holes of golf, the 17th and 18th at famous St Andrews, and generally had a fine time, and the trek also gave me the chance to have a bit of a look around in the rugby context – with the growing likelihood that an English club contract was a future option for me. But I also knew that the chance of a Wallaby jumper and the rekindling of better things in a difficult season was something worth clinging to. And I did cling to that. And sometimes it's amazing how things work out.

At the same time back home there was unfolding one of the most remarkable and intense times of my career. Almost as soon as I was sacked by New South Wales, I was to find myself back in the Wallaby team – and in the middle of negotiations for my future days in football, the huge bulk of which, thankfully, was handled by John Fordham.

On 22 May 2004, karma took a hand. The big rugby news, eight days after I had been cut by New South Wales, was that a serious knee injury suffered in the Brumbies Super 12 semifinal, would keep Wallaby No. 13 Stirling Mortlock out of football for several weeks. He would miss at least the first Test against Scotland and the Test against England. Suddenly I was back in the frame, back in the squad, back in Wallaby colours. Maybe there were more Tests to be played yet.

On the Sunday, Eddie Jones called me. 'I need to track down Matthew,' he said. 'We want to add him to the Wallaby squad.' Within the space of a truly extraordinary week, Burkey had been told he wasn't wanted by New South Wales and had been invited to join the Wallabies.

John Fordham

In the week before that first Scottish Test in Melbourne, the coach pulled me to one side and said, 'Can I talk to you?' As a footballer you always have a feeling where such a conversation is heading. 'Mate, I've got some bad news for you,' he said. 'You're on the bench. We're going to put Clyde Rathbone at centre.' Raths, of course, was a specialist winger, but a super player, an outstanding competitor and built like a brick you-know-what . . . and with youth on his side. Walking the razor's edge in my career, I had hoped to get a start. But I was becoming pretty good at rolling with the punches by now. There would be no rocking of the boat. I joined the bench brigade.

The message before the game was that the bench guys had better be ready to go – that some of us would get 40 minutes. I warmed up like a freak prior to halftime and after the break and the other boys were laughing and saying, 'Just relax!' I eventually got fifteen minutes and ran around like a chicken with its head chopped off, trying to make some sort of impact. But I kicked a goal in that match, which gave me some satisfaction. Soon after I had come off the bench after the long wait, Sailor scored in the right-hand corner. Walking back, I handed the ball to Roffie, who had been kicking. He gave it straight back. 'Mate, do you want to have a shot?' It was about a centimetre from touch. I suspect he might have been thinking of his average (ha ha). I hit it sweet, absolutely on the spot and the ball soared high between the posts. It was a quietly satisfying feeling – a nod to the doubters. At least I could still do *that*!

In the wake of the Test, and squeezed into the international season, I played my last-ever match for New South Wales on 25 June 2004 against a big, strong Pacific Islands team. I was named at outside-centre, and captain for the game, which seemed to me something of a token gesture, considering that I was one of only a few senior players there. And we got hammered 68–21 in a contest that left plenty of bruises.

It was my 115th cap for the Waratahs and my 32nd time as NSW captain (a record) in a game that seemed unlikely to produce anything much in the way of emotion, considering the very low-key build-up. Most of the media questions I fielded during the week were instead to do with whether or not rugby league's Andrew 'Joey' Johns would be playing rugby union, that being a major media issue of the moment. Johns, with his toughness and high skill level, could certainly have made the changeover successfully.

There was ultimately a huge ongoing squabble and debate over whether rugby administrators had stuffed up the attempted signing of Johns. Maybe. When I made the point that I thought Johns would be a great acquisition for rugby, there was a veiled accusation in the *Sunday Telegraph* – a hint that as I was in the same (Fordham) management stable as Johns, well, I *would* say something like that, wouldn't I? This theory was off the mark. I answered the question I was asked only from the perspective of someone who had played rugby at a high level for years and who therefore was entitled to have an honest opinion on the issue.

With all of that going on, the game against the Pacific Islands was almost an afterthought to me, a postscript. I had virtually accepted that the Queensland final-round Super 12 game on 8 May was the end of my NSW career. And I was deeply angry at much that had gone on. I wasn't too much in the mood for football, but as the national coach had said to me, it was a chance to get some game time.

We went into the match with just two backline moves on the schedule – and I fronted Andrew Friend about it at training. 'We've got to have some other plays,' I said. 'We've got to have something different – we can't do the same thing every time we get the ball.' 'This is it,' Friend said. 'This is what we're going to do.' My frustration certainly didn't add to my enthusiasm for the match. I had a couple of more senior allies alongside in Morgan Turinui and Nathan Grey, and during training I called a couple of different moves. One of them queried me doing that. 'Well, one thing's for sure,' I said. 'They can't drop me after the game!'

I did my best that night to steer an inexperienced Waratah side around the paddock against a big, physical opposition that played with unbelievable intensity and adopted a sort of 'Harlem Globetrotters' approach. They were a team who had stretched some of the best in the world – the Kiwis and the South Africans. After 24 minutes it was 42-nil and I was thinking, 'Holy s—, this is going to be 100-nil.' In the end we got bashed, but in the last hour of the match we got a few things together and managed to compete not too badly, although the scoreline pretty much indicated the way it had been. Nathan Grey was great that night.

There had been vague talk of 'doing something for Matt Burke' in association with the match. But it wasn't a night for great emotion or celebration. The crowd was pretty thin, and there wasn't much at stake. Fordo had earlier raised the idea of a farewell lunch, something I had initially been cool on – not being the sort of bloke who wants to pitch himself into the spotlight. But when this final game fizzled out the way it did, I thought: 'Well, I probably deserve a bit better than that, so why not do the lunch?' Chelsea Spindler, who ran the event, was the clincher. She was adamant I do the lunch, as it would get a great response.

What emotion there was attached to my final game had very little to do with NSW rugby, as it turned out, although the official match program, 'OH' ('Our House'), carried a nice front-cover photo and the line, 'Farewell to a Champion'. The real feeling on the night came instead from the guys in the Pacific Islands team. At the after-match function they sang Polynesian songs, which they do so passionately and well – and in a tribute that I won't ever forget, they gathered around me in a circle and sang. My dad recalls the words of their team manager that night: 'We don't know the name of your prime minister, we don't know the name of your foreign minister . . . but we all know Matt Burke!' I knew a few of them well through Super 12 and other games I had played, and I was deeply touched.

After my 115 matches for New South Wales, and as the longest-serving player in Australian rugby at that time, I had reached the first of what turned out to be a few finales that year.

There are things about that 2004 NSW season that still cut deep. When my immediate competition at standoff (Tim Donnelly) had a hot streak for couple of weeks after I had been injured early, it became very much a case of 'out of sight, out of mind' for me. It honestly seemed that they didn't want any part of me, which was very frustrating. Then we started losing games. When I came back and was playing okay, I was straight away back in the loop. It was a case of, 'Mate, what can we do here to get out of this hole?' And I felt like telling them where to go, because it had been so very apparent earlier in the season, when things were going well, that

I wasn't wanted at all. But when the wheel fell off to an extent, and shits were trumps, things changed.

For the second Test against Scotland, in Sydney, I didn't get a start. I watched the game on TV from the Burke lounge room. Mortlock was gone, and then Matt Giteau picked up a virus and was ruled out of that game. But even with illness and injury, I didn't make the cut. I was out of the loop for the England game in Brisbane, too – the match in which chance dealt a big hand when Wendell Sailor broke down just before the game and Rathbone came in to grab a hat-trick of tries and play brilliantly. Talk about 'seizing the day'!

But I was in the gold jumper again (for ten minutes!) against the Pacific Islands team in Adelaide as the Wallaby campaign continued. It wasn't much, but it was satisfying to be there. Joe Roff got hurt that day, busting up a knee, which was a cruel break – he was playing so well. I got to take another shot from the sideline – and landed the goal. I was now batting two (from touch) from two in this sporadic season. I was contributing to the Wallabies, and that felt good. And I suppose there was a little bit of 'in your face' in the way I felt – to the NSW decision-makers who had shut the door on me.

I got to know a fair bit about being a bench player that season. The regular warm-ups during a match are supposed to take you to a point where they actually simulate playing. At the Adelaide Oval, where we played the Pacific Islands, there seems to be a lack of drainage – and it had rained for four days before that game. The ground was heavy, and running on it seemed to drain away your energy. I spoke to the trainer who was running us: 'I've got to slow down. My legs are dead,' I told him. 'Well, how do you think the blokes out there are feeling?' he retorted. 'Look, my job is to add something fresh,' I told him. 'Not to go in there at the same pace.'

Warm-ups are crucial, and you need to get them right. In the first half you'll have the chance to watch the game for about fifteen minutes – then you'll warm up at fifteen minutes, 25 minutes and 35 minutes, with the last one carrying you through to half-time. In the ten minutes in the change room you listen to the coach do his spiel, which usually includes a word to the subs along the lines of: 'You're an integral part of this team. You could get on at any time now, so keep yourself ready.' At this point the bench players look at each other knowingly. They are thoroughly aware by that time who's going to get on and who's not. In the second half you go straight into another warm-up because you've been sitting in the dressing room for ten minutes, and then it's fifteen, 25, 35 minutes.

For the Tri-Nations match against New Zealand in Wellington in 2004 I was on the bench on a night when it poured with rain without a break. The heavens gave us a real pizzling. The warm-up routine proceeded through the match in the unrelenting downpour, and in the second half I was up at the five minutes, the fifteen minutes, the 25th-minute marks to go through the routine. Late in the game, I looked up at the clock and it was the 35th minute of the second half. I was the only bench player who hadn't got the call. And I made my decision. 'Nup, I'm not going to do this last warm-up.' Instead, I sat there and started to remove the tape from my wrists. It was a safe move . . . the call never came.

It was the worst feeling in the world. I hadn't been on the bench many times over the years, and never before had I failed to get a run. That night I was an outsider – drenched to the skin, and dirty on the world. But I would hold my head up and keep going.

Back in a warmer, drier Perth to face the South Africans in George Gregan's 100th Test, I got sixteen minutes at the end and it was the familiar story of trying to make an impact in a limited time. Fortuitously I got to play in George's record-equalling 101st game and record-breaking 102nd. Again, I had a sideline goal chance when Clyde Rathbone scored to take us to 28–26. Once more, I got a good piece of it and landed the goal. We held on, and won the game 30–26.

My career was now galloping towards its conclusion in Australia. It almost seemed as if time had speeded up, so quickly were things moving. In the lead-up to the game that would end it all for me on home territory – against the New Zealanders, fittingly – thoughts of my career, and of games I had played, darted in and out of my mind. It was a strange build-up for me – contending with this parade of nostalgia in my head, while focusing on what inevitably would be a tough game, and one to which I wanted to make a contribution. I put my head down and concentrated on just doing the normal things I did before any football match.

It turned out pretty well. We won the game, 23–18 – and coming off the bench I got reasonable spells at outside-centre, relieving Stirling Mortlock, who was having trouble with an ankle injury. I was into the match after twenty minutes, and that felt good – to be able to run out there and genuinely contribute, rather than running around 'headless' in the last few minutes. I made some tackles, got the ball in my hands a few times, and kicked a goal. For the first time in quite a while I came off at halftime feeling pretty good – as if I had actually done something. I got the call for the last fifteen minutes, too, and kicked another goal, taking us out to the five-point lead that we held until the end.

My memories of that last game on Aussie soil are very special. On both occasions when I took the field there was an enormous roar from the crowd of more than 80,000, which was very uplifting. At the end I was out there with my Wallaby mates and there was a fair bit of emotion, and kind words from all the guys. Reluctantly, I finished up on the shoulders of Matt Dunning and Jeremy Paul, who were laughing, knowing only too well that I don't like that sort of attention.

Kate came down to the sideline and I was able to see her and give her a kiss – a quiet acknowledgment between the pair of us that something in our lives had finished. I walked to the dressing room alone, and was there for a minute or two before the other guys arrived – and, yeah, I did get a bit emotional then, although there were no tears. Then they were all there and we were singing the national anthem. I had finished on a winning note – although we were without the Bledisloe Cup, which had been won by the All Blacks.

We headed to South Africa for the match that would end it all for me – well, as far as the Southern Hemisphere was concerned. It was a chance for something special. Victory over there would win the Tri-Nations Tournament for Australia and that would be a fine way to go out. Instead, we finished in collective defeat (23–19), and with me down in the dumps. There was no fairytale ending.

Coach Eddie Jones gave me just six minutes on the paddock, the last six – during which I had a shot at goal that missed. Afterwards, I was filthy. He had no obligation to put me on and I understand that – but the team wasn't going particularly well that day and maybe with the experience I have I could have made a difference. I don't know, and I never will now. I felt like a No. 10 batsman at cricket, who doesn't have a lot of opportunity. I guess my disappointment was tied in with the bigger picture – that I would have hoped for a better and more spirited finish to my time in Australian rugby. I have never felt so out of it.

In the dressing room, it was difficult to accept that very probably I would never play football with these blokes again. Our rendition of the national anthem was passionate that late afternoon – and I sat for a long time in the room, soaking up the environment, taking it all in. There were beers, and some kind words offered – but no tears. I appreciated Chris Latham coming up to me to say how much he had enjoyed playing and competing with me over the years. That night we had one of our traditional team 'court sessions', which I left in a very inebriated state. It being my last Test I filled *plenty* of categories that required me to have a drink.

It was now time to settle my future. It had become a pressing necessity. Never had I been more in need of a good and shrewd manager than during those tumultuous days. One branch of my career had ended (New South Wales), another had been rekindled unexpectedly (the Wallabies) – and the great unknown of my future loomed large just down the track, needing to be settled with some urgency. While I concentrated on my football, John Fordham simultaneously juggled the offers and the many steps that needed to be taken – which included having to apply pressure on the ARU so that I could get away.

The first thing that happened was that Queensland, our rugby enemy from the north, came up with an enthusiastic offer, but one that would mean a reduced salary. Their message was pretty much this: 'We understand his quality and we believe it would be great to have Matt among our blokes to help provide direction.'

I didn't take the offer, but when I saw Queensland Head Coach Jeff Miller sometime later, I thanked him. I told him that I genuinely appreciated the offer from up north – and that it had been good for my ego, too! At least *someone* wanted me . . .

If the option was to be taken up by NSW for Matthew to keep playing in the Super 12s, a clause in his contract stipulated that the base playing fee would be 'not less than' what he was currently being paid. The province (in this case, Queensland) offered the maximum amount it could pay, $110,000 – with the 'top-up' to come from the ARU. The ARU offered only $60,000.

That figure wasn't even in the ballpark compared with what Matthew could earn elsewhere. It wasn't a consideration.

Matthew was behind the clock in the quest to be linked with an overseas club. He had anticipated staying with New South Wales and so was behind the eight ball in what the players had christened the 'dash for cash' – the securing of contracts with Northern Hemisphere clubs.

There were various offers for Matt – three from South African Super 12 clubs, one from France, one from Ireland, and three more from UK clubs, apart from Newcastle, who emerged as favourites.

John Fordham

The Newcastle Falcons always had the jump on the others. Negotiations began early between the club's director of rugby, Rob Andrew, and Fordo – the pair being close friends, having first met when Rob played for Gordon in 1986.

When I had been in the UK on the three-match Barbarians tour, Jonny Wilkinson came down to London to spend some time and we went back up to Newcastle, where I met Rob Andrew and was able to have a good look at the ground, and the set-up. I liked what I saw. Subsequently, I had long talks with Andrew Blades about the prospect of going over there and he told me, 'Go – you'll meet a great bunch of people. They play a spirited type of rugby, and it's a fun town. You'll enjoy yourself for sure.'

The first thing was to get an early release from the ARU. Matt was contracted until the end of the year, and Newcastle's firm requirement was for him to obtain a release from the ARU and to be able to join the club by 1 September. There was an initial reluctance by the ARU to grant the release because the domestic season (Tooheys New Cup) hadn't yet finished. Under the ARU guidelines, an early release would be considered if:

- *the player is in the last year of his standard player contract;*
- *the player has played a minimum of 60 games for his province, or 30 Tests;*
- *the player has been a professional player for more than five years.*

John Fordham

Fordo subsequently campaigned hard through the media to get the ARU to do the 'right thing', and journalists Peter Jenkins (*Daily Telegraph*), whom I hadn't considered a supporter of mine (in the latter stages of my career, anyway), and Cameron Bell (*Sunday Telegraph*) took up the cudgels with strongly written articles. The pressure had its effect. The ARU suddenly announced its new 'early release' policy – and I was free to join the Falcons.

By the time I was in South Africa playing my last six minutes in a Wallaby jumper, the deal had long since been done. I was joining the Falcons. We would be gone within a week.

Back home, meanwhile, Kate was slogging away, doing her best to have everything ready so that we could leave for England the following week. I felt bad about not being able to give her more support, due to my Wallaby obligations in those final hectic weeks. But she understood what it meant to me – that I could still play Test rugby right to the end. Kate had packed up the unit, given birth to our second daughter, Edie, unpacked and set up our new house, and then arranged to send all our stuff either into storage or to the UK – all the while looking after the two kids! Kate did *all* the work – an enormous job of getting the Burke family organised.

The week that followed, before our lives changed, was helter skelter. There were people to see and places to go. At the NSW level there was nothing formal, although there was a players' dinner, with wives and girlfriends along, and presentations to Scott Staniforth and me. There I was given the huge honour of having the Waratahs 'Players' Player' trophy named after me for future years – the 'Matt Burke Cup'. Scott Staniforth and I were thanked and farewelled, with Nathan Grey talking about Scott and Chris Whitaker talking about me. Whits was quite emotional and he had even written a poem especially for the occasion. Coming from him, this meant a great deal to me.

In my speech that night I was able to say how I felt about my fellow players, whose support for me had been absolutely outstanding during the recent difficult times. I spoke about what it meant to me to play with such a great bunch of guys, and said that I regretted not getting to know some of the younger blokes as well as I could have – but that I hoped my own career might provide some sort of positive message for them.

The other big event of the week was a farewell luncheon at the Sydney Convention and Exhibition Centre attended by 1000 people, at which I copped plenty, as will be outlined in the next chapter! Wallabies Supporters Club representative Alan King, a bloke I had known since the days when I started in the Sevens, got up at that function and described my sacking and the handling of it by the Waratahs as 'disgraceful'.

The Friday before we left Australia, I hit the wall. I came down with a huge headache that dragged on over a couple of days. It may have been brought on by all the emotion, or I may have picked up a bug in South Africa. On the Saturday, as we loaded containers with all our furniture and effects that were to go into storage, I could barely lift my head. By departure day, the Sunday, I was starting to feel better – but now it was Kate who was feeling the worse for wear, which was no surprise considering all that she had taken on board. The families were at the airport, along with Whits and his wife and two kids, and there was the usual bustle and confusion, an excess baggage problem, and some hugs and maybe a few tears.

The decision to leave Australian rugby wasn't so hard in the end. The difficulty was almost entirely to do with the personal side of it – the fact of having been in our newly refurbished house for just eight weeks, and that now there would be the huge disruption of moving the family to the other side of the world.

When things were rosy for me in football here, the thought of leaving – of *not* finishing my career in Australia – worried me greatly. But it all gradually faded away. I harboured deep disappointment at the way some things had been done, and in the end I thought it best for me, for New South Wales and for Australian rugby if I moved on. I had really had enough of the bitchiness and criticism that was being published in the papers. The thought of going somewhere I was wanted, and just getting away from everything, became increasingly appealing.

One thing was certain: I had no intention of going to England to 'coast' through the remainder of my career. I assured the Falcons people that I was far too competitive for that to happen. My intention was to compete to the limits of my ability – right up to my last day in football.

Finally, we were off with the two little ones, on a flight that is never an easy experience. But we survived, enduring an additional three-hour wait at Heathrow for the connecting flight north. And at last we were in Newcastle – settling into a rented place that we would call home for a while.

At least we were there. The last part of my life in rugby was about to begin.

Chapter 28
ROAST BURKE FOR LUNCH

A few days after I played my last game in the Wallaby gold (well, six minutes of it!) and while I was on the brink of jetting off with Kate, Harriette and Edie on our new adventure, the friendships and threads of my life came together at a *huge* luncheon in Sydney. I'm still amazed by the number of people who came along to say goodbye. In the ballroom of the Sydney Convention and Exhibition Centre on Friday, 27 August 2004, family, friends, acquaintances, and even some people I didn't know, gathered at a function I won't ever forget. There were messages from the likes of Prime Minister John Howard and Steve Waugh. As I knew it would, considering some of the people involved, the 'Matt Burke Tribute Lunch' turned into something of a roast. It was a day of good feelings punctuated by the MC Richard Harry's rallying call for the afternoon: 'Mattie, Mattie, oi oi oi . . . Burkey Oi, Burkey Oi . . . Mattie, Mattie Burke.' The lunch offered some insights, plenty of emotion and a lot of fun. What follows is an edited version of some of the things said by those who got up in 'tribute'.

It all began with Dick telling the gathering: 'I could think of no better way to while away a Friday afternoon than to blow an enormous amount of smoke up Matt Burke's arse' And it sort of went on from there, a commentary on the life and times of M. Burke – all in great spirit and with humour, which is just the way I feel about playing the game of rugby union. The irreverence came after a more serious tribute, read out by Dick, from my friend and manager, John Fordham, something that I greatly appreciated.

Matthew Burke was always destined to be a great rugby player, and someone who would make an indelible contribution in so many ways to a game he first perfected as an athletically advanced student at St Joseph's College in Sydney. Such was his early maturity and skill level that young Burke skipped the normal process of graduating to grade rugby by way of Colts and powered straight into first grade for Eastwood in 1991. His Wallaby calling came quickly as a twenty-year-old in August 1993 against the South African Springboks. Exactly eleven years later, in August 2004, this point-scoring phenomenon played his 81st and final Test for the Wallabies against the same nation in Durban. During his spectacular career, we saw him become Australia's most capped and greatest fullback and second-highest point-scorer of all time. Matthew Burke, his versatility spreading to three positions, proudly wore Wallaby gold against sixteen international teams. Along the journey, he rewrote the record books both for world and Australian rugby. On numerous occasions he was the Wallabies' match winner, scoring all of Australia's 24 in a 1998 Bledisloe win against the All Blacks, and also 25 of Australia's 35 points in the World

Cup final against France in 1999. Wearing the sky-blue of the NSW Waratahs told a similar story as well. His record-breaking 115 appearances for the state team netted him 1175 points and fittingly enabled him to become the highest point-scorer in Super 12 history during his final year with the province. While the curtain gracefully falls on Matthew Burke's incredible rugby legacy in Australia, the welcome awaits him in the United Kingdom where his special qualities as a player and a person will be admired and enjoyed by a legion of new fans.

Dick Harry continued by listing various records I had established, including 'Most towel snaps against another guy's arse, Dublin, 1998'. I guess people were getting the drift as to how it might develop!

Proceedings continued with Phil Kearns recounting with glee the story I told earlier of NSW coach Greg Smith's theory, expounded at training one day, that, if according to statistics one bloke in twenty was a 'poof' then there must be one in the Waratah ranks. Said the coach to Kearns: 'We've got fifteen blokes running around here . . . look at Matthew Burke . . . look at his hair . . . I think he's our poof!'

Dick Harry: 'A very insightful man, Greg Smith. Now, as this is the official arse-kissing Matthew Burke ceremony, I've got to ask you: mate, what's your most enduring memory of Matthew Burke?'

Phil Kearns: 'Oh, it's his hair. I mean, it's perfect on every occasion. He would be at the bottom of a ruck or a maul, and he'd pop out and it would be perfect. We've always wondered if it was a wig. I think probably the most enduring moment for me is when he scored that try to win the Bledisloe Cup in 1998 and smashed his shoulder. I actually set it up for him, and he has never thanked me to this day for doing that . . .'

Dick Harry: 'It reinforces why we hate them [backs] so much.'

Phil Kearns: 'Now, I'm going to invite three guys up here on the stage to have a chat about Burkey. The first of them played 75 Tests for Australia in a number of positions across the backline. He was captain of the Wallabies on one occasion, versus the United States, where his opposition players scored the only try against the Wallabies in that tournament. Will you please welcome Jason Little? Number two is a player who played ten Tests for Australia, went to the mighty Newington College, but was really the black sheep because he actually played first grade at Newington before coming to the Wallabies. Most people know that you have to play *second* grade at Newington if you want to come to the Wallaby side. Whenever he is out on the drink, the share price of Southern Comfort goes berserk. Would you please welcome Scott Bowen up to the stage? And finally, one of the greatest players I've had the fortune of playing with. A wonderful player, a wonderful guy, played twenty Tests for Australia, sat on the bench so many times it was painful. He is the creator of the George Gregan voodoo doll. Can you please welcome Chris Whitaker?

'I emailed these guys about ten days ago and said "Guys, can you give me a bit of info so that I can lead you into a couple of stories so that it will make it a really good day today?" Nothing . . . I got nothing. And I pushed a little bit harder and Scottie Bowen responded. So, I got a little bit from Scott. I spoke to Whits on the mobile before I arrived here, and I said: "Whits, have you got something for me?" And he said, "For what?" I said, "We've got the lunch today." "Oh, shit. Is that today?" he said. And Jason rang me today at about eleven o'clock to confirm that he had nothing. So, we could be – oh, maybe 30 seconds up here. Now, Whits, you took over the captaincy from Burkey at the NSW level. Was he really a shit captain?'

Chris Whitaker: 'No, not at all. That was probably one of the toughest times I think the Waratahs have seen. The coach rang me and said, "Look, mate, we're thinking of offering you the captaincy." And my first thought was, "Well, what about Burkey?" And so I rang him up and he was sensational. Nothing but supportive. Right behind me the whole way, and throughout the year right behind the whole team, in the way he did things. So, really, he was still the leader of the team. Everyone looked up to him. Everyone still does, although I think in the end everyone got sick of his shit stories.'

Phil Kearns: 'So, Scottie, out of all of us here, you've known Burkey longer than anyone. You ran into each other at school level. Tell us about that.'

Scott Bowen: 'Well, Matt came from the rugby nursery, St Joseph's College. The late 1980s, 1989, was his first appearance for that First Fifteen. Many people wouldn't know he actually started in the five-eighth position. Earlier this year, I had a call from Bob Dwyer about Matt and the position that he perhaps should play this season and perhaps looking at him as a long-term five-eighth. I said to Bob, "Mate, it would be the worst decision ever made." Joey's don't lose too many matches from year to year, and in this game we played them at Newington and we won 10–7. Matt played five-eighth that day and it was probably the *last* time he played five-eighth. I played Matt at cricket as well, and I always tried to rattle him because he is a very composed person. When I was bowling, and I was a very ordinary bowler, I used to jog back to my mark, keep the pressure on top of him. He would play his shot, I'd call for the wicket-keeper to throw the ball back to me, and I'd jog back to the mark, ready to send the next one down. He had the composure to step away a couple of times, which gave me the real shits, and this went on and on to where my overs would end up taking about three or five minutes when I was trying to get through them. So, from a very early age he showed that great composure.'

Phil Kearns: 'Did you sledge him?'

Scott Bowen: 'All the time. If you have ever played golf with him, and I know you have, he hates the chat and it's something that I can rattle him with. I like to talk while I'm actually hitting the ball, and it's something that really frustrates him. So, certainly I chip away at him.'

Phil Kearns: 'Whit, Burkey is a master storyteller. Tell us about that.'

Chris Whitaker: 'He's got a couple of different names. One is "Mash", because, like the TV series *MASH*, Burkey's stories just keep reappearing. I think he gets into a problem when he starts telling a story and then it kind of doesn't go anywhere, and he realises that and tries to make something out of it and it doesn't work, as it started off as a shit story. Among the Waratahs now they are just called "Burkey stories".'

Phil Kearns: 'It's like talking to your grandma – you know, every tiny little detail of the story. And you just go, "Hurry *up*!"'

'He does – well, he did in a previous life – like a little bit of a punt every now and again. Does he still pop into the casino, or is he cured of that?'

Chris Whitaker: 'I think he still does. He's married now, so he might have changed his ways, but when we go away down to Adelaide or somewhere where there is a big casino you can usually find him there. He's a bit of a sole punter. He usually gets there by himself. If you say, "Can I come along?" and you don't know what you're doing, he definitely doesn't want you by his side. It's the same with *anything*, I think. Over the years he has put so much time and effort into the little things, for *me*, anyway, such as my golf. I'm probably one of the worst golfers you will ever see, and I find it frustrating playing with Burkey on a golf course, where he plays more rules than they do at the PGF. And then when it comes to my kicking, he tries to help me with *that*, too. He is so patient.'

Phil Kearns: 'Yeah, apparently he gambles with his children now . . . has a punt on the red or black . . . "I'll put my kid on it."'

'Now, Scottie, in his first NSW game you set him up pretty well. Against Wellington, three tries.'

Scott Bowen: 'He did thank me after the game. He's a very difficult subject because he has done so many things perfectly . . . You know, his whole demeanour is pretty good. I will get a "thank you" at some stage. It was against Wellington at Concord Oval. I think we had a fairly young side, you [Phil Kearns] were captaining the side ferociously up front on that occasion, and Matt scored three tries on his debut – an outstanding debut – and certainly started positioning himself for that run-in to the Wallabies later that year.'

Phil Kearns: 'Which he can thank *you* for.'

Scott Bowen: 'Well, sort of. I've got a lot of thanks for him with his goal-kicking. That helped me get selected in about 50 matches. In the old Greg Smith days, I used to have to go over and help Matt retrieve the balls, because Greg made it quite clear to me that I was only in the team while Matt could kick goals. So, I had to help out. I'd stay at North Sydney Oval to 9.30, 10.30 at night. However long it took Matt to practise, I would be there returning the footballs.'

Phil Kearns: 'That's very true. The alternative five-eighth was David Knox, who could kick goals, so that is absolutely a true story. Jason, anything to add? No? OK, let's move on.'

Jason Little: 'Actually, thanks for that introduction, Phil. I thought I had nothing to add until I saw Phil "Eddie McGuire" Kearns trying to do a panel interview.'

Phil Kearns: 'Gee, that's a cracker, mate – you've really got them rolling in the aisles now. He's super-competitive. When you're struggling for things to do in the airport when you are on tour, travelling, any old game would do. And he hates to lose.'

Scott Bowen: 'It comes back to the casino, I think, too. He puts the hours in there and finally gets the rewards. Whether it's 4 am or 6 am, he eventually goes home with the money in the pocket. I can remember at Zimbabwe Airport, sitting there tossing coins at a wall; we were filling in some time, and sitting there betting was the theme. Yeah, he's very, very competitive in everything he did and obviously was always a standout performer. He took *my* money.'

Phil Kearns: 'He's taken a *lot* of our money.

'So, what is your overriding memory of Burke? I mean, of all the things you could say about him, good or bad – hopefully, they'll be bad – what do you think about him as a bloke, mate, player? I mean, what *makes* him a great player?'

Chris Whitaker: 'I think you can be a good player, but I think you need a strut – and he has got that strut. If anyone has seen him after he has kicked a goal, he's got that perfect tee toss . . . then the arms go back and the hair goes back. So, I definitely think you need something like that to be a great player. He's probably one of the greatest.'

Scott Bowen: 'I think it's just that outstanding composure under any circumstances that has made him such a great player. It's going to be interesting, him heading over to Newcastle . . . Who's going to get the goal-kicking duties over there between Jonny Wilkinson and himself? He is obviously an outstanding player. Great athlete, as well. He's someone who could probably have taken on any sport and been successful in it.'

Phil Kearns: 'Jase, have *you* got anything. No? OK. He's going to Newcastle – maybe you can tell us about Newcastle?'

Jason Little: 'Thank you, Matthew, for the invitation to come up and be part of the panel. It's been fantastic. Actually, you were asking about quality players. I think Steve Waugh touched on it when he said Burkey has the great ability – and it *is* very rare among international players – to play better against New Zealand and South Africa than against Canada or the lower countries like the United States or Namibia. I think that is what sets him apart from just being a good player and makes him a fantastic player.'

Phil Kearns: 'Do you have one overriding memory of Burkey? Does any particular game bring back special memories?'

Jason Little: 'Actually, I don't think there is *one* – but I have similar memories of Burkey as you, and I think we got a bit of a glimpse of it in that video footage: the different changing hairstyles as he progressed. I will be interested to see when he gets back from Newcastle and stops dyeing his hair, what it looks like.'

Dick Harry (introducing Peter Fenton): 'Peter . . . so familiar to us all for that literary classic of self-sufficiency, "There was a young man from Nantucket". Ladies and gentlemen, Peter Fenton.'

Peter Fenton: 'Thank you, Dick. I had the pleasure of coaching Dick some years ago. He was a flanker and I said, "Go to the front row" – and, Dick, look what happened to you. I take some of the credit. When you write poetry, whether you write it for fun or for money (and I usually write for money and it turns out to be fun), you tend to go back to your childhood or your youth. When you are a boy you are very impressionable, and the people you go to watch are the ones who really get inside you. And most of my early times, I wrote about cricketers who I saw at the Sydney Cricket Ground in the late 1940s – Bradman and Lindwall and Miller and Neil Harvey, and so on. Now and again you see someone who prompts you to write poetry. And in 1991 young Matt Burke came down to Eastwood and I saw him train, I saw him trial – and we graded him in first grade, obviously. And it was very apparent that he would be a very, very good player. But just how *great* a player he would become was always a bone of contention. He was big, he was very, very fast, he had a lovely sense of balance – he was a beautifully balanced runner. But the one thing that really knocked me out about Matt Burke was that he was totally ambidextrous. He passed left to right as well as he did right to left. He could kick with both feet. Not just punting the ball, but drop-kicking the ball – even place-kicking the ball, which is a very, very rare phenomenon. To be able to do it means he has unbelievable balance, and I went away and wrote a poem inspired by this young boy. I didn't want to put his name in it, because I had seen similar players who had had too much pressure put on them by people saying, "Here comes the next whoever." I remember a kid I saw, Ian Craig, get 200 runs when he was only seventeen. I didn't mention Burkey's name. I just called the poem "The youngest cub". I wrote the last verse ten years later. I'm not going to say anything about you, Burkey, when I have finished the poem, except to say I'm pleased I got it right and you have been an absolute sensation.'

THE YOUNGEST CUB

The coach stands alone in the damp dressing room
As he watches his players prepare
And his eyes come alive in the dark and the gloom
As the youngest cub enters the lair.
And though he's the newest in all of the team
And this is his first major task,
He has talent galore or so it would seem
But the coach knows how much he should ask.

For well does he know that the lad's native skills
Will help but they won't be enough,

If the heat of the battle his confidence kills
If the task proves a little too tough.

For many a man will be born with the flair
To attack and to conquer the field,
But many a man when exposed to the glare
Will falter and stumble and yield.

He silently beckons the young man away
To a quieter part of the shed,
And again they go over the part he will play
As the youngster hears every word said.

For so many times the same words he'll employ
When a youngster's to make his debut,
'Relax, take your time, the game's there to enjoy
Your talent will see you come through.'

Now the coach settles back to watch how he goes
To see how he handles the heat,
But the lad is all class from his head to his toes
And his poise is an absolute treat.
He does things in a game you see once in a while
And he does them with consummate ease,
He kicks with both feet and he breaks with a style
That the toughest of critics must please.

Oh, he'll be a champion, no doubt of that
The crowd he will hold in his hands,
Barring bad luck or a chequebook so fat
They'll be chanting his name in the stands.

Ten seasons have passed since the boy took his bow
But with patience and courage and work,
He struts on the stage, there's no stopping him now
For the boy in the verse was Matt Burke.

Phil Kearns (introducing George Gregan): 'Now, niggle golf. Talk us through that, because you are the champion of niggle golf.'

George Gregan: 'Well, it is open slather, really. All the golf etiquette goes out the window. So, it's basically prison rules when you go out there from the first tee. Ripping the gloves at the top of the swing, putting it into reverse – all types of things. Throwing balls across the other person's vision at the top of their swing. Anything you can do to try and put the person off is fair game. And Burkes and I have had many a game like that, and I hate to say it doesn't rattle him much. A little bit of liquor or silence in those games is probably the best thing you can do. We've had some good times together on the course.'

Phil Kearns: 'What's he play off?'

George Gregan: 'Well, I think he's playing *now* the handicap that he probably should have been playing for the last eight years. He's off about six or seven now. He used to try to get it out to about ten or eleven. He would always be coming back shooting 73s, 74s, 75s. He's looking at me down there and holding his poise, because he knew exactly he should have been playing five or six for the last ten years and he's finally down to a handicap which I still think is a little bit higher than it should be. He is *always* taking my money.'

Phil Kearns: 'Valvoline. One of Burkey's nicknames is "Valvoline". How did that come about?'

George Gregan: 'Well, I think I pretty much led into it a little bit with the handicap scenario. He's a slippery character – quite oily. He's oily on the golf course and he has that demeanour – everyone thinks of him, you know, as that *Matthew Burke, the boy next-door.* Fantastic. Hair's always in good shape and all that type of thing. But he is a slippery character. Underneath that demeanour there's a very, very competitive, wants-to-win-at-all-costs, type of character. But a good guy to be around – and a great mate.'

Phil Kearns: 'Bad habits?'

George Gregan: 'Bad habits? Probably [the] MASH [thing] – that's probably one of his worst habits. But I love hearing his stories, because I like the banter that goes with them. So, I kind of let him go. I like saying, "I haven't heard that one, Burkes" – and he keeps rattling on. And it all starts up – everyone starts singing the *MASH* tune. I find that funny. But it's hard to get those stories out of him now.'

Phil Kearns: 'Oh, God, he can bore for Australia when he tells a story. Now, the World Cup semifinal, 1999. What was it – 18-all, I think, at the end of fulltime? Burke and Janni de Beer goal for goal. He had to step up and slot that last one. What was going through your head? I mean, I've got to hand it to Burkey . . . We couldn't have a better bloke.'

George Gregan: 'It wasn't me, mate [as captain]. It was Ealsie.'

Phil Kearns: 'But, mate, you were in the team.'

George Gregan: 'I was. You were there, too. But Burkes – you couldn't rely on a better bloke in that situation. I think in crisis under pressure there is no better guy to throw the ball to. It's amazing. He would just knock it over. And that has been a hallmark of his career, I think. Gary Pearce [who spoke earlier] pretty much set out how important he was to the team with those numbers. Every time he ran out, it gave you a certain peace of mind as a captain. When I have been the captain and he has been the kicker, it has just been a real nice feeling knowing that he will strut up and kick the goal.

'It's a thankless task, kicking goals. I honestly believe that they win games, they don't lose games, and he has won so many games for Australia with that right boot of his, and it's a tough job.'

Phil Kearns: 'You have seen lots of really good players over your career, but what separates the good from the greats?'

George Gregan: 'My first images of Burkes, not that he would have picked it up, was probably in 1990 when he came down to Canberra playing against Marist. He was outside-centre that day. They had a pretty red-hot team and they just did a number on this Marist team, and I can remember seeing Burkes. All those things that Peter Fenton said about him – balance, time to do things – he just had it all. And I remember thinking, "Gosh, *that* guy can play. Who's that?" Before you know it, he's running out for the Wallabies, he's playing for New South Wales at a very young age – and it didn't surprise me at all, because I got a glimpse of him in 1990 as a schoolboy.'

Phil Kearns: 'Is there one image of Burkey as a player or on the field that you remember at an international level? Do you remember just sitting back and thinking, "My God, that bloke's good"?'

George Gregan: 'Probably the 1996 game. Everybody probably remembers. We got off to a red-hot start against the Blacks and we ended up fading and losing it in the end. I think we got off to about a twenty points lead, and he scored this amazing try where I think he caught a high ball or a kick return and he basically dummied, jinked, ran 80 metres – it was the sort of stuff you see when you are watching the Under 7s, you know, the guy who has just got it all. He did that at Bledisloe level, and running around guys like Zinzan Brooke. He just went coast to coast and scored this amazing try. And in that game, too, I remember we got a penalty about 55 metres out. He pointed it at the post and knocked it over – and it sounded like a cannon going off. At 55 metres you would think it would be *just* going over the posts, but it was still going up as it went through and that to me highlights the sort of player Matt

Burke was. He was a real talent and a great guy to be in a team with. I was fortunate to play a lot of Tests with him.'

My own speech, which concluded the day, was largely one of thanks – to all the people who had worked to put together a fantastic function; and, more broadly, to all the people who had supported and guided me in my career. But I was able to fire off a few shots in return, too – to the likes of Kearns, Harry and Gregan. We had footage of Phil in the midst of a big stink in a match, and of Dick Harry complaining to a referee that an opposing forward had grabbed him by the testicles. 'It gives you an insight into what forwards really do on the field,' I told the audience. I also told a yarn about a video of support Phil had sent from home to the touring Wallabies before a big match. Within the team at that time we had a saying, 'Keep 'em nude' when we were working at keeping an opposing side scoreless. In the video, Phil was standing in beautiful warm Australian sunshine with his shirt off as he conveyed his good luck message. Then the camera gradually panned out, and he was standing there completely starkers. 'Keep 'em nude!' said Kearnsie. And we had footage of George with hair, which brought a good laugh. 'Like Jay Jay of *Good Times*,' I said.

I went out of my way to clarify a small matter in regards to Scott Bowen, and Bob Dwyer, who was in the audience: 'Bob, do you remember when we were back in Canada on one of our first trips, and it was freezing cold and you were doing an interview under the goal-posts? We had finished training and were taking some goal shots, and Scott kicked a ball and it hit you flush on the head. Scott walked away, and as I was the next person lining up, you yelled at me and gave me "the eyes". Bob, I just wanted to tell you it wasn't me.'

Members of my immediate and extended family were in the audience, and I tried to express how important they had all been to me. I thanked my mum and dad for the sacrifices they had made for me – and for never being pushy and just providing guidance. To Kate, I said: 'I love you so much . . . You are the major reason I played the game.' I tried to find the words to express how much I appreciated the support she had provided in my life for so long, and particularly in the last couple of years when things had been very tough at times. 'When I'm injured, I'm the worst person in the world to live with,' I admitted.

And I thanked the NSW and Australian rugby unions for the chance to play the game, and to travel the world. I thanked the players with whom I had shared the journey, and made the point that rugby is a players' game. I thanked the audience – and told them I was overwhelmed that so many people had come along to say farewell.

'I have had no regrets about playing the game,' I concluded. 'I've had injuries, but I've had a fantastic time, too. I think more than anything else, I've had fun.'

With that, I closed it down, called fulltime. It was time for a beer, I suggested.

It had been a wonderful occasion and, best of all, it had raised $60,000 for the Humpty Dumpty Foundation. The events of the lunch swirled in my head for a long time afterwards, and I know that the day will always stay in my mind.

It was 48 hours later that Kate, Harriette, Edie and I were on a plane, flying across the world to begin a new life.

Chapter 29

LAST FLIGHT OF THE FALCON

As I put these final words together, I am now 32, living in England's northeast, 20,000 kilometres from home – and am very likely in better physical shape than I have ever been. I don't feel like a footballer at the end of his run. And yet there has been a pervading mentality in Australian rugby that when a player gets to 30 his use-by date has arrived and it's a case of, 'See you later. It's time to go and get a *real* job.' I felt the sting of that in 2004 when New South Wales showed me the door with these words: 'You're not at a consistent level anymore. The other blokes are catching up to you. Yeah, you're still ahead of them – but they're catching up.'

I think that, in general terms, the attitude within Australian rugby to senior players has been misguided. Why discard experienced senior blokes just when they can play such a vital role in 'mothering' the young players of the next generation? Years on the board shouldn't matter if a player can still come out and do his stuff at the weekend. And there is a case for some more flexibility regarding the match preparation of senior guys. If a player needs a week with a lot of time in the swimming pool owing to a knee that has blown up, and then if the same bloke can come out and deliver the goods on the field at the weekend, he should be there. Producing the goods on match day should be the only criterion. A classic example is a bloke like rugby league's Cliffie Lyons, who played – and at a sustained high and creative level – into his late thirties. Although he was never regarded as much of an achiever on the training paddock, Cliff could do it in the 80 minutes of the match, so he was entitled to be there – and he always was. I think that playing football is a psychological thing, more than anything else. Whatever your age, if you're up to it mentally, you'll be there physically.

I was intrigued to read the words of Lions coach Clive Woodward on the subject in an interview he did with the *Sydney Morning Herald*'s Ben Kimber on 11 December 2004. Kimber wrote:

With captain George Gregan and five-eighth Stephen Larkham, two veteran players who appear set to continue through to Paris 2007 (World Cup), when Gregan will be 34 and Larkham 33, Woodward believes the presence of players with significant experience, despite their age, would be a crucial factor, as it was for England last year. 'No concerns at all (with the age of players). I'd say the opposite,' he said. 'We thought it was fantastic when we went down there and were called Dad's Army, because I knew what shape these guys were in physically, the Leonards, the Johnsons, the Backs. I'd say from Australia's point of view, with players of the quality of Larkham and Gregan going to go on, as far as Eddie Jones is concerned I'd be saying that's fantastic. It'd be like Martin Johnson and Lawrence Dallaglio saying, "Yeh, I'm going to keep playing for England." I wouldn't be saying, "Are we sure?" I'd be jumping up and down for joy . . . there's no doubt in my mind.' Woodward believes so strongly that age is no barrier, he is even considering calling his retired World Cup heroes back to international duty to join him on his next project, the British and Irish Lions tour of New Zealand, in his capacity as Lions coach.

I can only agree with these sentiments. I was appreciative, too, of some later words from former Australian rugby league coach Chris Anderson, with whom I had crossed paths a couple of times in the UK after he had jumped codes to coach Welsh rugby side Newport Gwent Dragons. In an interview published in the Sydney *Sunday Telegraph* in February 2005, Anderson offered a kind assessment of my form in England. He said: 'The best union player I have seen over here so far is Matt Burke. He is quality. He's hurt us the two times we played them.'

It hasn't been easy for Kate and me to start a 'new life' here in Newcastle with our two small children. But we're getting there. On our arrival, we moved into a rental property, and we juggled one car, between what I had to do training-wise with the Falcons and Kate's commitments with the kids, as she worked to hold the whole thing together. And we missed the social and family net-work that can make life easier for a young family. But early on, Kate and I found a gym close to home and that became a bit of a haven for us.

There were small advances, step by step and day by day – and we were helped considerably by Mark Mayerhofler, ex NZ Crusader and All Black, and his wife, Jayne, who had been through the same thing and gave us support and practical advice. I'm sure that anyone who uproots and moves to a new country has to make the same adjustments.

I am a lucky man. Kate and I have our two beautiful daughters – Harriette, born in September 2002, and Edie, born in March 2004. And I have a beautiful wife. There is a cliché about there being a woman behind every successful man. But as far as I'm concerned, it's the other way around. First, there is a great woman . . . and *then* there is the bloke (in this case, me!). Kate has been a source of inspiration for my life and my football career these recent years. She used to joke that she was third on the list; it was footy, the car . . . and then her. It was never *really* like that – she is No. 1. Kate's guidance has been invaluable in my football career – she has provided the clarity that sometimes can only come from someone who is one step removed. When you're right in the middle of the rugby world, you can get caught up in your own crap without really noticing. It's good to come home and talk about things – and to get the benefit of another perspective. In the year and a half before we took the step of moving to the UK – a time when I was getting screwed around a bit – she was a continuing source of pragmatism and common sense.

And she helped me through the bad times, because she lived them as well. I made no fuss at the time, but the period before I was dumped by New South Wales in 2004 wasn't easy. There were comments and newspaper stories that Kate had to wear as much as I did – stuff along the lines of I was too old and too slow. 'Piss him off,' they virtually said. And this was from blokes who knew little about the sport and what it takes to play for your country. There were sleepless nights then. But Kate was a tower of strength throughout it all. I suppose I sought solace from being with my family when things weren't going too great. And it was always there . . .

My life has broadened and deepened in recent years. Once there had been footy – and that was about it. But I have realised that being able to come home after a tough day to a kiss from my wife and a cuddle from the kids makes everything else pale into insignificance. My family is the biggest part of my life.

Life hasn't been too easy for Kate, being married to a professional footballer. Because of my job, I have missed a fair bit, leaving Kate to take care of everything at home. I found the touring life hard, being away from her and home and the kids. But it's the way it is for all of us who choose this career path – and it's the world's best job, so I can't complain too much. When the Waratahs made their decision that they had no further need of me, one of the attractions of the offer from Newcastle in the UK was the knowledge that the four of us would at least be together as a family most of the time. The English competition requires only fairly limited touring and only the occasional camp. I can be home by four o'clock each day, so I have time to play with my kids and watch them grow.

But, in order to support the girls and me, Kate has had to step away from her own career, which is no small thing. Essentially, she made the uncomplaining decision to live *my* life and follow *my* dream – and that's a tough call. I'm a lucky bloke.

In Newcastle the settling-in period continues. It's hard to get a good sandwich or a good coffee around here, and in the months from September to December the weather gradually went from mild to freezing. I took the car for a wash one December morning, and when I drove out of the place, it was snowing. But the people are friendly and welcoming. And walking into a football club meant that I was automatically part of something good – of mateship and camaraderie, and of a shared experience with 30 or so other blokes who would become my mates. For me it has been a lot easier than for Kate and the girls.

Training with the Falcons is a very different experience from what it had become at home. At Newcastle the regime is much less structured than at the national level. There are no fitness tests, no set program in terms of the weight program – you just turn up and do your stuff and then you head on. You could do four lifts one day, and 40 the next. All of it is under the tutelage of a bloke called Steve Black, who has been a real revelation to me. Blackie talks about the importance of enthusiasm in football and about how the pace of training should equate to the pace of the game. The only problem is that I have trouble understanding him at times, owing to his rich Geordie accent!

I like the Steve Black approach a lot. It's such a break from the statistics-based system I had been used to in recent seasons, where we had stats coming out of our ears. The figures would be thrown at us relentlessly: 'Mate, you're 4 per cent down on your fitness this week and you're 1.7 per cent down on your strength.' Blackie's approach is more holistic. If a player has had a sleepless night because of a baby, and struggles at training, he will take that into account. He cares little about a player's age – he is basically of the belief that you should play as long as you want to, as long as you're still up there mentally and physically. This is music to my ears!

Blackie approaches each individual differently, rather than taking a 'collective' approach to the team. His ideas are interesting and full of common sense, and seem to bring results despite the doubters over here. (Three Newcastle players tested first, second and fourth in the autumn fitness trials for the England side.) He doesn't believe in pre-training stretching. The stretching is done afterwards, when you're warm. Much of the work revolves around speed. Within three or four days of meeting Steve Black, I was enthusiastically on board with his beliefs – and keen not to let him down. He has a certain aura about him.

The team has been great – and very welcoming to the colonial interloper. In a defensive drill in the first week of training, I found myself being instructed where to go by a prop – and I couldn't help laughing, only because it had never happened to me before. The skills of the team are fantastic, and there is a big emphasis on catching, passing and kicking.

And the matches?

This first season for me is, of course, still very much a work in progress, albeit with some early successes for the Falcons – and notably in the prestigious Heineken Cup, which we kicked off with four straight wins. The style of play is inevitably shaped by the weather here each season – and I suppose it always has been, since competition rugby started back in the nineteenth century. At the start of the season you can play dry-weather rugby; but as winter blows in and the snow and rains and freezing days come, the game has to be played to suit. At that time it becomes virtually ten-man, or even eight-man, rugby. At the back-end of the season, when spring comes creeping back, there is the chance to play a more expansive game again. It's the annual challenge of UK rugby.

I suffered a shoulder injury not long after we arrived, and that required a week's break – but from then I got into a pretty good groove, playing fullback. In three successive games at home (Kingston Park), I was able to get the 'Man of the Match' vote, including one for a three-try effort in a match against Leeds that left me with a busted nose. My run of good form and good fortune led to jokes about the name of the award being changed to 'Matt of the Match'.

When I had been here not too long at all, there was even talk of my being conscripted into the touring Wallaby squad – although I can say now that it was never going to happen, despite the headlines that appeared. 'Burke set to reprise Test role,' said one newspaper. 'Injury stricken tourists may be forced to call on Burke,' said another.

The story surfaced in a flurry of concern after the Wallabies had lost to France in Paris. In the wake of that match, John Fordham took a call from rugby journalist Peter Jenkins, who told Fordo that Australian coach Eddie Jones had told him that my recruitment to the tour was under consideration. This was following the serious injury suffered by Steve Larkham against the Scots, and when Mat Rogers' immediate future was under a cloud because of a pending enquiry into an Edinburgh nightclub incident.

Fordo subsequently sent an email to Eddie Jones, in which he wrote: 'Eddie, there is a lot of media coverage here speculating on whether Matthew Burke will be approached by Wallabies management to play against England. Our response has been based on:

1. We have not been approached by the ARU or Wallabies management.
2. Matthew's contract with the ARU ended several months ago.
3. He is contracted to the Newcastle Falcons.'

Fordo then asked Eddie if he could throw any light on the situation.

Eddie Jones's curt reply was: 'John – we will be in touch if we need Matt.'

Fordo was less than impressed. He said later: 'In the circumstances, even if he had received an approach [from Wallabies management] and notwithstanding how much Matt had treasured the honour of playing for the Wallabies, he would not have played.' His words reflected exactly the sentiments I had relayed to him.

When John told me of Eddie's response to his email, I felt like saying to the coach: 'Hang on! If you need me, will *I* go? *That's* the question.' And the answer to that is: 'No, I wouldn't have played.' I hadn't finished my time in Australian rugby in the happiest of circumstances, and as far as I was concerned the ending there had been exactly that – an ending. My allegiances now lay with the Newcastle Falcons, who had shown faith in me.

In the end the Wallabies didn't ask. They had blokes in the squad just itching for a run – players hanging out for the sort of opportunity that was being presented. The Wallabies, of course, went on to beat England – and that was great.

My thoughts on Eddie Jones, Australian coach from 2001 when Rod Macqueen stepped down after the Lions tour of Australia, are somewhat mixed – but favourable overall. When he took over the reins from Macqueen he was a breath of fresh air, as a new coach inevitably is. Inheriting a good Australian side, he probably let the team run its own course in the early stages of his tenure. He then started to cut the cloth his way, to shape the direction of the team in line with his coaching beliefs – which is exactly what coaches do.

Eddie is most definitely from the school of coaching that embraces percentages as the source of all knowledge in the game. He's certainly fixated on stats and loves the percentages and having the hard-copy printout in front of him. With Eddie it wasn't a case of 'How did you feel?', but 'Here's how you went.' His style is a management one – of working towards targets using almost mathematical formulas, which, if his team can get them right, will mean that no one can beat them.

He's a terrific worker – a round-the-clock worker, sometimes to the detriment of people around him who can't keep up with his frantic pace. From my point of view he was, in the main, an enjoyable coach to play under. I think he's a coach who actually *taught* players – in a game in which, as I have mentioned earlier, talented players are sometimes just left to drift along. I found him a fairly personable kind of bloke – and a coach who would talk to you and ask you questions, although I'm not entirely convinced that he took much of the response on board. But he had a genuine interest in his players and he would communicate with them, and that was positive.

He was up front with all his players. Even the senior blokes weren't immune and many tasted the coach's wrath. He had the ability (which maybe many coaches share) to yell and scream. And he could be hard on the younger players. It wasn't pleasant for *anyone* to be on the receiving end of the renowned 'Jones stare' when things weren't going well. However, I always had the feeling that his bark was worse than his bite.

It's a big job, being Australian rugby coach, and Eddie gradually changed from his earlier, more relaxed days to being an angry man at times, swapping barbs with other coaches. I hope he still gets enjoyment out of the job. His commitment was never in question; he was relentless in his search to find ways to make his team improve. He was a coach for building and looking forward – rather than one who looked around at what other people were doing.

And always, perhaps like all good coaches, he was guarded – not giving too much away about himself, or his plans. Some coaches love the limelight, and love nothing better than to talk about how they constructed a game. Eddie Jones, now one of the major figures in world rugby, was never one of those.

My time in England, training and playing alongside another giant figure on the world rugby stage, Jonny Wilkinson, has given me insights into a man who has gained godlike status in his home country. Jonny, of course, is fly-half at the Newcastle Falcons and one of the great all-time goal-kickers. A wag observed in the press that there was no point in my taking goals to Newcastle when Jonny was around.

I have never seen anyone practise and work at their game the way Jonny does, although injury badly checked this season for him. The things he achieves on the football field don't come by chance, I can assure you. I recall a day not long after my arrival in Newcastle with the family when we had a scheduled 9.30 meeting at the club. Jonny was practising his kicking when I drove into the car park before the meeting. He came in for the meeting – and then went straight back out on the field, continuing the practice session. After a morning session of ball work for the backs, he practised again before a team photo shoot. After lunch he was back out there again, before our scheduled afternoon training session. The session ran for about two hours, and at the end of it – as I drifted to the car park with some of the others, ready to head home – Jonny Wilkinson was still out on the field, practising.

It is that intensity and dedication, backing natural ability, that explains Jonny's success in the game. It makes clear why in a high-pressure game like the 2003 World Cup final, he could knock over a field goal on his wrong foot. That was no chance kick; beyond doubt there had been thousands of them at Kingston Park on too many afternoons to count. It's good for fans to understand that when they see someone like Wilkinson do what he does, it's not down to chance. He is a professional and a perfectionist – and what the fans see on match day is only a very small percentage of what goes into his football life. It applies to all of us who play professional football – admittedly, in differing degrees: there is a huge amount of work and repetition that goes into any achievement that might reveal itself in the 80 minutes of game day.

Wilkinson is a player who always goes the extra yard. Maybe there are people who resent all the attention he gets, but it's fair to suggest that if they did the work he does, perhaps *they* would be getting the attention. The way training is these days, by the time you finish a normal session and do the weights and the other things that professional footballers do, you've got nothing left in the tank. Jonny seems to have remarkable recuperative powers – to be able to do all that and then to go back out there *again* to do more. His success is the result of unstinting hard work, and good luck to him.

Jonny Wilkinson is a nice bloke, too. Intense? Yes, for sure. With him, when it's football time, it is *absolute* football time. There is no mucking around. People tend to hang off his words when he talks of the game, which is as it should be, as he has a great knowledge of rugby and much to share, and he likes a joke as well. I know this for sure: if rugby happens to be your game, you'd rather have him with you than agin' you!

So, that's my story. As an icy wind blows in off the North Sea, rattling the windows, it's amazing for me to think that it's come to this. It doesn't seem so long ago at all that I was a four-year-old kid running around on the soccer field with the Carlingford Redbacks in Sydney. Now, because of another game, I'm here half a world away from home, with my wife and children – and contemplating the long northern winter, which may offer up some of the toughest challenges of my life in football.

But I'm looking forward to it all. My rugby journey has been like a dream, taking me around the world again and again, and to some of the greatest sporting arenas on earth. Now the final touchdown is here, far away from where it all began – but it's a valuable new experience to add to those countless memories I have of playing rugby.

I will spend two seasons with the Newcastle Falcons, hope for some good successeses for the club along the way – and then, if the Burke game plan works out, hang up my boots and get on with life.

'What then?' people have asked. 'Will you stay in rugby?'

Well, it won't be in coaching – not at senior level, anyway. I get a great deal of enjoyment out of coaching kids, and maybe there'll be some of that along the track. But being a high-intensity senior professional coach? I doubt it very much. Coaches at the higher levels lead pressured lives these days – and the turnover is high. I think back to an old adage: just because you are a sportsperson, it doesn't mean you should own a sports shop. It applies in football, for sure. Just because you've played 80 Test matches doesn't mean you can automatically convert to being a successful coach.

No, that won't be my pathway. But, of course, I'll always be somewhere around rugby. Through the years I have received so many things from the game in terms of the direction my life has taken, I'll never be far away from it. But my thinking now is that after I play my last game, I'll step back for a time and look at life on a much wider screen. Later, though, I'll be back to rugby for sure – probably just as a punter sitting in the stand or on the hill, watching the next generation . . . and the next . . . on a Saturday afternoon.

I have loved many things about this game. I have loved the fundamental, recurring challenge it offers players. It is satisfying and important to have the chance to test yourself each week, physically and mentally. My personal philosophy through all the years I have played has been never to be content with mediocre performance. The aim always has been to be consistent, and to elevate that consistency and improve each week. And always to know with certainty that when I played a poor game – and all of us manage those – I could do better. That would then become the challenge the next week.

Someone once asked me what I would wish for on the day that I finished as a rugby player. And I replied that my hope would be that I could look back knowing that I might have made some sort of positive contribution to the seasons of Australian and NSW rugby that made up the years of my career. And I would wish as well that perhaps with the things I had achieved, I had inspired some youngsters to take up rugby and to go on and play it with enjoyment – because they had seen me playing the game and having fun.

That would be enough.

Appendix 1

MATTHEW BURKE'S AUSTRALIAN RUGBY UNION TEST STATISTICS

Position	Opposition	Test	Date	T	G	PG	FG	Total
Wing	South Africa	3rd	8/93					
Fullback	France	1st	10/93					
O/C	Ireland	1st	6/94	1				5
Fullback	Ireland	2nd	6/94					
Fullback	Italy	1st	6/94	1				5
O/C	Italy	2nd	6/94					
Fullback	Canada	World Cup	5/95					
Fullback	Romania	World Cup	6/95	1	2			9
Fullback	England	World Cup	6/95					
Fullback	New Zealand	Bledisloe	7/95			1		3
Fullback	New Zealand	Bledisloe	7/95		2	3		13
Fullback	Wales	1st	6/96		6	3		21
Fullback	Wales	2nd	6/96	1	2	2		15
Fullback	Canada	1st	6/96	3	9	2		39
Fullback	New Zealand	Bledisloe 1st	7/96			2		6
Fullback	South Africa	1st	7/96		1	3		11
Fullback	New Zealand	Bledisloe 2nd	7/96	1		5		20
Fullback	South Africa	2nd	8/96			1		3
Fullback	Italy	1st	10/96		4	4		20
Fullback	Scotland	1st	11/96		2	5		19
Fullback	Ireland	1st	11/96		1	5		17
Fullback	Wales	1st	12/96	1	2	3		18
Fullback	England	1st	7/97	1	1			7
Fullback	New Zealand	Bledisloe	7/97		1	2		8
Fullback	England	Cook Trophy	6/98	1	4	3		22
Fullback	Scotland	1st	6/98	1	4	4		25
Fullback	Scotland	2nd	6/98		2	3		13
Fullback	New Zealand	Bledisloe	7/98	2	1	4		24
Fullback	South Africa	Tri-Nations	7/98			1		3
Fullback	New Zealand	Bledisloe	8/98	1		1		8

Position	Opposition	Test	Date	T	G	PG	FG	Total
Fullback	South Africa	Tri-Nations	8/98			5		15
Fullback	New Zealand	Bledisloe	8/98	1				5
Fullback	Ireland	2nd	6/99					
Wing	England	1st	7/99					
Fullback	South Africa	1st	7/99	1	3	2		17
Fullback	New Zealand	Bledisloe	7/99		1	1		5
Fullback	South Africa	2nd	8/99			3		9
Fullback	New Zealand	Bledisloe	8/99		1	7		23
Fullback	Romania	World Cup	9/99	1	5			15
Fullback	Ireland	World Cup	10/99		2	2		10
Wing	USA	World Cup	10/99	1	5	1		18
Fullback	Wales	World Cup	10/99		3	1		9
Fullback	South Africa	World Cup	10/99			8		24
Fullback	France	World Cup	11/99		2	7		25
Wing	France	1st	11/00			6		18
Wing	Scotland	1st	11/00	1	3	3		20
Wing	England	1st	12/00	1	1	4		19
Fullback	British Lions	1st	06/01					
Fullback	British Lions	2nd	07/01	1	1	6		25
Fullback	British Lions	3rd	07/01		2	5		19
Fullback	South Africa	Tri-Nations	07/01			4		12
Fullback	New Zealand	Tri-Nations	08/01	1	2	3		18
Fullback	South Africa	Tri-Nations	08/01			3		9
Fullback	New Zealand	Tri-Nations	09/01		1	4		14
Fullback	Spain	1st	11/01		10	1		23
Fullback	England	1st	11/01	1	1	1		10
Fullback	France	1st	11/01			2		6
Fullback	Wales	1st	11/01			7		21
O/C	France	1st	06/02		2	5		19
O/C	France	2nd	06/02	1		1		8
O/C	New Zealand	Tri-Nations	07/02			2		6
O/C	South Africa	Tri-Nations	07/02		3	3		15
O/C	New Zealand	Tri-Nations	08/02			2		6
O/C	South Africa	Tri-Nations	08/02		2	3		13
O/C	Argentina	1st	11/02			3		9
Fullback	Ireland	1st	11/02			3		9
Fullback	England	1st	11/02		2	4		16

Position	Opposition	Test	Date	T	G	PG	FG	Total
O/C	Italy	1st	11/02		3	1		9
Fullback	South Africa	Tri-Nations	07/03		2		1	7
Fullback	New Zealand	Tri-Nations	07/03	1		2		11
O/C	South Africa	Tri-Nations	08/03					
Wing	New Zealand	Tri-Nations	08/03					
O/C	Argentina	World Cup	10/03					
O/C	Romania	World Cup	10/03	2				10
O/C	Namibia	World Cup	10/03	1				5
O/C	Ireland	World Cup	11/03					
O/C	Scotland	1st	06/04		1			2
Fullback	Pacific Islanders	1st	07/04		1			2
O/C	South Africa	Tri-Nations	07/04		1			2
O/C	New Zealand	Tri-Nations	08/04			2		6
O/C	South Africa	Tri-Nations	08/04					
Total				29	104	174	1	878

Australian Wallabies

Tests 81 caps

Fullback 55 caps

Outside centre 19 caps

Wing 7 caps

Points 878

NSW Waratahs

Games 115

Points 1172 – 36T, 184G, 207PG, 1FG

Super 12 Points 959

Appendix 2

MATTHEW BURKE'S RECORDS

MOST POINTS IN TESTS IN A CALENDAR YEAR
'96 Season – 11 Tests (6T, 27G, 35PG)   189 points

MOST POINTS IN A TEST AGAINST NEW ZEALAND
'98 Season – MCG (2T, 1G, 4PG)   24 Points

MOST POINTS IN A WORLD CUP FINAL
'99 Season v France (2G, 7PG)   25 Points

MOST POINTS IN A TEST AGAINST BRITISH LIONS
'01 Season – Colonial Stadium (1T, 1G, 6PG)   25 points

MOST PENALTY GOALS IN A TEST AGAINST BRITISH LIONS
'01 Season – 6, Colonial Stadium   18 points

MOST PENALTY GOALS IN A TEST AGAINST WALES
'01 Season – 7, Millennium Stadium   21 points

MOST POINTS IN A TEST
'96 Season v Canada, Ballymore (3T, 9G, 2PG)   39 Points

MOST POINTS IN TESTS AGAINST BRITISH LIONS
'01 Season – 3 Tests (1T, 3G, 11PG)   44 points

MOST POINTS IN A TEST SERIES OVERSEAS
'96 Season – 4 Tests (1T, 9G, 17PG)   74 points

MOST POINTS IN A BARBARIAN GAME
'96 Season – 1 game (2T, 4G, 2PG)   24 Points

MOST POINTS IN A TEST AGAINST ITALY
'96 Season – Padova (4G, 4PG)   20 Points

MOST POINTS IN A TEST AGAINST SCOTLAND
'98 Season – SFS (1T, 4G, 4PG)   25 Points

MOST POINTS IN A TEST AGAINST ENGLAND
'98 Season – Suncorp (1T, 4G, 3PG)   22 Points

MOST POINTS IN A TEST AGAINST FRANCE
'99 Season – World Cup Final (2G, 7PG)   25 Points

MOST POINTS IN A TEST AGAINST WALES
'96 Season – Ballymore (6G, 3PG)   21 Points
'01 Season – Millennium Stadium (7PG)   21 Points

MOST POINTS IN A TEST AGAINST SPAIN
'01 Season – Madrid (10G, 1PG)   23 Points

MOST POINTS IN A MATCH AGAINST NZ MAORI
'02 Season – Perth (1T, 3G, 2PG)   17 Points

MOST PENALTY GOALS IN A TEST AGAINST NEW ZEALAND
'99 Season – 7, Stadium Australia   21 Points

MOST PENALTY GOALS IN A TEST AGAINST SOUTH AFRICA
'99 Season – 8, Twickenham, World Cup   24 Points

MOST PENALTY GOALS IN A TEST
'99 Season – 8, v South Africa, Twickenham   24 Points

MOST GOALS IN A TEST
'01 Season – 10, v Spain, Madrid   20 points

SCORED ALL THE TEAM'S POINTS IN A TEST
'98 Season v All Blacks, MCG (2T, 1G, 4PG)   24 Points
'00 Season v England, Twickenham (1T, 1G, 4PG)   19 Points
'00 Season v France, Stade De France (6PG)   18 Points
'01 Season v Wales, Millennium Stadium (7PG)   21 Points

MOST POINTS IN TESTS AGAINST NEW ZEALAND
Achieved in 16 Tests   170 points

MOST TESTS AT FULLBACK FOR AUSTRALIA
55 Tests

TOP SCORER FOR AUSTRALIA AGAINST:
Wales – 5 Tests (2T, 13G, 16PG)   84 points
South Africa – 16 Tests (1T, 12G, 36PG, 1FG)   140 points
New Zealand – 17 Tests (7T, 9G, 41PG)   176 points

TOTAL POINTS IN TESTS FOR AUSTRALIA
81 Tests 29T, 104G, 174PG, 1FG   878 Points

Statistics compiled by Bob Burke